·THE CULINARY HERBAL

·THE·
CULINARY
HERBAL

GROWING & PRESERVING
97 FLAVORFUL HERBS

SUSAN BELSINGER & ARTHUR O. TUCKER
WITH PHOTOS BY SHAWN LINEHAN

TIMBER PRESS · PORTLAND, OREGON

Published in 2016 by Timber Press, Inc.

Timber Press
The Haseltine Building
133 S.W. Second Avenue, Suite 450
Portland, Oregon 97204-3527
timberpress.com

Printed in China

Text and cover design by Anna Eshelman

Library of Congress Cataloging-in-Publication Data

Belsinger, Susan, author.
    The culinary herbal: growing and preserving 97 flavorful herbs/Susan
Belsinger, Arthur O. Tucker; with photos by Shawn Linehan.—First edition.
        pages cm
    Includes index.
    ISBN 978-1-60469-519-9
    1. Cooking (Herbs) 2. Herb gardening. I. Tucker, Arthur O., author. II. Title.
    TX819.H4B393 2016
    641.6'57—dc23   2015013386

To the McCleary girls—grandmothers, mothers, daughters, sisters, cousins, aunts and nieces—the circle of life

—S.L.B.

To Sherry, our children and their families, and Rex, for putting up with me all these years

—A.O.T.

CONTENTS

THE
CULINARY HERBS

PREFACE

COLLECTIVELY, WE HAVE more than a century of experience in gardening and cooking. Art started growing things when he was six as the child of what would later be called hippies (but in the late 1940s were merely considered poor survivalists), and he has dabbled in herbs ever since. Susan cooked at her grandmother's side, starting as a little girl and throughout her childhood, but she didn't have her first garden for growing herbs until she was twenty, and she taught her first cooking class at that age.

Art, a recently retired professor of botany at Delaware State University, still occasionally teaches botany and horticulture, and he continues to enjoy researching and writing about herbs. He learned to cook when young because, with two busy parents who were just trying to keep the family afloat, he got tired of eating bologna sandwiches. While he grew up on traditional Pennsylvania German dishes, Julia Child on TV was an epiphany, and he hasn't stopped since.

Susan has written countless books and articles on gardening, herbs, and cooking, often focusing on the garden-to-kitchen aspects—grow, harvest, and create recipes. Recently referred to as a "flavor artist," she has shared her passion for herbs and cooking through teaching and inspiring others with sensory experiences. Art has been her mentor, guiding her in the botany, science, and chemistry of all facets of herbs.

Herbs brought us together, first as colleagues, then as friends. We both love growing herbs and other plants, spending time in our gardens, and visiting other gardens. We especially like to prepare and eat good food. Over the years, we have come to respect each other's highly developed sense of smell and taste. When we are together, we go on ad infinitum about botanicals, sensory experience, and cooking— we are flavor and fragrance junkies.

We have written this book for gardeners who like to cook and cooks who want to grow the best-flavored culinary herbs, as well as for the everyday herbal enthusiast. In the book, we share our passion for cultivating and cooking with herbs, from the traditional ones to little-known plants and backyard weeds, to pass on our knowledge about the flavors and fragrances of herbs.

THE
MODERN-DAY
CULINARY HERBAL
AN INTRODUCTION

WHY DO WE PUT HERBS INTO OUR SOUPS, casseroles, desserts, and beverages? Because herbs add depth of flavor to any food and enhance and round out aromas and tastes. Herbs are broadly regarded as green plants that are used for culinary, medicinal, and ornamental purposes. Generally, herbs are not used on their own as a dish, but combined with other foods to add flavor, nutrients, and medicinal virtues. We practice all three of these uses every day, and we are passionate about using herbs in the kitchen. For decades, we have been wooed and enchanted by these inimitable fragrant and tasty plants. We know them by their appearance, their leaves, their shapes and color, and their flowers and seeds—and we know them intimately through sensory experience. We have written this book to share our knowledge about growing and cooking with herbs, so that you can cultivate these various plants and create and enjoy foods graced by them.

In this culinary herbal, we go beyond popular herbs such as parsley, sage, rosemary, and thyme, and venture farther afield. While we do include many herbs that are easily cultivated in our gardens, we also discuss a number of wild herbs often considered weeds that we forage from our backyards, meadows and fields, and the woods' edge. We also include plants that are not typically considered herbs. For example, although elder is considered a shrub or tree, garlic is a bulb, and arugula or chile peppers are usually found in the vegetable garden, these plants are grown and harvested for seasoning. We have gathered together this collection of herbs specifically for their culinary attributes. We give you descriptive details of cultivation, aroma, and taste for nearly 100 herbs, as well as examples of the many foods and dishes in which they are used.

Ancient herbals were the medicinal manuals for their eras. They offered recipes for treating all sorts of maladies as well as for tonics, and some of the plants were even toxic and dangerous to consume. Depending on the author, plant descriptions were sometimes included in these herbals.

This book is a modern-day herbal. Rather than exploring the medicinal properties of herbs, this book is a gardening-and-cooking culinary herbal, focusing on the smells and tastes offered by certain plants. We have sorted through many species and varieties of culinary herbs and selected our favorites to cultivate for cooking. Having spent a large part of our lives growing, smelling, tasting, and eating herbs, we offer our opinions on which herbs lend the best fragrance and flavor.

ALL ABOUT SMELL AND TASTE

Everyone talks about how things taste, but we don't often hear people discussing how a certain dish smells. And yet flavor is derived from both taste and smell.

Smell

Smell is not only a precursor to flavor, but it is an integral part of flavor. Without smell, you cannot sense and savor the full flavor of a food. In fact, flavor is about 90 percent smell.

Here is a simple experiment you can do right now to understand this proposition. Pick an herb leaf, but do not rub it or sniff it. Hold your nose closed with your fingers and do not let go. While holding your nose, take a little nibble of the herb leaf. Do you taste anything? No? While still holding your nose, take another nibble to be sure. Same results? Now let go of your nose and breathe. You will be amazed to experience the herb fragrance and flavor filling your nose and mouth. Now you understand the smell-flavor relationship. We do this experiment with children and adults to show them the power of our olfactory sense. Try it with your friends and family.

In our olfactory memories, we each have tens of thousands of smell memories, beginning when we were born. An infant instinctively knows who its mother is by her scent. We know when our neighbors are grilling outdoors by the odor of lighted charcoal or searing meat, and we know when they are mowing the lawn by the aroma of freshly cut grass wafting through our open windows. When driving down the road, your nose lets you know when you go by an Italian restaurant or a fried chicken diner. You don't even have to think about it—it is an imbedded olfactory memory. While each individual has innumerable smell memories, we have many fewer taste memories.

Taste

While most of us have learned that our tongue has four kinds of taste buds—sweet, sour, salty, and bitter—a few other cultures add a few more tastes. In India, proponents of the Ayurvedic system include "pungent" as a taste, and we agree heartily with this, since we consider garlic, chile peppers, and even mustard as pungent. To this taste might be added the opposite—cool—like the menthol in peppermint. And then there is *umami*, which is a Japanese word that might be translated as "a pleasant, savory taste" or "a deliciousness" that some describe as brothy. Umami is recognized by our taste receptors that taste glutamates (such as MSG, monosodium glutamate) and is found in foods or food combinations like aged or fermented foods, soy and fish sauces, seafood, cured meats, mushrooms, seaweed, and some vegetables and cheeses. We have tasted umami in recipes combining some of these ingredients, soups, and even fine wines. And sometimes, "mouthfeel" is added as a taste by some researchers. Mouthfeel is the curious coating that occurs in the mouth when you consume lactone-rich foods, such as coconut dishes.

So, let's say we add pungent/cool and umami to the basic four tastes, and that gives us six tastes. When you think about it, that isn't very many, but every food and every herb that we eat can be categorized into these six basic tastes or a combination of them. By adding an herb like sorrel to a soup or sauce, its tart, lemony flavor and mineral salts will add a sour and salty flavor to the dish. And adding chile peppers or garlic to a dish will make it pungent. Since herbs contain concentrated flavor and natural minerals, we can often use less salt in foods containing them.

Today's society craves sweet and salt, and fast foods have exacerbated the overuse of these two tastes. When we create a dish, we look for a balance of flavors and try to incorporate all of the tastes—sweet and salty, bitter and sour, and pungent/cool and umami—so that we can enjoy the full range of sensory stimuli. With the other dimensions of flavor offered by herbs, we do not need so much sweet and salt in our diets. In addition, bitter and sour stimulate our digestive juices, to aid in digestion.

Sensory experience

When we smell an herb, we rub its leaves to release the essential oils and inhale deeply, usually with our eyes closed. We do this again and again, so we can capture the bouquet in our olfactory receptors. The same goes for tasting: We take a nibble and let the taste roll across our tongue and permeate our taste buds, and we taste again. We find that the more we do this, the more in tune we are with the sensory experience, and our senses of smell and taste become heightened. In this manner, we can create for ourselves the utmost sensory pleasures. We also feel that anyone can do this if they take the time to smell and taste and think about it. The more one practices, the more acute your senses become.

ABOUT THE BOOK

Through the years, we have cultivated many herbs. We have our favorites, which are tried and true, and we share them with you in the book. This way, if you are a beginning or even a somewhat experienced gardener or just have a small space, you can choose the best herb plants to grow.

The main section of this book includes profiles of selected culinary herbs. In these plant descriptions, we explore how each individual herb smells and tastes. We mention foods or dishes from around the globe that highlight or go well with that herb's flavor. We discuss whether the herb is best used fresh or cooked, and how to prepare it. Each plant profile also provides information on cultivating that particular herb, and offers suggestions on harvesting and preserving it. For some herbs, like chervil or lovage, we recommend just growing the straight species. For other herbs, like the basils or mints, we suggest five or six favorites.

While we have not included plants that primarily have medicinal applications, the culinary herbs, besides adding flavor, often have medicinal virtues, so we occasionally mention some of those attributes.

Although we have included many tender perennial herbs, we have not included tropical herbs and spices, since these plants need to grow in a hot climate or a greenhouse to produce flowers, seeds, roots, or tubers. We have greenhouses and we have grown turmeric, cardamom, tea, coffee, allspice, and other tropicals. Even with a greenhouse, though, we have not seen them flower and produce seed or fruit; we grow them mostly for the pleasure of having them.

Among the selected culinary herbs, we have included those that are sometimes called potherbs. These plant materials, such as nettles, lamb's quarters, and purslane, are on the borderline between common culinary herbs and vegetables, and can be gathered from the wild or cultivated. They are often used for seasoning, but also their leaves, stems, and flowers can be cooked and used for food by themselves, and many potherbs are excellent additions to salads.

After the plant profiles section of the book, we provide general information on growing herbs. We explain how to start herbs from seed, cuttings, and layering (bending down branches and covering with soil so they root), how to grow herbs in containers or indoors, and how to maintain healthy herbs. We then discuss particulars on preserving the harvest, including what techniques you can use, from drying to freezing. We also offer our master recipes for capturing, storing, and cooking with the essence of herbs.

Generally Recognized As Safe (GRAS)

Just because something is "natural" does not mean it is intrinsically "good." Poison ivy is natural, and comfrey leaves, which may contain chemicals that cause liver cancer, are natural. In the United States, flavoring ingredients are regulated by the Food and Drug Administration under the Food Additives Amendment, section 409, of the 1958 Food and Drugs Act. The Flavor and Extract Manufacturers' Association (FEMA) provides an expert panel to determine those flavors and levels that are granted exemptions from the coverage of section 409 and whose use in food is "Generally Recognized As Safe" (GRAS). This subject is summarized in the Code of Federal Regulations, chapter 21, parts 182 and 184.

In 1972, the National Academy of Sciences' Food

▶ **HARDINESS ZONES**

USDA hardiness zones are based on average annual minimum temperatures. Knowing a plant's hardiness zone rating will help you determine whether it will survive in your climate through the cold winter. The lower the zone number, the colder the winter temperatures. To see temperature equivalents and to learn which zone your garden is in, see the U.S. Department of Agriculture Hardiness Zone Map at planthardiness.ars.usda. gov/phzmweb/.

For Canada, go to planthardiness.gc.ca/ or sis.agr. gc.ca/cansis/nsdb/climate/hardiness/index.html.

For Europe, go to uk.gardenweb.com/forums/ zones/hze.html.

For hardiness ratings for the UK with USDA equivalents, go to rhs.org.uk/Plants/Plant-trials -and-awards/pdf/2012_RHS-Hardiness-Rating.

Protection Committee reviewed GRAS chemicals, and since then the FEMA expert panel has reviewed flavor ingredients and published periodic updates in *Food Technology*. In Europe, a classification of "Nature-identical" is similar to GRAS, and the European Community (EC) is preparing inventories of flavoring materials. In the book's plant profiles, we have listed the GRAS status for an herb only when we consider it pertinent.

What does this mean for you, the consumer? Consider safrole, the principal component of sassafras. An extract or oil of the root of sassafras (*Sassafras albidum*) contains 74 to 85 percent safrole, which causes liver cancer in mice, rats, and dogs. Safrole is viewed as a precarcinogen. On the other hand, there are herbs (like sassafras) that have been consumed for millennia by cultures without ill effect, and investigations of the chemistry of these herbs do not reveal any obvious toxic substances. Many of these herbs, as they increase in popularity, might be nominated for GRAS status someday, but in the meantime, we can only list them as in limbo and point out any concerns.

THE

CULINARY

HERBS

Trachyspermum ammi seeds

AJOWAN

Trachyspermum ammi (T. copticum)

The seeds (actually fruits) of this annual smell of thyme when crushed and are used to impart the flavor of thyme in Indian savories, particularly *ompadi, namkin boodi,* and *sev*. In Ethiopia, the fruits are used to flavor *alicha,* which is a meat stew; wet bread; and *katikala,* an alcoholic drink. The essential oil of the fruits is antifungal because of the presence of thymol, a simple phenol that burns the tongue almost immediately when a single seed is tasted alone. Just before the strong thyme taste penetrates the tongue, there is a brief instant when the fruity flavor of coriander seed registers on the palate. Use sparingly.

In spite of its wide use in Indian food for centuries and its documented health benefits, ajowan has not achieved GRAS status (perhaps because no one ever lobbied for it).

We grow the straight species. Native to Asia, North Africa, and Europe, ajowan enjoys the heat of summer.

CULTIVATION AND PROPAGATION
You can find ajowan (sometimes referred to as *ajwain*) at food stores specializing in Indian foods. Because of the lax growth and uneven germination of ajowan, plant seeds 3 to 6 inches apart or even closer. Seedlings appear within seven to fifteen days. Application of organic nitrogen is beneficial. Additional potassium and sulfur may be needed, depending on soil tests. Collar rot and root rot (*Athelia rolfsii*) affect ajowan, and the spice beetle (*Stegobium paniceum*) attacks the stored seeds.

HARVESTING AND PRESERVING
Plants flower in about two months, and harvesting can begin when the flower heads turn brown. The plants are then dried in sheds and the fruits separated from the chaff on large sheets of paper. We simply put the loose harvested plants into large paper bags and store them in a warm outdoor shed for a few days until they are dry, then beat them to separate out the fruits. The chaff is lighter than the seeds, so a vacuum nozzle lowered slowly into the bag to the right height above the seeds will suck up the chaff and leave the heavier seeds (shake the bag slightly while doing this). Seeds can be stored in airtight containers in the freezer for up to one year.

Flowers of ajowan (*Trachyspermum ammi*)

Amaranthus tricolor 'Red Stripe
Leaf' (or 'Red Leaf')

annual, 1 to 8
feet tall

hardy in
zones 3 to 10

full sun

can withstand
dry conditions

well-drained
soil, pH 7.0

AMARANTH

Amaranthus species

The aroma of amaranth is herbaceous and green (even if it is red), and it tastes like a mild, leafy green similar to spinach or orach. Small leaves can be snipped for salads at the beginning of the growing season. As the plant matures and the leaves get bigger, they can be harvested and used like spinach. They are good fresh as long as they are tender, and can be used as wilted greens and in soups and casseroles. If the leaf stems are tough, remove them and just use the leaves. Very large leaves late in the season tend to taste bitter and be too tough to eat.

Amaranth is such a showy plant it can be grown as an ornamental. The entire plant can be eaten, and some species are used medicinally. Leaves are used as a potherb and a vegetable, while the seeds, a good source of protein, are used as a grain crop. When choosing seed, note that some amaranths are grown mainly for their leaves, while some just for the seeds (often referred to as grain amaranth).

The tiny, shiny, dark brown to black, protein-rich seeds can be dried and cooked like a breakfast cereal. They are glutinous in texture once combined with liquid, and take fifteen to twenty minutes to soften. They can be added to soups or sauces, and cooked with oatmeal or other cereals and grains. The seeds can be whirred in the blender and used in smoothies, or pulsed with flour and added to baked goods from breads and muffins to cookies and pancakes. Whole seeds can be popped like popcorn, making tiny little popped grains.

The selections discussed here can be used for their leaves as well as their seeds. The red-colored amaranth (*Amaranthus hypochondriacus*), sometimes referred to as prince's feather, adds bright color to the garden and the salad bowl. It is also used as a colorant for food and as a dye. The Hopi Indians use A. 'Hopi Red Dye', which has bright red foliage and flowers, as a dye plant. They use the red leaves in salads, and the flower bract to color

While green amaranths blend in with other herbs, red amaranths are showy in the garden.

The golden-brown seed heads of green amaranth (*Amaranthus retroflexus*) can be 3 to 4 feet in height.

piki, the thin Native American blue corn pancakelike bread, and corn bread.

Green amaranth (*Amaranthus retroflexus*) has green leaves with yellow-gold flowers. It is used medicinally for its astringent properties, and as a green dye. For gardeners with small spaces, *A. hypochondriacus* 'Pygmy Torch' is much smaller, growing to 15 to 18 inches. Tricolored amaranths are striking plants in the garden with showy red, green, and creamy yellow foliage; try *A. tricolor* 'Red Leaf', *A. tricolor* 'Aurora Yellow', or *A.* 'Molten Fire'.

CULTIVATION AND PROPAGATION

Amaranth is easy to grow. Once the soil has warmed in spring, sow amaranth seeds 8 to 10 inches apart. Seedlings look similar to lamb's quarters and pigweed, so sow them in a bed in rows so they can be easily identified. Transplants should be spaced about 12 inches apart. Amaranth prefers warm weather and can withstand heat. Plants grown in tropical climates for grain can be fairly heat and drought tolerant. While amaranth tolerates dry conditions, leaves are more prolific and better tasting when the plant is well watered. If nitrogen and phosphorus are added to the soil, the plant will grow taller and produce more foliage and seed. Once it flowers, the blooms will remain until first frost or harvest.

HARVESTING AND PRESERVING

In the first part of the growth stage, harvest the small foliage for salads. As the leaves get larger, cook them for wilted greens. Once the plants are in full flower, the foliage tends to be too tough to eat. The blooms are beautiful ornamentally in the flower garden or the vegetable or herb garden. For medicinal purposes, once flowers have formed, the whole plant (*Amaranthus retroflexus*, *A. tricolor*, *A. spinosus*) is cut and dried.

For seed harvest, once the flower heads have formed seed, try shaking or gently rubbing a flower head; if the seeds fall off easily, it is time to harvest them. When ready to save seed, cut the flower heads (leaving a few for the birds), hold them over a large bucket or washtub, and rub them to remove the seeds, letting them fall into the container. Sieve them through a screen to remove the chaff. Or, flower heads can be placed in paper bags to dry, which will catch the dropping seeds. Once dried, they will also need to be sieved. Seeds can be saved for next season's plantings, or used in the kitchen. Be sure seeds are completely dry before packing them into labeled jars. It is best to refrigerate seeds to retain freshness; use within six months.

Angelica archangelica

biennial to
short-lived
perennial, to 6
feet tall

hardy to
zone 4

full sun (in areas of
cool summers) to
part shade (areas
of hot summers)

keep moist but not
constantly wet

loamy soil,
average pH 6.3

ANGELICA

Angelica archangelica

While we do not recommend consumption of raw or dried angelica parts because of the furanocoumarin (a chemical compound that may cause skin sensitivity to sunlight) content, the essential oils and extracts of angelica roots and seeds are GRAS at low levels and can be used to enhance other flavors. Angelica seeds and roots smell woody with hints of peppermint and pine. Roots and seeds are used in making a number of popular herbal liqueurs and are sometimes used in gin.

The stems—sliced, candied, and colored with green food coloring—are popular in England for cake decoration and as a confection. These are apparently safe because of the long time involved in cooking and candying.

We grow the species. Native to northern and central Europe, west to the Netherlands and Iceland, and south to Central Ukraine, angelica prefers cool summers.

CULTIVATION AND PROPAGATION

Angelica is easily started from seeds (actually fruits) planted immediately after ripening in late summer in garden beds. As for most umbellifers (plants with clusters of flowers), freshness of the seed is of utmost importance. Seeds from the plant's primary (central) inflorescence typically produce the highest germination rate. Light is necessary for germination, so the seeds should be planted in shallow holes and barely covered with fine sand. Fresh seeds may be stored dry at around 41 to 43°F (the refrigerator) for up to two years. Seeds may also be germinated indoors if shallowly sown in moist soil at 72°F day temperature and 64°F night temperature under artificial light; the plants should be 5 inches from cool white fluorescent lights at a day length of sixteen hours. Transplant young seedlings grown indoors to the garden four to six weeks after germination, when they are 3 to 4 inches high; plant seedlings with 12 inches between them, in rows 2 to 3 feet apart.

The soil should be evenly moist, well drained, slightly acid, and high in organic matter.

HARVESTING AND PRESERVING

Before harvesting, keep these two warnings in mind. First, collectors of wild angelica (which frequently naturalizes in cooler climates) often confuse this plant with poison hemlock (*Conium maculatum*), the poison that killed Socrates. Second, all parts of angelica—the fruits, leaves, and roots—are scented with a sweet aromatic oil, and these parts also contain a number of furanocoumarins. Even when not combined with light, these compounds are documented to be toxic and can cause genetic damage and possibly cancer.

Leaves and flowering stalks may be harvested from the plants in the second year of growth. Viral and fungal diseases may attack the leaves in late summer, making the leaves unappealing. If you want to harvest the roots, remove the flowering stalks to prevent loss of growth or quality. Harvest the roots in the fall of the second year of growth or the following spring. After digging, the roots should be washed to remove attached soil. Dry the roots slowly in a clean room with good air circulation; we don't recommend rapid oven drying because it can cause loss of oil.

Anise (*Pimpinella anisum*)
flowers, foliage, and dried seeds

annual, to 2 feet tall

seedlings can withstand minor frost

full sun

keep moist but not constantly wet

loamy soil, average pH 7.2

ANISE

Pimpinella anisum

When crushed between your fingers, anise seeds smell sweet, mildly fruity, and then like licorice candy. If you pop a tiny anise seed in your mouth and bite it between your front teeth, you get an immediate hit of black licorice candy flavor. At first, it might seem slightly sweet, although the aftertaste has a definite bitterness.

Anise seeds (really fruits) are used to flavor licorice candy. The sweetener extracted from the root of the licorice plant has almost no aroma, so "anise-scented" more accurately describes the scent of licorice candy and similar odors.

Anise seeds are also used to flavor liqueurs (anisette, ouzo, raki) as well as some meat dishes (lamb shanks), ice cream, candy, chewing gum, condiments, teas, and pastries (*pizzelles*). Because they are similar in flavor, anise seeds are sometimes confused with fennel seeds, which are used in sweet Italian sausage. But the seeds are not identical in appearance; anise seeds are much smaller than fennel seeds.

We grow the species. Probably native to Asia, anise is easily cultivated worldwide.

CULTIVATION AND PROPAGATION

The seeds of this lacy-leaved plant, similar in appearance to dill, should be sown in warm soil in spring. The plant requires at least 120 frost-free days to fruit properly. Choose a spot in full sun with well-drained, friable garden loam. Anise is susceptible to drought, so irrigation may be necessary. Plant seeds about ½ inch deep in rows 18 to 30 inches apart, one or two seeds per inch. Germination occurs in seven to fourteen days at 70°F. Carefully thin seedlings to 6 to 12 inches apart; anise transplants poorly. New growth is spindly, and plants tend to flop unless soil is firmed at the base of the plant.

HARVESTING AND PRESERVING

While the seed in the umbel is still green, pull the plants out of the ground or cut off the tops by hand, tie into bundles, and stack in conical piles with the fruiting heads toward the center. Thresh after drying and separate the seeds from the chaff. The home gardener can expect a harvest of 1 to 2 tablespoons of seed from each plant. Store dry seeds in airtight jars in a dark cupboard until next year's harvest.

Agastache foeniculum

hardy short-lived perennial, 3 to 5 feet tall

 hardy to zone 4, preferring cool summers

 full sun to part shade

keep moist but not wet

 soil rich in organic matter, pH 7.0

ANISE HYSSOP

Agastache foeniculum

While commonly called anise hyssop, the odor is more similar to French tarragon, though sweeter, with a hint of basil. The foliage and flowers taste similar to the aroma—sweet, with the taste of licorice candy, tarragon, and basil—and just a bit floral.

All of the thirty or so *Agastache* species are good for honey production and make great ornamental perennials. The flowering plants go well with the silver-leaved species of mountain mint (*Pycnanthemum* species), which flower about the same time in the July garden and also provide good bee forage. The young, broad, bright green leaves of *A. foeniculum*, tinged purple in cool weather, are attractive with spring bulbs such as yellow daffodils.

Agastache species do not have GRAS status, even though the leaves of many species have been used for centuries as a substitute for French tarragon, infused in syrups and cordials, or brewed into tea, and the flowers have been used with fruit, in desserts and confections, and mixed in salads. Both the leaves and flowers make good additions to potpourri.

Agastache foeniculum is most often grown, though *A. mexicana*, *A. rugosa*, and *A. scrophulariifolia* provide similar flavors to French tarragon and basil, though may include plants scented of peppermint or pennyroyal.

CULTIVATION AND PROPAGATION

Agastache species need little more than partly shaded to sunny, well-drained, slightly acid to near-neutral soil. The seeds (actually tiny nuts, or nutlets) are most easily started by broadcasting; established clumps readily reseed themselves, often in tiny nooks and crannies or the middle of the garden path. Seeds may also be sown in the greenhouse, with transplants in six to eight weeks. Clumps generally last two to three years, becoming very woody at the base and eventually dying. Since reseeding is not a problem, anise hyssop will persist in your garden yet never really become weedy; it is easy to move about. The soil should be evenly moist, well drained, slightly acid, and high in organic matter.

HARVESTING AND PRESERVING

For tea, harvest leaves early in the day during a sunny, rain-free spell close to when the plants will be flowering, then dry the leaves and store them in glass jars. Anise hyssop leaves and flowers make an unusual vinegar for salads and a tasty cordial if you like the taste of sweet licorice. Our friend puts anise hyssop in his vodka, which he keeps in the freezer, for a preferred libation. Leaves are sometimes candied as a confection for desserts; after the egg white and sugar mixture has set and dried, store them in tightly closed containers at room temperature or in the freezer for three to six months. Flowers are often harvested fresh as edible flowers for salads, beverages, syrups, and desserts.

Eruca vesicaria

annual or
perennial, 12 to
30 inches tall

hardy in
zones 5 to 10

full sun, part
shade in hot
climates

keep moist but
well-drained

loam, pH 6 to 7

ARUGULA

Eruca vesicaria (E. sativa)
Diplotaxis species

This leafy salad green has become a very popular herb to add to salad mixes with good reason. Though the aroma is green and herbaceous, perhaps slightly pungent, the flavor packs a punch and dances all over the tongue. It is at once a savory herbal green, a bit nutty, slightly bitter, and spicy, and it can sometimes be downright hot. Arugula is related to mustard and nasturtium and can have that same kind of peppery bite. Other words used for the flavor include radish, peanut, horseradish, bacon, and smoky.

Arugula (commonly sold under this Italian name), sometimes called rocket, is used most often as a salad green combined with lettuces, endives or chicories, radicchio, spinach, and other baby greens sold as a gourmet mix called mesclun (from the French) and *misticanza* (in Italian). Italians also eat arugula solo as a salad simply dressed with lemon juice, olive oil, salt, and pepper. It is a good source of vitamins A and C as well as iron. Medicinally, it is used as a tonic herb.

It makes a wonderful salsa verde, providing flavor and texture when tossed in salads with other vegetables, especially tomatoes, avocadoes, and roasted potatoes or beets, and it goes well with citrus fruits, pasta, grains, cheeses, chicken, and on pizza. Arugula can be used as a potherb and wilted with other greens, or added to soups or egg dishes. The taste is muted when it is cooked, though it still has a richness and depth unlike any other green. It is best cooked briefly: add it at the end of a stir-fry or soup, simmer, then toss it with pasta before serving or whip it into garlic mashed potatoes. The small, yellow or cream-colored, or sometimes purple-veined flowers make excellent, spicy garnishes.

Common arugula

For wider leaved salad greens, with white blooms that have purple crosses, we grow *Eruca vesicaria* 'True Italian' and *E. vesicaria* 'Runway'. They are good-tasting (though they do get pungent in hot

We enjoy the delightful appearance and flavor of these spicy arugula flowers.

temperatures and little precipitation), sturdy plants, which grow back quickly after harvesting again and again. If allowed to go to seed, they will offer volunteers in the next season. *Eruca vesicaria* 'Astro' is fairly new to the market and similar to 'True Italian'.

Wild arugula

The so-called wild arugulas (*Diplotaxis* species) are perennial and have narrower leaves and smaller, yellow flowers. Both *D. tenuifolia* 'Sylvetta' and *D. tenuifolia* 'Rustic' are good choices to grow. These arugulas tend to be more rangy, with leaves that are a bit chewier and more pungent even when young. They come back every year and spread, but they are easily controlled—just whack them back and eat them.

Wild arugula (*Diplotaxis tenuifolia*) has narrow, deeply serrated leaves and small yellow flowers.

Diplotaxis tenuifolia 'Dragon's Tongue', another recent introduction, is comparable to *D. tenuifolia* 'Rustic'. *Diplotaxis erucoides* 'Wasabi', introduced by Renee's Garden Seeds, grows closer to the ground in rosettes. If you like it hot, these leaves are the spiciest arugula yet—think wasabi!

CULTIVATION AND PROPAGATION
Plant seeds of annual arugula (*Eruca vesicaria*) outdoors in full sun to part shade (in hot climates it lasts longer in part shade or shade and doesn't get quite so pungent), ¼ inch deep, in well-worked and moisture-retentive soil, as soon as the soil can be worked in spring. Thin gradually, harvesting for salads, so plants are at least 6 inches apart. Like many salad greens, arugula doesn't like hot weather and will want to bolt (send up a flower stalk and go to seed). Sow annual seed in early spring, then again in late spring to early summer, and in late summer to early fall, about four weeks apart, to insure continuous harvest; it is a rapid grower. Or allow

them to behave like those perpetual patches—let them drop seed and return next year where they will.

Wild arugula (*Diplotaxis tenuifolia*) is a perennial plant that returns every year and spreads as it ages. It is easily grown from seed, sometimes too easily, and rapidly reseeds itself. It is rangy and gets quite big when it flowers but has the advantage of withstanding the heat of summer. Grow both annual and perennial arugulas if you have space in your garden.

HARVESTING AND PRESERVING
Arugula leaves mature at six to eight weeks and can be thinned or harvested as baby salad greens as early as three weeks. To harvest, cut larger outer leaves first, or cut the entire plant back about 1 inch above the ground and it will grow back. Once the weather becomes hot, the leaves also taste hotter. Cut them back before flowers appear. You can keep this plant going under a row cover in cold weather. This salad green is best eaten fresh and in season.

Ocimum basilicum 'Genovese'

BASIL
Ocimum species

Basil is a spectacular, tender herb with many species that offer an array of sublime fragrances from licorice to lemon, cinnamon, and spice. Though all the basils are wonderfully aromatic and flavorful herbs, it is the sweet, green, bush basil that is the most beloved. *Ocimum basilicum* is the king of aroma as well as flavor. Part of its immense popularity is that as an annual, which we can only experience during the heat of summer like a summer-ripe tomato, circumstances increase its desirability, and so we have to grow and harvest an abundance of it while it is in season. The marriage of basil and tomatoes is transcendent; a handmade pesto is perhaps the best sauce possible, incurring delightful flavors on the palate; and the sweet lemon fragrance and flavor of lemon basil creates an unforgettable, ethereal gelato.

There are so many different basils to choose from, you'll have to decide how much garden space to allot to these useful culinary herbs. It is challenging to know which basils to choose, so we will discuss some of our favorites.

Sweet, green bush basil

If we could only have one basil plant, it would most certainly be *Ocimum basilicum* 'Genovese Verde Migliorato', most often sold as 'Genoa Green', 'Genoa Green Improved', or just 'Genovese'. Susan, having lived in Italy for two years, feels that this basil is closest to the favored basil she cultivated and consumed there in large quantities. It is her number one choice for making pesto and combining with tomatoes.

The fragrance is heady with a clean, green aroma with anise hyssop and mint, followed by hints of citrus, cinnamon, and clove. The flavor is well rounded, full of spice, licorice, and mint, and is just slightly pungent.

Besides the traditional pesto and *antipasto di pomodoro e mozzarella*, basil is wonderful with any summer vegetable or salad; on sandwiches and pizza, in soups, sauces, salsas, and vinaigrettes; with pasta or grains; in a Bloody Mary; and in baked goods and even gelati.

Other sweet, green bush basils we recommend are *Ocimum basilicum* ' Italian', *O. basilicum* 'Napoletano', *O. americanum* 'Genoa Profumatissima', and *O. basilicum* 'Italian Pesto'.

Lemon basil

We really haven't met a lemon basil we didn't like. These basils are predominantly lemon flavored and do not have the anise taste that the others do. *Ocimum basilicum* 'Mrs Burns' Lemon' is our first choice—a sturdy, dependable plant with lovely lemon aroma and flavor. It grows a bit taller and has somewhat larger leaves than the common lemon basil.

The fragrance is perfumy with a big lemon nose, resinous and oily, with a hint of cinnamon and a floral note. The flavor is clean and assertive lemon zest followed with light spice and a hint of mint.

Lemon basils are delightful in everyday beverages like lemonade and iced tea, as well as in libations and syrups. They make a delicious mayonnaise or vinaigrette; complement summer vegetables, chicken, and fish; are good in any baked good from cookies, pies, and cakes to puddings; and are perfect with seasonal fruits and in your favorite ice cream.

Other lemon-flavored basils we recommend are *Ocimum ×citriodorum* 'Lemon' and *O. ×citriodorum* 'Sweet Dani'. Common lemon basil, which often has smaller leaves, provides a respectable lemon fragrance and flavor, though it is a little dull compared to 'Mrs Burns' Lemon'. 'Sweet Dani', with compact, shorter

'Mrs Burns' Lemon' basil is our pick of the lemon-flavored basils.

This upright, cinnamon-scented basil is sold as 'Greek Columnar', 'Aussie Sweetie', and 'Lesbos'.

plants than other lemon basils, has a big lemon bouquet and a strong lemon flavor.

Cinnamon basil

Cinnamon-scented basil plants have bright green leaves with dark purple stems, so they stand out in the basil bed. Although their aroma and taste do not work for pesto, their spiciness is wonderful in baked goods. The aroma is clean and spicy with hints of cinnamon, sweet grass, mint, and a bare whiff of anise. The flavor combines spice with citrus zest, giving a perfumed taste backed by just a touch of anise and mint, resulting in a final warm pungency on the tongue.

Cinnamon basil is perfect in stewed tomatoes, tomato sauces, and some soups; delicious in cinnamon rolls, cakes, cookies, breads—all manner of baked goods where cinnamon would be used; and in beverages, rice pudding, custard, ice cream, and with fruit—especially apples and pears.

Other cinnamon-flavored basils we recommend are *Ocimum ×citriodorum* 'Lesbos' and *O. ×citriodorum* 'Aussie Sweetie'. Be sure to sniff and taste them, since some have a dominant licorice flavor.

Thai basil

These basils are essential to Thai cooking, with their graceful bouquet and assertive licorice taste; they typically have a well-rounded balance of flavors. Plants look more like an ornamental, with a tendency to have rounded flower heads rather than spikes.

The fragrance of most Thai basils is a big, rounded aroma of spice

that is sweet with licorice and some mint. They have a strong, perfumed flavor with hints of licorice, mint, and spice. These assertive basils stand up to spicy, flavorful dishes from soups and stir-fries to curries; are often used with noodle dishes, vegetables, meat, chicken, fish, and seafood; and whole leaves are frequently served as an accompaniment to many meals.

Other anise-flavored or Thai basils we recommend are *Ocimum basilicum* 'Thai' and *O. basilicum* 'Queenette'.

Purple or opal basil

Because of their extraordinary color, the purple or opal basils are wonderful to add to a green herb garden or to the flower bed. But we find them lacking in flavor for most culinary uses. We do use the leaves to capture the garnet color in opal basil vinegar, while also adding a robust green-leaf basil to lend flavor support.

A few of the more handsome and sturdy varieties are *Ocimum* 'Dark Opal' (*O. basilicum* × *O. forskolei*), and *O.* 'Osmin', which retain their true color throughout the season. The dark leaves of *Ocimum basilicum* 'Purple Ruffles' have showy, ruffled edges.

CULTIVATION AND PROPAGATION
To grow the most interesting basil varieties, start them from seed. Sow seed indoors, four to six weeks before transplanting. This method gives you a head start, compared to direct sowing in the garden, allowing for plants to mature earlier and provide more harvests. Since basil is a tropical plant, it must have sun and

Thai basils have shiny green leaves and showy dark purple blooms like those seen here on 'Siam Queen'.

warmth from seedling to maturity, and you must provide the seeds and seedlings with the right conditions for germination and growth.

Indoors, it is not hard to provide warmth, but natural light is not enough to develop sturdy seedlings. If you don't have a greenhouse to propagate seed at home, you will have the best success if you begin the seedlings under lights.

HARVESTING AND PRESERVING

The most important thing about growing basil is keeping it cut back so you will have a continual harvest of fresh leaves throughout the season. We are diligent about this, so we get a huge yield of leaves throughout the harvest season, and we keep the basil's flavor and aroma at its peak, rather than letting the plants flower and become bitter. In our zone 7 gardens, we set basil out in mid to late May. When we transplant the new tender plants, we cut them back just above the bottom two sets of leaves. This early pruning seems a bit drastic, but it will provide for more growth early on.

Depending on the weather and the growth of the plants, we prune the plants back in this manner about every four weeks, so the next pruning takes place in mid to late June. This pruning and harvesting process is repeated every month— or when the plants show any sign of a flower bud—throughout the growing season. This way, we harvest 15 to 25 cups of basil leaves per plant and have tasty basil in September rather than bitter spent leaves.

People often tell us that they have trouble growing basil successfully. The first thing we ask them is whether they kept it cut back. If you just pinch off the tips or the flowers, the plant will keep trying to make flowers in order to set seed. The leaf yield will be small and the plants will become bitter tasting. So keep those plants pruned, and eat basil. With proper, regular pruning, each basil plant can be harvested five or six times during the growing season.

We like to make aromatic herbal pastes with our basil and freeze them, because that preserves optimum flavor. We also dry basil and make vinegar.

The opal or purple basils add vibrant contrast in the herb garden and their leaves make a beautiful ruby-colored vinegar.

Laurus nobilis

tender evergreen perennial shrub or tree, 10 to 50 feet tall

hardy in zones 8 to 9; needs protection from frost and cold

full sun; can take a little shade in very hot climates

keep moist but not wet

well-drained soil, average pH 6.2

BAY LAUREL

Laurus nobilis

Bay laurel (*Laurus nobilis*), sometimes called Grecian bay, is the bay to cultivate for culinary uses. Run your thumbnail down the center vein on the underside of a fresh bay leaf, close your eyes, and inhale. The fragrance of fresh bay is heady. In the first inhalation, you smell a combination of honey and balsam with hints of spice like nutmeg and clove. That is followed by a suggestion of citrus, lemon or orange. At a second inhalation, you detect floral notes like vanilla, or perhaps rose. The flavor is similar to the fragrance—aromatic and complex. First you notice balsam and slightly honeysweet tastes, with a slight bitterness. Then you pick up hints of vanilla and spice with a bit of clove, black pepper, and flowers.

Fresh or dried bay leaves can be used in making a traditional French bouquet garni (tied bunch of the herbs parsley, thyme, and bay leaf) used to flavor any savory item from stocks, soups, stews, sauces, and gravies to marinades and stuffings. With the sweet and spicy flavor elements that bay has to offer, it also can be used in desserts like custards, puddings, and sauces as well as sweet doughs, syrups, and cordials, and compotes with fruits and especially with chocolate.

Bay leaves, fresh or dried, are generally removed from cooked dishes before serving because they are thick and leathery and the edges can be jagged and sharp when broken. It's better not to endanger diners, since on rare occasions people have choked on them.

CULTIVATION AND PROPAGATION

Bay is best rooted from suckers or tip cuttings (cuttings from near the base of the plant root are easiest; those from the top can take months). Seed germination has varying results. Although native to Asia, bay laurel grows throughout the Mediterranean region. It likes the good drainage and rocky amendments of the soil there, the hot sun, and even moisture. It can get over 50 feet tall, but with regular pruning it can be kept at 10 to 12 feet tall. A row of bay shrubs makes a handsome hedge.

Bay will not get as large when grown in a container. It is a good container plant, which is especially handy for those who live in colder climates; the pot can be moved inside for the winter and back outdoors for the summer. The plant will become potbound and should be transplanted every two to three years.

HARVESTING AND PRESERVING

When harvesting bay leaves, which can be done as needed throughout the season as soon as they harden after emerging, do not just pick off a leaf. Plucking single leaves weakens the plant. It is best to snip off the stem tip, or a branch if you need to prune, and then pluck the leaves from that stem.

Keep freshly harvested leaves in a ziplock bag, folded over rather than zipped closed, on the inside door of the refrigerator. They will stay green and fresh for about three months. Even if they dry, they will be far superior to bay leaves bought at the grocery store, which can be up to two years old. Fresh bay leaves make a delectable syrup.

Nigella sativa dried
flowers and seeds

short-lived
annual, to 12
inches tall

does not
withstand
frost well

full sun

 keep moist but
not wet

 loamy soil,
average pH 6.9

BLACK CUMIN
Nigella sativa

Although the flowers of *Nigella sativa* are delicate and beautiful, they are not eaten nor is the dill-like foliage. Black cumin seeds have a complex flavor that is pungent, peppery, nutty, and sometimes acrid with an aroma reminiscent of lemony carrots or nutmeg. In India, the seeds are widely used in many spice mixtures, such as *panch phoron* (Bengali five spice) and curry blends, masalas, and kormas. When they aren't used in spice blends, they are most often used whole, not ground, and are added to stews, casseroles, and vegetarian recipes like lentil dishes. In northern India, black cumin is used to flavor the traditional naan bread baked in the clay tandoor ovens. In Egypt and the Middle East, the seeds are sprinkled on cakes, pastries, and breads. In Syria, cheese is mixed with black cumin seeds. The wide use of black cumin seed today is tied to its long history of use; it is mentioned in the Bible, Isaiah 28:25 (variously translated as dill, fitch, or fennel).

In the garden, *Nigella sativa* looks like a dwarf version of its close relative love-in-a-mist (*N. damascena*) or wild fennel. The flowers of black cumin are very similar to those of love-in-a-mist but a paler blue, almost white, carried above finely cut, fennel-like foliage.

We grow the species. Native to western Asia, southeastern Europe, and the Middle East, black cumin is easily grown almost anywhere.

CULTIVATION AND PROPAGATION
You can obtain seeds at stores stocking Indian or Middle Eastern foods. Black cumin seeds should be broadcast or sown in rows in tilled garden loam in late spring. Plants should be sown on site since they do not transplant well. Flowering occurs about two months later, followed by hollow, ½-inch-long, horned seedpods.

HARVESTING AND PRESERVING
When the pods turn tan and are dry, harvest them, and crush them in a large paper bag to release the seeds, about fifty per pod. Gently lower a vacuum nozzle inside the bag until you can pick up the light chaff and leave the heavier seeds. Store the seeds in labeled jars until the next season's harvest.

Borago officinalis

short-lived annual, to 28 inches tall

seedlings do not withstand frost well

full sun

keep constantly moist but not wet

loamy soil, average pH 6.6

BORAGE

Borago officinalis

Borage is cheery, in an awkward way. It is a bit clumsy of stem, with a sprawling footprint, but it bears beautiful star-shaped, blue or blue-pink flowers that sparkle against its large, coarse, hairy, green leaves. Both leaves and flowers have very little scent to the human nose, although the flowers attract pollinators.

Borage has long been employed as bee fodder, and the cucumber-flavored leaves have been eaten like spinach or were used to flavor aperitifs such as Pimm's Cup. Small leaves were sometimes eaten raw, while the larger leaves were steamed, which wilts the objectionable hairs. But recent research has found that both flowers and leaves contain pyrrolizidine alkaloids, which cause liver cancer when consumed in high concentrations, and hydrocyanic acid, so we no longer consume borage sandwiches, though Susan occasionally grabs a handful of small leaves and wilts them down with other potherbs. We still candy the blossoms, which are among

the prettiest candied flowers, and Susan floats the mild-flavored, slightly vegetal-tasting borage flowers on cucumber soup, Pimm's Cup, and perhaps a summer citrus punch, and uses them to garnish tzatziki and cream cheese spreads.

In spite of the alkaloid content, we also cultivate borage because it is a delight in the herb or flower garden and for its historic use. Seeds and plants of the species are available in many herb catalogs. Rarely, seeds of white- ('Alba' or 'Bianca') or pink-flowered borage surface in some specialty catalogs.

CULTIVATION AND PROPAGATION

Borage germinates quickly from broadcast seed in spring, and grows rapidly to about 28 inches with coarse 8-inch leaves and blue flowers appearing in June or July. Borage prefers well-drained, stony soil in full sun and only a moderate amount of water. In conditions to its liking, borage will reseed.

We delight in the lovely little blue star-shaped blooms of borage.

The white-flowered borage is a dainty and elegant cultivar.

Arctium lappa leaves and roots

hardy, coarse
biennial, 3 to 7
feet tall

hardy in
zones 2 to 10

full sun to
some shade

keep moist, but
grows wild in
waste areas

sandy loam,
neutral to
alkaline soil,
average pH 6.0

BURDOCK

Arctium lappa

Burdock (or gobo) is considered a bitter herb. The small leaves are green tasting and bitter. The first-year root is rather mild in flavor with some bitterness and starch under-tones, a bit earthy, nutty, and sweet. Freshly dug root smells of the earth, starchy like a potato but with wild elements added. The long roots, which can reach over 2 feet, have a brown outer covering and white interior and are dug in the first year, and stems are peeled and cooked like asparagus. The bitterness in the outer peel promotes digestion, so do not peel the root.

The small leaves can be eaten in salads, though they are usually cooked in two changes of water to remove the bitterness and added to soups or stir-fries. Large leaves get very tough and bitter. The root is tasty and nutritious. Use it as you would a carrot or parsnip—steamed, boiled, and mashed, or sliced and added to soups, stews, or casseroles. Both stems and roots are sliced and candied in maple syrup or sugar syrup.

Arctium lappa 'Gobo' is raised as a root crop in Japan, where it is sometimes soaked in water first to remove some of the bitterness, and then cooked in soups, stews, and stir-fries. Common burdock (*A. minus*) is found throughout the United States and Canada, and in some areas it is considered to be an invasive. It is also edible, though it is a smaller plant with smaller flowers and burrs.

CULTIVATION AND PROPAGATION

Many of us don't have to plant *Arctium lappa*, also known as greater burdock, since it grows wild and abundantly in northeastern North America. If you wish to cultivate it, seeds contained in the dried burrs can be easily germinated. Since the plant is very hardy and self sows readily, plant appropriately.

Because burdock sends down such a deep taproot, you should prepare a bed digging down at least 2 feet deep in loamy, sandy soil. Plant it in spring for a fall harvest and in fall for a spring harvest. First-year roots are the best to eat; during the second year, the plant flowers and sets seed, and the root becomes pithy.

HARVESTING AND PRESERVING

While leaves can be snipped when small, the long root has to be dug, and this can be quite a job. You need a shovel, digging fork, or even a digging bar or post-hole digger in order to dig down deep enough to get the whole root. After digging the root for the first time, you will realize that a very sandy soil can be a blessing.

If you want to dry the root, cut it into small, bite-sized pieces and put it in the dehydrator to dry, in an oven with the light on, or on screens in the sun (if you are in a place without much humidity). Be sure the pieces are completely dry before storing in labeled jars. Use it in soups or stews, or make it into a tasty root purée. Sliced fresh root can also be added to maple or sugar syrup, and simmered until tender. It should be stored in a clean glass jar, in the refrigerator. It is also eaten as a confection that aids digestion.

Calendula officinalis

fairly hardy
annual, 8 to 24
inches tall

will perish with
heavy frost; can
withstand minor
frost

full sun; part
shade where
temperatures
are hot

keep moist but
not wet

moderately
loamy soil,
average pH 6.6

CALENDULA
Calendula officinalis

The aroma of calendula (or pot marigold) flowers is honeylike, followed by a slightly spicy and then a woody odor, and just a little bitter, pungent aroma. If you bury your nose in the blooms, inhale, and think about it, there is a heady suggestion of rhubarb and angelica flowers, fruit, and just a hint of celery seed. The foliage, when rubbed, has a similar though much stronger smell, with concentrated resinous notes. The flavor is a bit challenging to describe; it varies with the cultivar and its cultivation. Petals are mild tasting, herbal, and slightly sweet, and some have just a hint of bitterness. An infusion of flower petals tastes like a gentle herbal tea. (An herbal infusion is the steeping or soaking of an herb in liquid, usually water, although it can be vinegar, alcohol, cream, or milk, to extract its flavor or aroma.) A longer infusion, which turns a golden orange color, is reminiscent of the liquid from cooking pumpkin or winter squash: it's sweet and veg-etablelike, perhaps a little woody.

Although the leaves are edible, they are very bitter, so just the flower petals are eaten. Calendula petals can be used in both savory and sweet dishes. Brought to America and used by the colonists to color butter and cheese, dried calendula petals have been called the poor man's saffron, and are used in place of the expensive spice for taste and color. The name pot marigold refers to calendula's use in the soup pot; it was often used to flavor and color broths. Infuse fresh or dried flower petals in milk to make puddings and custards; add them to herb butters and cream cheese for their bright yellow-orange color; incorporate them into batters for corn bread, bread, and cakes for color and mild flavor; cook them with grains like rice, in dishes like couscous, or in soups; and add fresh petals to vegetable salads, egg salad, and deviled eggs. Some fresh petals can be a little tough, and dried petals, even if cooked or infused, can be chewy, so you might want to mince or purée them before adding them to a recipe.

There is no better herb for heal-ing the skin than calendula because it helps boost cell growth. An oil infusion or salve made with the dried petals is good to use on dry skin, chapped lips, skin irritations,

'Calypso Orange' calendula is compact and valued for its reputedly high anti-inflammatory properties.

'Erfurter Orangefarbigen' calendula is grown commercially in Europe for its highly regarded medicinal virtues.

rashes, or to heal scars, but do not use it on open wounds.

We have grown several cultivars for years with good success: 'Calypso Orange', 'Erfurter Orange-farbigen', 'Flashback Mix', and 'Pacific Beauty'. 'Calypso Orange' has the highest faradiol content, which is responsible for calendula's anti-inflammatory activity. We have not grown a calendula that we didn't like. Mix it up—try blooms with petals in hues of bright orange, tangerine, school bus yellow, pale yellow, cream, pink, and even multicolored.

CULTIVATION AND PROPAGATION

Calendula is easily sown from seed. Seeds can be started indoors, or can be sown directly into the garden soil. Sow or transplant 10 to 12 inches apart. Since calendulas are cool-season annuals, blooms are bigger when grown in cool weather, so plant in early spring; they often have a resurgence of growth in the fall. In hotter zones, calendulas can suffer from too much heat and will stop flowering, so plant in part shade with moist soil as a possible counterpoint to the heat. There are heat-resistant cultivars.

HARVESTING AND PRESERVING

During the summer, to gather calendulas for cooking or drying, visit them at least every other day. Harvest flowers that are in full bloom or that have bloomed the day before. Bring them inside and leave them whole or remove the petals from the center disk (which tastes very bitter). Place the flower heads in a small baking pan or sprinkle the petals in the pan. Place them in an oven with a pilot light or with the light turned on (this will heat the oven to 100 to 110°F which is perfect for drying flowers). Turn the flower heads or occasionally fluff the petals that are drying, and add the new batch to dry. Every week or two, put the well-dried petals into a labeled, dark glass jar and store them in a dark place away from heat. They will keep until the next harvest season.

'Flashback Mix' contains blooms in many shades of cream to yellow to orange, often multicolored.

This old cultivar 'Pacific Beauty' is dependable and comes in orange or yellow.

Caper (*Capparis spinosa*) sprigs, with foliage, small flower buds, large fruits (seedpods), and brined capers

tender perennial
shrub, to 5 feet
tall

hardy to
zone 9

full sun

withstands
drought when
established

well-drained
soil, average
pH 7.5

CAPER

Capparis spinosa

Capers are usually eaten pickled. Pickled capers usually have the odor of the vinegar and herbs (like French tarragon) used in the pickling process, though they smell vegetal and slightly suggestive of an artichoke. The flavor of capers is reminiscent of salty, bitter green olives, a bit sharp, with a quality similar to pickled grape leaves.

In Mediterranean countries, caper plants grow wild on rocky cliffs by the sea, hanging over stone walls and emerging from cracks in old buildings—even hanging from the ruins at the Parthenon. The seeds have been most likely scattered by birds. The plants are evergreen in the hot summer months and produce caper buds throughout the season, so they should be harvested daily. Numerous cultivars are listed in the literature for Greece, Italy, and Spain, and are becoming available at selected nurseries. They may take extra effort to locate but are worth the search. Traditional cultivars include 'Nuciddara' and 'Testa di Lucertola' from Italy and 'Comun' and 'Mallorquina' from Spain.

In the past, when cooks wanted the flavor of capers but could not locate them, home gardeners would pickle young, green fruits of nasturtium (*Tropaeolum majus*). These can be a surprisingly good substitute. The taste is less bitter, though, and more sharply pungent.

CULTIVATION AND PROPAGATION

While most people have tasted capers, few realize that you can grow your own. But unless you live in a very warm climate, capers are treated as a tender perennial and grown in pots so they can be overwintered in the greenhouse.

Capers are borne on a shrub that has long, sprawling branches that can trail down or form a gentle mound to 5 feet and potentially 10 feet across. Flower buds, the capers, appear in each leaf joint from spring to fall, and a well-grown plant older than four years can yield more than 20 pounds of capers per year. If allowed to open, the buds produce an attractive 2- to 3-inch white blossom with four crepelike petals that lasts only a day. The fruits are tiny green pears with long stems.

Capers are propagated by cuttings or roots because of the variability of the seed. The named cultivars should be propagated only by cuttings.

HARVESTING AND PRESERVING

Raw capers are not palatable and must be pickled in the same manner as cucumbers before consuming. The home gardener may harvest the tender, young flower buds, which are ready when they are round, fat, about the size of a dried chickpea. Harvest them just before they bloom; that window is about

These caper flower buds are
ready to harvest.

one day from fat round bud to open flower, so they need to be checked every day early in the morning. Once they are harvested, wash and drop them into salted vinegar, along with the others that have been gathered throughout the season.

Alternatively, mix caper flower buds with salt overnight and then drop them into vinegar. The addition of French tarragon definitely improves the taste. The tiny buds (designated *nonpareil*) usually have more flavor than large ones (*capot*). In the Mediterranean area, small leaves or sprig tips are often added to the caper jars, though that is not seen much elsewhere. The immature fruits, or *taperons*, are also sometimes pickled, but the taste is more bitter and considered unpleasant to many; at any rate, it is an acquired taste. The young shoots may be consumed as a vegetable like asparagus.

Caraway (*Carum carvi*) sprigs,
with green seed heads, foliage,
flowers, and dried caraway seed

annual or biennial, to 59 inches tall

seedlings can withstand frost

full sun

keep moist but not constantly wet

light loamy soil, average pH 6.4

CARAWAY
Carum carvi

The seed of the caraway plant is closely associated with foods of northern and eastern Europe, especially rye bread. The smell and taste of rye bread and caraway go hand-in-hand—one does not think of one without the other. The aroma of ground caraway seed resembles dill seed and is pleasant, slightly woody, and resinous with a suggestion of celery seed. The flavor echoes the smell, except there are suggestions of citrus rind and earth and perhaps a little nuttiness.

For most dishes, the seed is crushed to release the oils but not ground. Caraway is also used in Swedish *limpa* bread and Irish soda bread. And it is delicious in coleslaw, potato salad, beef or lamb roast, liqueurs (like *Kümmel*), salad dressings, soups, applesauce, and baked fruit. A popular cake made in the British Isles is flavored with caraway seed and is enjoyed with tea. Caraway foliage is sometimes added to cheeses, salads, soups, or stews, but the flavor is rather bland. We often sprinkle sliced cheese with caraway, and it really is without equal in sauerkraut.

While caraway is commonly a biennial, annual forms are also available. In most seed catalogs, the biennial form is normally available, and most catalogs do not offer named cultivars or seed lines. The annual forms require a longer growing season than the biennial forms, and have a lower essential oil content in the seeds. The biennial forms tend to be dark brown seeded, while the annual forms tend to be light brown ("blond") seeded. The seed line called 'Mogador' is light brown and long seeded; 'Dutch' cultivar seeds are darker. 'Karzo' is recommended for the highest seed yield and highest essential oil content.

CULTIVATION AND PROPAGATION
Caraway seeds are sown from mid-spring to midsummer in full sun and well-tilled, humus-rich soil with good moisture retention. The optimum temperatures for germination are 59°F for eight hours and 50°F for sixteen hours. Germination may be increased to nearly 100 percent by soaking the seeds for three to six days and drying for four hours before planting.

Space plants 14 to 24 inches apart between and within rows. During the first year after sowing, the biennial form produces a 1-foot-high mound of fine leaves. Flowering occurs early the next summer, with 2-foot-tall hollow stems topped with white flowers. Seven weeks of cold temperatures, 46°F in the daytime and 41°F at night, is optimal for flowering, but rootstocks with a diameter less than ⅓ inch require longer vernalization (exposure to cold temperatures). Seed yield is directly correlated with the amount of sunlight between flowering and yield.

Because of the waste of space for a biennial crop like this, vegetables such as peas are sometimes intersown for maximum use of land. Caraway is subject to attack from a number of fungal diseases. The most injurious insect is the caterpillar of the caraway moth.

HARVESTING AND PRESERVING
Harvest plants with a sickle as soon as the oldest seeds mature. Partially dry the plants in sheds in large brown paper bags before threshing to avoid loss of seed. For the home gardener, a large plant will produce about ⅓ cup of seeds. Store thoroughly dry seeds in glass jars in a dark cupboard until next season's harvest.

Nepeta cataria

short-lived herbaceous perennial, to 3 feet tall

hardy to zone 4

full sun

keep moist but not constantly wet

well-drained loamy soil, average pH 6.6

CATNIP
Nepeta cataria

As the name indicates, cats like to nip catnip. To humans, the leaves smell slightly musky and herbaceous, with a hint of mint and perhaps a mere suggestion of chamomile, and the taste is similar to the aroma though a bit bitter. In herbal literature, catnip has been recommended as a sedative tea and used for cramps, although it has no GRAS status. Besides the comforting medicinal virtues of a cup of catnip tea, the leaves and flowers have been used to flavor sauces, soups, grains, and meat dishes. The herb appears often in Italian cookery, where it is used to season pasta, rice, grain dishes, and salads. The colorful flowers can be scattered judiciously in salads.

In addition to being attractive plants and useful in the kitchen, catnip will attract cats to your garden, and if you enjoy watching their antics, you'll witness a free feline circus! Cats will come from all around to roll in the catnip, even in winter. Unfortunately, they may crush the catnip plants and also valuable plants nearby, so beware. Interestingly, the crushed leaves and oil are among the most effective mosquito repellents available because of the fragrance. Almost all nepetas contain nepalactone, the organic compound that entices cats.

The straight species is most commonly available. The chief variant is lemon catnip (*Nepeta cataria* var. *citriodora*), which has the same sort of aroma and taste as other catnips but has a gentle lemony dimension that subdues the musky camphor notes. You may find such attractive examples as *N. mussinii* and *N.* 'Six Hills Giant', which have smaller foliage and abundant, blue-purple blooms.

CULTIVATION AND PROPAGATION
This short-lived perennial herb is usually grown from seed. We recommend starting seed indoors or in the greenhouse, and then putting transplants in the garden. Germination is best at 68 to 86°F, with seeds planted sixty to sixty-five days prior to transplanting. Cuttings are also easy to root and will quickly establish a uniform patch.

Well-drained soil suitable for garden vegetables is recommended for catnip. Fully acclimated transplants 6 to 8 inches tall should be planted two weeks before the last frost and spaced 9 to 12 inches apart in rows every 30 to 38 inches.

HARVESTING AND PRESERVING
Leaves can be harvested anytime during the growing season when you want to use them for tea or a recipe. Plants may be harvested two to three months after planting, when about 25 percent of the blooms have turned brown, which is an indication of optimal oil levels. In early morning, just after the dew has evaporated, harvest the stems 3 to 5 inches above the crown. Regrowth will occur from basal buds, and a second harvest may be made later in fall. Dry leaves to use for tea or feline fun and store them in labeled glass jars until next year's harvest.

Anthriscus cerefolium

short-lived
annual, to 28
inches tall

can withstand
frost

full sun to part
shade

keep moist but
not wet

soil rich in
organic matter,
average pH 6.7

CHERVIL

Anthriscus cerefolium

No herb, except perhaps tarragon, is quite so French as chervil, an association that is not surprising for a nation known for its celebration of fine food and the subtle use of herbs. At first sniff, chervil leaves have the fragrance of parsley, with a tarragonlike undernote. And indeed, many gourmets have described the flavor as resembling a refined combination of French tarragon and parsley, with perhaps a slight suggestion of pearlike fruit. Fresh chervil is among the four herbs comprising the classic blend *fines herbes*, with parsley, chives, and tarragon. This French quartet is used fresh or only briefly cooked. The small white flowers have a similar, milder flavor like the leaves and can be used as a garnish in lighter dishes, salads, and even fruit.

Chervil is a short-lived but rather cold-hardy annual. The species is most commonly available. However, if you can find it, the chervil cultivar 'Brussels Winter' tolerates cold well and is a little slower to begin flowering.

CULTIVATION AND PROPAGATION

Some home gardeners characterize chervil as finicky. Successful cultivation of the plant depends on timing, because it grows best in cool, moist soil in full winter sun or in part shade in late spring and fall. Chervil also prefers soils that drain well and have a nearly neutral pH. Good soil drainage and fertility are important factors for achieving large, productive plants. As far south as zone 7, chervil is best grown as a fall or winter crop. In the colder reaches of this growing area, we advise using a cold frame or similar winter protection.

Chervil flourishes in cool spring and fall conditions, especially when midday temperatures hover between 40 to 50°F, when plants will become lush and richly textured and may reach over 12 inches in diameter. When warm weather arrives, overwintered plants stop producing foliage and send up flower stems 24 to 30 inches high topped by umbels of small, white blossoms that produce seed before the plant dies. In areas where summers are hot, chervil does best in part or full shade, although the combination of heat and shade seems to render the plants weak and susceptible to spider mite infestation.

Chervil produces dark brown, 1-inch, splinterlike seeds (really fruits) that may be sown directly in the garden. When an early start is needed to catch the most desirable weather, start plants indoors and transplant into pots. Bare-root seedlings of chervil transplanted directly in the garden often fail, but pot-grown transplants take hold quickly during cool growing conditions. When taking advantage of warm soil to start the seedlings indoors or in a greenhouse, allow four to five weeks from seeding to transplanting. Chervil seed will not germinate in soil that is too warm; this characteristic keeps chervil seed scattered in spring from germinating during summer heat when the plants are most likely to struggle or die. Seeds sown in early spring or late fall when soil temperatures are cooler germinate in about fourteen days.

HARVESTING AND PRESERVING

Drying and the heat of cooking can easily destroy the delicate flavor of chervil leaves and flowers, so the herb is best used fresh from the garden. Use chervil to make a tasty herb butter.

Stellaria media

spreading annual
that often
overwinters, 6 to
12 inches tall

hardy in
zones 3 to 8

sun or part
shade

keep moist

moist soil,
pH 6.0

CHICKWEED

Stellaria media

This wild green, which grows in abundance in our gardens, provides us with a lovely green ground cover with tiny, star-shaped white flowers. It is also a valuable food with medicinal properties. It is native to Europe, and has spread throughout North America. And indeed, as the name suggests, chickens do love it. The small, bright green leaves have a sweet, fresh, green scent, which is pealike. The stems have hairs on them. The flavor is mildly sweet and green tasting, a little earthy, with suggestions of minerals, and chickweed does contain nutrients and trace minerals such as calcium, potassium, and some iron. The flower buds and tiny flowers are edible too, so just harvest them along with the leaf tips.

New spring growth, and recurrence of new growth in the fall after summer's heat (unless summers are mild where you live and then you might have it all season), are the best times to enjoy chickweed. Big, new lush growth is best. Later in the season when plants get stressed or start to form seeds and their production slows, chickweed can get stringy and tough and the leaves are much smaller.

This potherb is delightful raw in salads, on sandwiches, added to salsa verde, spreads, or dips, or cooked briefly, in the greens pot, soups, sauces, or stirred into eggs, stir-fries, or pasta.

We are fortunate to have tasty, nutritious chickweed volunteer all over our gardens, in all seasons except winter. When gathering any food from the wild, be sure that the area has not been sprayed with pesticides and that you have properly identified the plant. There are many other weeds that grow in proximity with chickweed, and two in particular resemble *Stellaria media*: scarlet pimpernel (*Anagallis arvensis*) and mouse-ear chickweed (*Cerastium vulgatum*). Scarlet pimpernel is a poisonous plant that differs from chickweed in that it has scarlet flowers and a square stem, is hairless, and has small dark spots on the underside of the leaves. Mouse-ear chickweed can be eaten, and looks similar to *S. media*, though leaf growth tends to be sparser. It has hairs on both the tops and undersides of the leaves and the stems are hairy and sticky, whereas chickweed only has hairs on the stem.

CULTIVATION AND PROPAGATION

If you do not have this prolific herb growing in your garden, it can be sown from seed. The plant grows in rosettes and travels across the ground spreading outward, and upward if it is crowded. Harvesting the tips will encourage growth.

HARVESTING AND PRESERVING

Although the entire aboveground plant can be harvested as a fresh green for salad or for cooking with other greens as a side dish, or added to soups or sautés, the inner stems of this spreading plant are tougher, with smaller leaves, and tend to hold more grit. Therefore, snipping bite-sized lengths (about 2 inches) of the tender tips with scissors is the most efficient way to harvest chickweed for the kitchen. It requires less cleaning and the new leaf growth at the stem ends is bigger and newer, therefore more tender. The older stems can be downright chewy because of their tough, threadlike inner core. Also, tip pruning encourages more new growth on the tips.

Harvest stem tips for drying and medicinal preparations. Chickweed promotes healing and soothes itching, so it is used as a poultice and in salves for the skin. Leaves dry quickly spread on screens or in baskets. If it is humid where you live, dry them on baking sheets for a few hours in an oven with a pilot light, or turn the oven light on. Check them every hour or so and remove them immediately once they are dry. Store in labeled dark glass jars for about three months for culinary purposes and about six months for medicinal applications.

Cichorium intybus
leaves and flowers

common
perennial, 1 to 3
feet tall

hardy in
zones 3 to 9

full sun

keep soil moist

well-drained
soil, optimum
pH 5.5

CHICORY

Cichorium intybus

The leaves, flowers, and roots of this naturalized roadside weed are edible. Leaves and flowers have an herbaceous, slightly bitter aroma, and the flowers smell mildly sweet. Small leaves and flowers can be eaten in salads; both are bitter tasting and mildly astringent, so they should be combined with other salad greens or ingredients. Gather flowers early in the day when they are open. Leaves and blooms wilt rather quickly and do not last as a cut flower.

The leaves are also often used as a potherb. The fresh roots have long been cooked as a food though they are earthy and rooty tasting, a bit bland, and slightly bitter. In many parts of the world, chicory root is dried and roasted as a beverage. Although some regard chicory root as a substitute for coffee, it is really used best as an additive to coffee. Young roots are best, since older roots are even more bitter.

We like to gather the wild, naturalized *Cichorium intybus* (common chicory) leaves and flowers. There are also many domesticated types (endives) that you can grow for their broader leaves; they are somewhat bitter, but cooking lessens that characteristic. There are loose-leaf heads such as the tall 'Treviso'

types, the 'Sugarloaf' types that grow more like a romaine lettuce, and the 'Chioggia' types that have a more rounded head. There are also some upright plants that resemble dandelions and are sometimes called Italian dandelions; you can cultivate them and they are bitter but good. All add a pleasingly bitter dimension to salads or wilted vegetables.

CULTIVATION AND PROPAGATION

You will find this plant along fields, roadsides, and railroad tracks. If cultivating it, plant it in somewhat moist, well-drained soil, especially if you want healthy root growth. It will tolerate sandy and even claylike soils, as well as acid to alkaline soils. The cultivated varieties prefer loamy soil and cool weather, so they can be grown as fall-winter-spring crops.

The art of blanching Belgian endive (also known as *witloof*, meaning "white leaf," in Dutch), which is a member of the genus *Cichorium*, has been practiced in Europe and North America for many years. Forcing the leaves to grow without light reduces the bitterness, and these tended heads are considered gourmet additions to salads or as cooked vegetables.

HARVESTING AND PRESERVING

The eye-catching blue-purple flowers of common chicory open just after sunrise, last only 4 to 5 hours on hot, sunny days, and then close about noon. If it is cooler and cloudy, they will remain open for pollinators all day. So if you want them on your salad and it is sunny and hot, harvest them early in the day. Prepare them, as well as small leaves, for lunch, or wrap them in damp paper towels and refrigerate until suppertime. Leaves can be dried for soups and stews.

If harvesting the root, dig down deep to get the long taproot. Trim the root, scrub the dirt away, and slice. The root can be roasted on baking sheets until dry and golden brown, which gives it a caramel-like flavor. Once cooled, it can be ground and added to coffee or enjoyed on its own as a beverage. It has also been added to beer, especially stouts.

Capsicum annuum 'Fish'

shrublike perennials, 15 inches to 4 feet tall

hardy only in frost-free areas

full sun

keep moist but not constantly wet

loamy, friable soil, average pH 6

CHILE PEPPER

Capsicum species

The aroma and flavor of the capsicums are as varied and bright as their myriad vivid colors. The range in the pungency of chiles from mild to wild is created by the capsaicin content, the hot element in the ribs and seeds of the chiles. A poblano pepper might have just a hint of heat, while a habanero or a fish pepper can be downright incendiary. The term "nose-twister" (as Louise Beebe Wilder refers to nasturtiums in *The Fragrant Path*) is an apt description of what happens when you inhale the aroma of a chile pepper. For "chileheads," smelling the pungency foretells the heat to come on the tongue and then of the endorphins that are secreted, giving you a feeling of well being and creating the desire for more. You can become addicted to chile peppers, and you can build up your chile tolerance from not-so-hot to hot-hot-hot!

Chiles originated in the Americas and are used in cooking around the world. There are many species and cultivars you can choose from. Fresh, they are chopped and used in salsas, escabèches, guacamole, kimchee, and salads of all kinds. They are cooked in chili with beans and meat, sauces, soups, stews, stir-fries, noodle dishes, marinades, pickles, jelly, and jam. Once roasted to remove the skins, they are peeled and stuffed with cheese, meat, or vegetables to make rellenos and poppers, or chopped and simmered in sauces, chilis, soups, and stews. Chiles are delicious with eggs and cheese and baked in corn bread or biscuits. Beans without chiles are like a day without sunshine.

Many types of chiles are dried, some left whole for cooking with beans and in stews, while others are ground and made into ground red chile powder for making red chile sauce for enchiladas or tacos. This ground chile is combined with herbs and spices to make the blend called chili powder, which is used to make chili con carne or chili with beans.

Warning: Handling uncut capsicums without gloves is okay, but in the kitchen when cutting chiles, wear disposable gloves.

Capsicum annuum **'Fish'**, also referred to as fish pepper, got its name in the late nineteenth and early twentieth centuries, when cooks grew it, especially in southern North America and northern South America, for use with seafood—from crabs and oysters to terrapin—and especially in cream sauces. This variegated-leaved plant has come back into favor, not only as a handsome specimen in the garden, but also because of the small striated peppers that go from cream and green to yellow to orange and red as they mature. The flavor is slightly fruity and very hot, so 'Fish' chiles are a good choice for making salsa and especially a concentrated, fermented sauce like Tabasco. Since they are fairly thin-walled, they dry well and make good ground red chile pepper flakes.

Capsicum annuum **'Poblano'** is a large, thin-walled, dark green pepper. It is most often roasted and peeled to make *chiles rellenos* or to be used in green chile sauce or stew. It has a delicious, deep, hearty flavor that is enhanced by roasting. Generally, their heat is mild to medium, although some can be quite hot. These require a longer growing time to maturity than, say, a jalapeño. When matured to deep red and dried, the poblano becomes a mahogany-colored *ancho* and is used to flavor soups, stews, and chilis. It is an essential dried pepper for making chili powder.

'Anaheim', **'New Mexico'**, and **'Numex Big Jim'** are all good choices for roasting and making rellenos and green chile sauce. The first two have medium heat, while the latter is mostly mild and quite large. The 'Anaheim' and 'New Mexico' chiles, once matured to red, are used to make *ristras*, which are strings of chiles strung by their stems with heavy twine and hung up to dry. These are ground after they are dried and made into

'Lemon Drop' chiles

ground red chile used in making sauces and chili powder.

***Capsicum annuum* 'Serrano'** is an essential chile to grow—one we could not live without. Although this pepper is not very big, it packs a piquant punch and has a very pleasant chile taste. Some serranos can be hotter than others, depending on how and where they are grown. Serranos can be eaten green (used like a jalapeño) or red; when red, they are good for drying and using in chili powder, soups, and sauces.

Jalapeños and serranos can be used interchangeably in recipes, though the jalapeño is crunchier and juicier, tasting more like a green bell pepper that is hot. While the jalapeño is larger and has thicker walls, the amount of heat added to a dish, chile for chile, is about the same. Because jalapeños have thick flesh, they are challenging to dry. Most often they are smoke dried and are then called chipotles. Researchers recently have developed jalapeños with no heat, which is an oxymoron. So read seed packets and plant labels to avoid disappointment.

***Capsicum chinense* 'Fatali'** is one hot chile; as the cultivar name infers, "fatal." These handsome, elongated, wrinkled fruits turn from yellow to red and are extremely hot in both stages. When they are cut open, their aroma, besides being nose-twisting, has a fruity fragrance with hints of apricot and citrus, which carries through in the flavor. They are tasty in salsas, especially ones made with tropical fruits, guacamole, escabèches, and with eggs and cheese.

'Lemon Drop' is a Peruvian chile that is delightfully citrus-flavored with a good amount of heat. This tasty yellow capsicum can be used like a 'Fatali', but it does not have nearly the pungency.

Habaneros (*Capsicum chinense*) have a reputation for being high up on the scale for heat, and deservedly so. These lantern-shaped peppers range from very hot to incendiary and come in colors from yellow and orange to scarlet red and brown. Habs, as they are affectionately called, have a fruity aroma and flavor, with hints of apricot and just a touch of citrus and smoke. Use them carefully in salsas, marinades, shrubs, and in beans, sauces, soups, and chilis. 'Chocolate', 'Caribbean Red', 'Scotch Bonnet', and 'Rocotillo' are all good selections. A family of four only needs one or two habanero plants, unless they are serious chileheads.

CULTIVATION AND PROPAGATION

A primary consideration for growing chile pepper plants is how much space you have in your garden for them. Depending on variety, each plant needs 2 to 3 feet around it, full sunlight, and good soil. Chiles are good container plants if the containers are roomy enough.

Select chile plants at a nursery, or start seed indoors in small pots, in moistened, sterile, soilless potting medium with one part perlite to two parts spaghnum peat moss. Cover the seeds lightly with about ⅛ inch potting mix, and spray or mist with water. Once seeds germinate, place in a spot where they get a minimum of eight hours of sun a day (or under grow lights). After four to six weeks, the plants should be ready to be hardened off, a process in which you put the plants outside for a time each day and gradually acclimatize them to outdoor conditions for about two weeks before planting into the garden.

Chile peppers grow best in loamy soil with plenty of humus. The plants benefit when their beds have organic matter, such as compost or aged manure, worked into the soil. A little greensand or wood ashes, good sources of potash, are also good additions. Good drainage is essential, whether chile plants are grown in the garden or in containers.

Although all capsicums from bell peppers to chiles can be harvested when they are green, if left on the vine, a mature pepper turns red when it is ripe. Chile peppers can be quite hot in their green stage, as well as in the red, ripe, mature stage, although the red stage is sweeter tasting.

HARVESTING AND PRESERVING

Once they are big enough, pick green chiles to use anytime during the growing season. It is good to harvest chiles throughout the season to encourage more fruit. When most of the chiles on the plants have matured to red, it is time to harvest and dry them or to pull the plants and hang them to dry. Dry air, hot sun, and warm nights provide the ideal conditions; with low moisture and even sunlight, chiles can dry in less than one week. In regions with high humidity and where sunlight and temperature are uneven, chiles can be dried in the sun, but they must be brought indoors at night or if it rains. Peppers can mold if they become wet or damp during the drying process.

Smaller chile peppers dry well if the whole plant is pulled and hung upside down in a well-ventilated place. Small fruits can also be dried if they are spread in a single layer in large, flat baskets or on screens, and turned every day so they dry evenly. They can also be strung through the stems and hung to dry.

Bigger peppers with thicker walls take longer to dry. Spread them on baskets or screens to dry, or make ristras and hang in the hot sun to dry.

A completely dried chile should feel leathery rather than brittle and be free of moisture. Drying time will vary greatly according to the size of the pepper, thickness of the flesh, and the weather. In humid areas, capsicums can be partially dried in the sun and finished off in a 150 to 175°F oven. Spread them on baking sheets and cook, turning them occasionally. Drying in the oven can take from one to forty-eight hours, depending on the size and moisture content of the chiles. The aroma in the house will be mouthwatering. Remove the smaller chiles as they dry and let cool. Store dried chiles whole in tightly closed glass jars and label them. Thoroughly dried chiles will keep in jars out of direct light for at least a year.

'Rocotillo' chiles

Allium schoenoprasum

	❀	///	☀	💧	⁘
Common chives (*Allium schoenoprasum*)	herbaceous perennial, to about 12 inches tall	hardy to zone 5	full sun	keep moist, well drained	loamy soil, average pH 6.3
Garlic chives (*Allium tuberosum*)	short-lived herbaceous perennial, to about 2 feet, flopping	hardy to zone 5	full sun to part shade	keep moist, well-drained	loamy soil, average pH 6.3

CHIVES

Allium species

Common chives (*Allium schoeno-prasum*) have a distinctive, herbal, green taste with decided onion overtones. Sometimes, cut onion tops, scallion tops, or Japanese bunching onion tops are substituted for chives, but they cannot match the flavor. If your so-called "chives" are extraordinarily large and carry too much leeklike flavor, suspect a substitution. Many plants of genus *Allium* have pungent tall, narrow, green leaves and similar pink to purple blossoms.

The marriage of chives from the Old World and potatoes from the New World was truly inspired. Baked potatoes with sour cream and chives are a standard offering in North American restaurants. Some potato salad recipes are incomplete without chives. The leaves of chives are used for soups, salads, and vegetable dishes, and are among the traditional four French *fines herbes* along with tarragon, parsley, and chervil. The buds and blossoms are also edible and fairly pungent, and may be pickled in vinegar, used in a flavorful butter, and scattered fresh as a tasty garlic-flavored garnish over any dish from vegetables, grains, and pasta to pizza and meats.

We usually grow *Allium schoeno-prasum* 'Fine Leaf', because of the flavor in the fine, hollow leaves. Other chives cultivars include 'Corsican White', 'Grosser Riesen', 'Mittelgrosser Schnittlauch', 'Feine Schnittlauch', and 'Forescate'. A cultivar of large chives is 'Fruhlau'.

An Asian counterpart to European chives is garlic chives (*Allium tuberosum*). As the name denotes, garlic chives combine the delicate, herbal note of chives with a robust note of garlic. Versatile garlic chives can be used like chives, onions, or garlic, though the taste is most similar to garlic but just a bit less pungent. Garlic chives are especially good in stir-fries. Add them during the last few minutes of cooking to avoid stringiness. Garlic chives have white flowers.

Chinese and Korean growers have a number of different, local cultivars available, but, sadly, the choice in the rest of the world is usually the straight species (*Allium tuberosum*). But if you search in gourmet herb catalogs, you may be

Common chive umbels

Garlic chives have white flowers that bloom from midsummer to late summer.

able to find our choice, 'Nira', which has big, bulky plants for ease of harvesting and is the most attractive for a floral arrangement.

CULTIVATION AND PROPAGATION
Chives grow easily in full sun in a moist, near-neutral garden loam. Chives may be grown from seeds, and clumps should be divided every three to four years. Chives' native habitat is stream banks and damp meadows; the herb will not withstand prolonged drought. Give top dressings of nitrogen during the season, according to the vigor of the crop and level of production you want to get. Organic mulch improves the yield, and wheat straw is particularly recommended.

While garlic chives may enliven a stir-fry, they are sometimes unwanted in the garden. The prolific seeds seem to sprout everywhere, and kneeling on a clump of garlic chives surprises both the senses and the laundry bill. You can practice deadheading (removal of the blossoms before seed-set), but because individual clumps are often short-lived, you may want to allow some seeds to form.

The traditional Chinese method of growing garlic chives is to direct-sow fresh seeds into beds 3 feet by 15 feet in 4-inch-deep drills as soon as the ground can be worked in the spring. You will get faster and more even germination from pre-germinated seed: soak seeds overnight in warm water, strain off water, wrap in clean, wet cloth, place them at 65 to 76°F for four to five days, sow, and cover with a thin layer of straw. The following spring, transplant in clumps of twenty to thirty seedlings 4 to 6 inches apart in rows 20 inches apart. In China, the leaves are commonly blanched under clay "chimney pots" and top-dressed with ½ to 2 inches of sand to produce delicately flavored yellow leaves. A well-grown clump can yield more than 8 pounds of chives per year.

HARVESTING AND PRESERVING

At home, harvest both common and garlic chives as needed, taking the outside leaves first rather than shearing the entire plant. In commercial production where this is not feasible, the entire clump of plants is cut 2 inches above the ground.

The clump regenerates only after several weeks, and then with very tender new growth. Cutting also encourages new bulblets and discourages flowering. Chives may also be forced for fresh leaves during winter. One study in Germany found that the base and center of the leaves were "juicier and crisper," while the tips were "strawy/fibrous and drier."

Common chives are best used fresh, although they can be snipped into a freezer container and kept in the freezer for three to four months. Both flowers and foliage make a tasty herb butter, and the flowers make a lavender-hued vinegar.

Garlic chives are also best used fresh. The leaves can be harvested the second year, with three harvests per season. After the third or fourth year, chive plants deteriorate. Garlic chives may also be forced for winter production. Garlic chives can be used to make garlic butter or garlic vinegar.

The five stages of cilantro (*Coriandrum sativum*): cilantro leaves, lacy leaves, flowers, green seeds, and dried seeds. These dried seeds are an Indian type, which are oval in shape rather than round like the commonly found coriander seeds.

annual, to 3
feet tall

seedlings can
withstand
light frost

full sun

keep moist but not
constantly wet

light loamy
soil, average
pH 6.6

CILANTRO

Coriandrum sativum

Cilantro is the Spanish word for the leaves of the coriander plant and is the plant name generally used throughout the United States. This herb has two faces: one is the leaf that smells of stinkbugs to some, and the other the fruit that smells of a flowery, citrus spice. Green fruits smell and taste of the foliage, along with a resinous citrus endnote, but acquire a spicy, floral aroma and a chestnut-like color when dry.

While the inimitable odor of the leaves may be off-putting to some, the taste becomes muted when cooked and provides a deep flavor rather than a sharp accent to accompany food. The leaves are sometimes described as tasting soapy or cloying, but they are better described as green and herbaceous, slightly resinous. The leaves are used in cuisines around the globe, from Latino-inspired recipes like salsa and guacamole to African dishes to spicy Thai foods and Chinese fare. They combine well with spicy and pungent food, especially chile peppers.

We usually grow the species (*Coriandrum sativum*) for the leaves, not the seed (or fruits), called coriander, the spice. Therefore, seed lines that have large leaves and are slow to bolt are especially desired. 'Calypso' is the slowest to bolt, and the plants provide a high yield of leaves. 'Santo' and 'Slo-Bolt' are also slow-bolting and bear a good yield of leaves; 'Slo-Bolt' withstands warm weather well. These cultivars do not send up their seed stalks as quickly and generally last three to four weeks longer in the garden.

CULTIVATION AND PROPAGATION
Coriandrum sativum is a crop for cool spring weather. Moderating heat with shade cloth will also extend the period of foliage harvest.

Cilantro is grown from seed sown in near-neutral garden loam where it will receive full sun. Seeds sown

**Cilantro blooms with green
seeds forming.**

directly in the garden have a low
germination rate, usually less than
50 percent. Germination can be
enhanced above 60 percent by rubbing the seeds until the fruit halves
separate, then soaking them for
three to four days and letting them
dry for eight hours before planting.
For the home gardener, the seed
can be broadcast or planted in rows
or raised beds; allow 9 to 32 inches
between rows.

Sow seed as soon as the soil
can be worked in spring and after
danger of heavy frost is past.
Germination begins about four days
after sowing, when the rubbing and
soaking method is used, or after
about twenty-five days otherwise.
Cilantro does not successfully

compete with weeds, so mulch or cultivation is important. Keep evenly moist during growth. Also, early fall cilantro plantings will produce leaves for several weeks, even after the first light frosts. Use a floating row cover on fall cilantro to extend the harvest season.

HARVESTING AND PRESERVING

Leaves are harvested about one month after sowing. Foliage is usually hand-harvested by shearing the outermost leaves. New growth will come within a few days from the center of the plant. Leaf harvesting continues until the central flower stem rises and leaf production ceases. The white flowers can be harvested for salads and garnishes.

The leaves do not dry well, but can be preserved by freezing or making an aromatic paste.

Harvest coriander stems when about half the seeds have changed from green to tannish-gray or when the seeds on the central umbels are ripe, preferably in the morning when dew acts to prevent shattering. Then place in paper bags to dry thoroughly. Shake the bags to remove most of the seeds from the stems, but some manual removal may be required. The dried leafy parts are easily removed with a gentle lowering of a vacuum cleaner nozzle into the bag. Store cleaned coriander seeds in labeled jars out of direct light for a year, until the next growing season.

Dianthus plumarius 'Ipswich Pinks'

herbaceous perennial, 3 to 31 inches tall

hardy to zone 5

full sun

keep moist but not constantly wet

light loamy soil, average pH 7.0

CLOVE PINKS

Dianthus species

The fragrance of clove pinks, as the name suggests, is intensely clove-like. An alternate old name, "sops in wine," comes from the use of clove pinks blossoms to flavor wine in the sixteenth and seventeenth centuries. The taste of these blooms is mildly sweet, with hints of clove, sometimes vanilla, or is vaguely minty; the foliage from these edible flowers is not eaten. These days, clove pinks have limited use for flavoring wine, but have a particularly decorative edible flower. Use the petals as a decoration in a *Maibowle* (a traditional German punch of white wine or white grape juice flavored with sweet woodruff and decorated with strawberries and flowers) or on cakes and serving platters of desserts.

Dianthus caryophyllus has been frequently hybridized with the closely related *D. plumarius*, grass or cottage pinks, which has flowers with deeply cut, ragged petals. Don't worry about the genealogy; just let your nose be your guide when these popular flowers are in bloom. We particularly recommend the very old hybrid 'Gloriosa' for its intense clove perfume and exceptional vigor. It is a double pinks–carnation hybrid with a darker "eye."

CULTIVATION AND PROPAGATION

Many species of *Dianthus* are particularly adapted to well-drained alkaline soil in full sun to zone 5, sometimes even to zone 3. Clove pinks and grass pinks have low, spiky blue-green foliage and make effective edge plantings or ground covers, particularly in rock gardens. Propagation, especially of *D. plumarius* 'Ipswich Pinks' and 'Gloriosa', is primarily from cuttings or layering. Because the stems of pinks are hollow, the cuttings are sometimes called pipings. Pipings may be taken any time of the year, but they root best during cool weather. Seed propagation is easy, although it will not perpetuate the named cultivars.

HARVESTING AND PRESERVING

Harvest fresh flowers when at the height of fragrance; they are best used fresh. Flowers can be made into a syrup or candied. Drying preserves only a little of the fragrance.

Plectranthus amboinicus

succulent, sprawling tender perennial shrub, to about 3 feet tall

 extremely sensitive to frost, not hardy above zone 9

 full sun

 keep moist but not constantly wet

light loamy soil, average pH 6.0

CUBAN OREGANO
Plectranthus amboinicus

Also called Puerto Rican oregano, Indian borage, or Spanish thyme, Cuban oregano may be substituted for Greek oregano (*Origanum vulgare* subsp. *hirtum*). However, the large (up to 2¾ inches), fleshy, fuzzy leaves are not easily manipulated by cooks accustomed to using crushed, dried oregano leaves. In parts of India, the leaves are dipped in *pakora* batter (a spicy Indian batter the consistency of pancake batter) and fried. Cuban oregano is often used to flavor salsas.

The thick leaves smell stinky to some noses—like cilantro (it has some similar elements)—though it does smell similar to common oregano with fruity and musky notes. The crunchy, juicy leaves taste like a resinous oregano with mucilage; use in small amounts.

The straight species (*Plectranthus amboinicus*) is typically cultivated for cooking use. As a fragrant ornamental, 'Well Sweep Wedgewood', with a cream-colored center, is very attractive. 'Variegata' has leaves edged in white.

CULTIVATION AND PROPAGATION
Like the other members of genus *Plectranthus* (including Swedish ivy [*P. australis*]) and the closely related colorful coleuses, this low, perennial shrub requires full sun and fertile garden loam with constant moisture. Under optimum conditions in the garden, Cuban oregano can reach 39 inches in height, but plants in pots rarely reach half that. Winter temperatures should not be below 40°F, so in cooler areas, plant in pots and overwinter preferably in a cool greenhouse.

HARVESTING AND PRESERVING
Cuban oregano is best eaten fresh. The fleshy, young leaves can be harvested constantly. They do not dry well.

Eryngium foetidum

tender biennial, to about 16 inches tall

cannot withstand frost

full sun

keep moist

friable garden loam, average pH 5.6

CULANTRO

Eryngium foetidum

Culantro is a heat-tolerant plant that can serve as a substitute for cilantro; the fragrance and flavor are comparable. The plant is native to Mexico and South America but is grown around the world. It is particularly popular in Latino and Caribbean cuisine, and is widely used in Southeast Asia and India. The thin, spiky leaves and green leafy flower bracts are a bit milder than cilantro, with a suggestion of the soapy taste and a green, herbaceous, slightly resinous aftertaste. In addition to heat tolerance, culantro retains its flavor well when dried, in contrast to cilantro leaves, which taste like tissue paper when dried. The leaves are adorned with soft spines that wilt with cooking.

Only the straight species is available at most herb nurseries, although different selections are available in Asia.

CULTIVATION AND PROPAGATION

Culantro is easily cultivated in moist garden loam if started early indoors and transplanted after any chance of spring frost. After spring-planted cilantro has ceased to produce leaves because of heat, culantro will continue to grow. It also does well as a container plant. So in cooler areas, plant in pots and overwinter preferably in a cool greenhouse.

Slugs and snails have a peculiar affinity for culantro and can become a major problem if preventive measures are not taken. Mealy bugs may also infest the tightly packed leaves and are virtually impossible to eliminate. So discard the parent plant and sow the mature seeds.

HARVESTING AND PRESERVING

Culantro, like the other herbs that can be used as cilantro substitutes, is best used fresh. Storage at 50°F in plastic bags will extend its shelf life to two weeks, compared to four days at ambient supermarket conditions. Blanching quickly in hot water at 205°F, prior to drying, helps to preserve the green color. Dry leaves on baking sheets in the oven with pilot light or light on until thoroughly dried. Store dried leaves in labeled, glass jars out of direct sunlight for three to six months.

Cumin (*Cuminum cyminum*) foliage
and flowers with dried cumin seed

annual, to 20 inches tall

 can withstand slight frost

 full sun

 keep moist but not constantly wet

 light soil, average pH 7.3

CUMIN
Cuminum cyminum

Cumin seed is an integral part of curries, chilis, beans, and Mexican cuisine. It is also used to flavor meats, pickles, cheeses, sausages, salsas, soups, and stews. The odor of ground cumin is warming, sweetly fragrant, slightly fatty, and resinous, The inimitable flavor combines all of the wonderful aromas, especially the resinous, spicy, and nutty qualities, followed by soft, mellow, green, and earthy notes with just a suggestion of citrus oil.

We grow the straight species, which is the only one usually available.

CULTIVATION AND PROPAGATION
The fruits (the seeds) of cumin lose their viability quickly after one year, so seed lots should be tested for germination success. Good seeds will have at least 70 percent germination. Cumin is commercially cultivated in India in garden loam with fine tilth of a near-neutral pH.

For the home garden, germination is improved by soaking seeds in running water for twenty-four to thirty-six hours before planting to remove germination inhibitors.

Cumin is a cool-weather crop, so it must be planted in early spring or early fall, since it requires three to four months of growth to produce mature seeds. Cumin is picky: plants refuse to grow in spots that are too windy, too wet, too dry, too cold, or too hot. Plant seeds 2½ to 3 inches apart.

Cumin plants seldom exceed 6 to 8 inches in height and are spindly with threadlike leaves. They can become engulfed by weeds if the gardener is not diligent. Cumin can be grown easily in large pots.

HARVESTING AND PRESERVING
Harvest when the fruits start to turn brown, and then dry them. Gather the plants in a large paper bag, hang to dry in a shed, and then shake and bruise the plants to release the seed. Remove the chaff easily by slowly lowering a vacuum nozzle into the bag, sucking in the chaff and leaving the heavier seed behind. Store the cleaned seed in labeled jars out of direct light for up to a year. Before using cumin in a recipe, we generally toast the seeds lightly and then grind them.

Bergera koenigii

tender shrub to small tree, 13 to 20 feet tall	hardy to zone 9	full sun	keep evenly moist	garden loam

CURRY LEAF

Bergera koenigii (Murraya koenigii)

Curry leaf is an essential ingredient of curries in India and throughout Southeast Asia. It is also used in soups, chutneys, and with fish and meat dishes and vegetables. The smell of curry leaf has been described as distinctly currylike with overtones of gasoline. We do not recommend consuming curry leaf by itself because the strong resinous and savory spice flavor is too intense, but it mellows considerably when combined with other fresh spices like cumin, coriander, turmeric, or ginger. Use the whole leaves in soups, stews, curries, and marinades, wherever the flavor of curry is desired, then remove the leaves before serving.

Seeds and plants of the species are available through specialty herb catalogs. Named cultivars are available in Asia, though they are rare elsewhere.

CULTIVATION AND PROPAGATION
Outside tropical areas, you can easily cultivate curry leaf in most garden soils in containers, with no particular restrictions except that it be kept free of frost. So in cooler areas, plant in pots and overwinter preferably in a cool greenhouse.

HARVESTING AND PRESERVING
Harvest curry leaf fresh since leaves lose their flavor when dried. The leaves can be frozen in ziplock bags for up to three months.

Dandelion (*Taraxacum officinale*)
leaves, flowers, and root

hardy
perennial, 6 to
12 inches tall

hardy in
zones 3 to 10

full sun but
will grow in
part shade

keep moist,
though will
grow in most
disturbed soils

rich soil, pH 6.5

DANDELION

Taraxacum officinale

The smell of a dandelion flower is slightly sweet, mildly floral, and very suggestive of honey and hay. The taste of the flower petals is at first a little bit sweet, but upon chewing (since the petals are slightly fibrous), they taste pleasant, like a mild leaf lettuce. The leaf, on the other hand, has a green, somewhat acrid smell. The taste of smaller leaves is green and mildly bitter with a hint of tartness; even small leaves are chewy. As the leaves get older, they become more bitter and tougher in texture.

Dandelion greens contain vitamins A, B, C, and D. Dandelion is very high in beta-carotene and contains the minerals calcium and potassium, some phosphorus, iron, and zinc. Small leaves can be used raw in salads, while bigger leaves can be wilted and eaten like a potherb, or added to soups. The Pennsylvania Germans of the eastern United States serve the newly emerged dandelion greens with a hot bacon and vinegar dress-

ing over potatoes—a wonderful combination of flavors.

When the plants form flowers, harvest the tasty golden morsels for your scrambled eggs or stir-fries. They are not as bitter as the leaves and offer an interesting texture to food. After the flower petals appear, they can be removed from their bitter, green bracts, and petals can be strewn over green salads; egg, tuna, and chicken salads; and in soups to lend appetizing color and healthful plant pigments. They can also be used to make dandelion wine.

The common dandelion is everywhere, ours for the gathering. Just be sure you gather them from fields and lawns that have not been sprayed or fertilized with chemicals.

CULTIVATION AND PROPAGATION
Most folks don't have to cultivate dandelions. In fact, a vast number of Americans spend endless hours and a small fortune trying to remove them from their lawns. *Taraxacum officinale* is found

throughout North America and other temperate regions of the world, dotting lawns, vacant lots, fields, and roadsides with their recognizable yellow blooms.

This perennial has a thick taproot that plunges deep into the earth as soon as it germinates. If dandelions are cultivated in garden soil, both the roots and greens will grow much larger than they will in a grassy lawn. Small leaves appear in rosettes, then flower buds appear, followed by flowers; these grow from the long taproot and the heart, which is just above the root. All of these parts of the dandelion are edible; just be sure to taste them for bitterness. Leaves are least bitter early in the spring.

HARVESTING AND PRESERVING

During the late winter and early spring, gather the leaves from the center of the plant in one hand and cut with the other hand through the crown of the plant just above ground level; the central leaves are the most tender. It is best to gather the greens just before or right after the plants bloom, since once they bloom, leaves can become quite bitter and tough. Wash the leaves in water with a bit of vinegar added to remove grit, then rinse and spin dry in a salad spinner. Nibble a leaf or two to learn whether the grit is thoroughly washed away and to test the bitterness level of the harvest. If necessary, remove the tough midrib from the leaves. You may also need to cut off the lower portion of the leaves if they are very bitter. You can parboil the leaves to reduce bitterness, but remember that the

presence of a bitter flavor stimu-
lates the digestive juices, aiding the
liver. The leaves are best eaten fresh
or cooked, right after harvesting,
though they can be blanched and
drained, cooled, and frozen or dried.

Dry the flowers whole and store
in labeled jars out of direct light
until the next growing season.
Remove the bitter bracts and use
the dried petals in soups, with
grains, or in veggie burgers.

The root is dug in late fall or
spring. It is bittersweet, full of
nutrition, and can be used like
carrots or parsnips in soups, stews,
and stir-fries. The roots can also
be dried for a few days and then
roasted, ground, and used as a
coffee substitute (similar to using
chicory). In this form, the root is
rather bitter and a bit nutty tasting.
Store roasted roots in a jar and
grind them as needed.

Edible daylily (*Hemerocallis fulva*) flower buds, mature flowers, and tuberous roots

perennial with
fibrous roots,
10 inches to 3
feet tall

hardy in
zones 3 to 10

full sun, needs 6
hours daily, though
it will grow in
some shade with
fewer blooms

keep moist,
well drained;
can withstand
drought

loamy, slightly
acidic soil, about
pH 6.5

DAYLILY
Hemerocallis fulva

Although the common daylily is native to Eurasia, the tawny-orange flowers of the clone (the exact genetic copy) 'Europa' are found on roadsides and in fields across North America. The open flowers smell slightly floral, rather like a mild herbaceous honeysuckle though not quite so sweet. The flower buds and the flowers vary in taste depending on where they are grown. Their flavor is vegetal, occasionally floral, with a suggestion of zucchini or green bean and sometimes a hint of asparagus.

Flower buds have been used for centuries in Chinese cuisine in soups and stir-fries. They can be sautéed and eaten alone or tossed with pasta or grain dishes. They are also good pickled and dried for future use. Flower petals with their crisp texture can be used as crudités for dipping, scattered whole or chopped on salads, in herb butters, soups, and egg dishes. Whole blooms can be battered and sautéed in oil, or filled with cheese or rice, then dipped in a batter and sautéed, or used as a container and filled with a dip, cheese or grain salad, and served fresh as a lovely floral presentation.

The roots can also be dug and eaten; they are tuberous and somewhat fibrous. The roots are tasty and sweet, a little bit nutty, and crunchy. Small, tender roots can be chopped and used on salads, while larger ones can be boiled for about ten minutes to soften them and then eaten like a vegetable with a little butter or olive oil, salt, and pepper.

Hemerocallis fulva 'Europa' typically appears in shades of orange, sometimes colored with a little bronze, yellow, or red. We most often choose to eat this daylily. There are thousands of *Hemerocallis* hybrids available, from 3-foot-tall to diminutive selections, with trumpet-shaped blooms to many petaled flowers, and in an amazing array of colors. Taste the flowers before using—some can be bitter or metallic, depending upon where and how they are grown.

Daylilies are mildly diuretic and can have a laxative effect if eaten in large quantities.

CULTIVATION AND PROPAGATION
These hardy perennials are not very picky about growing conditions, although they prefer sun and

Common daylily grows wild along roadsides and shores.

enriched loamy soil. They appear along highways, hillsides, and old house foundations in dry conditions. Since they have fibrous roots, they spread easily, and need to be divided when the clumps get too large and have fewer blooms. Just dig them up, divide, plant each portion in a hole about twice the size of the roots, spread out the roots, and add enriched soil. Plant the crown just below soil level, just barely covering it with 1 to 2 inches of soil, and water well. They appreciate being mulched to keep the weeds down, although they tend to do well on their own even if neglected.

Use only unsprayed daylilies; gathering from roadsides where there is a lot of traffic exhaust is not recommended.

Daylily buds can be harvested from about 1½ to 2 inches in size until the day before they open. They can be cooked or dried for future use. Dry on baking sheets in an oven with a pilot light or the oven light turned on until they are free of moisture. Store in labeled glass jars out of direct sunlight until the next season. Flowers can be harvested daily—they only last one day. Pick them, and swish in a bowl of water to remove bugs and dirt. Remove the pistils and stamens and place the flowers facedown on a tray or plate lined with a cloth or paper towel, so they drain and remain open until ready to use. Covered lightly, they will last a day in the refrigerator.

To harvest the roots, dig up an established clump and shake off the dirt. Select the roots you want to use, and replant the rest. Scrub the roots and chop them to prepare them to be sautéed or boiled.

Dill (*Anethum graveolens*)
flowers and foliage

annual, 18 to 48 inches tall	seedlings can withstand minor frost	full sun	keep moist but not wet	garden loam, average pH 6.5

DILL
Anethum graveolens

Dill seeds (actually fruits) and foliage, known as dillweed, smell of a spicy caraway and fennel, and are somewhat pungent with undertones of mint and citrus. The fruits smell more pungent than the foliage, which tends to be more "green."

Anyone familiar with dill pickles knows the flavor of dill, which is a combination of parsley and fennel with a bit of celery, and a pungent bite with a slight burnt taste, especially so in the seed, along with oily resinous overtones.

Dill's cultivation humbles and mystifies many home gardeners, in large part because of the dual uses of the plant. In young plants, dill's blue-green, feathery foliage with its delicate and perishable aromatic tones is used fresh (as dillweed) to flavor fish and chicken, soups and sauces, egg and potato dishes, cheese and yogurt, and most especially spring green salads. As the herb matures, foliage production ceases as long stems shoot up, edible flowers bloom, and dill's second product, pungent seeds, appear. These enhance vinegars, pickles, breads, crackers, cookies, cakes, and pies.

We prefer three cultivars: 'Bouquet', 'Dukat', and 'Fernleaf'. 'Bouquet' is the most prolific for bountiful flower production. 'Dukat', or its improved form 'Superdukat', flowers a week later than 'Bouquet' and has high essential oil content. 'Fernleaf', a selection by Burpee Seed Company from Turkish seeds, is unique in that it grows to only 18 inches tall, a size that makes it ideal for cultivating in containers. In these cultivars, if you can get the plants to reseed themselves, the resulting plants will be generally stronger than the original ones. The cultivars 'Mammoth' and 'Elephant' grow 3 to 4 feet tall, with large flower heads, and are recommended for late flowering.

CULTIVATION AND PROPAGATION
Dill responds to cool weather and long days, so as soon as nights reach a minimum 25°F temperature,

direct seed in a smooth, well-prepared plot from early spring to late summer. Sow seeds in separate plantings a few weeks apart to have a continuous seasonal crop of dill-weed for salads and making pickles.

Soil should be light and neither too sandy nor too stony; a medium to heavy, well-drained, organic soil is preferred. You can enhance germination by soaking seeds for four days with 50 milligrams per quart of ascorbic acid (vitamin C). Seeding after late summer will produce few leaves and mostly seeds.

The home gardener should plant fifteen to twenty seeds per foot of row, and thin to three or four plants per foot, with rows 1 to 3 feet apart. Use the thinned seedlings in the kitchen. Seed takes seven to nine days to germinate, and flowering begins forty to sixty-seven days after germination, depending on sowing time, soil, and weather.

Young potted plants transplant readily. The age of the plant determines how quickly the plant will end foliage production to begin making seeds.

Dill is sensitive to water stress, so overhead sprinkling may be used from the time of seeding to 2 feet in height. Then switch to soil irrigation to reduce disease and risk of seed shattering. Early fall dill plantings will produce leaves for several weeks, even after the first light frosts. Use a floating row cover on fall dill to extend the harvest season. Late-fall sowings will germinate the following spring. Dill may be grown in the greenhouse but requires full sun.

HARVESTING AND PRESERVING
Harvest dillweed throughout the season. Harvest seeds as soon as they start to turn brown.

Store dried seeds in jars until next season. For dillweed, freeze-drying is recommended instead of hot-air drying, but even freeze-drying causes a loss of 75 percent of the aroma compounds. When you have an abundance of foliage, make herb butter or aromatic herbal paste, which can be frozen, which better conserves the flavor of dill than drying. Dillweed is best used fresh. Home gardeners usually snip foliage as needed. Use it to make vinegar and herb butter. And pickles, of course.

Blue elder (*Sambucus nigra* subsp. *cerulea*) leaves and berries

shrub to small
tree, 4 to 20
feet tall

hardy in
zones 4 to 10

full sun, but
also grows in
part shade

keep moist to
intermittently
wet

neutral to
alkaline soil,
average pH 6.0

ELDER
Sambucus species

The fragrance of elderflowers is delicate—sweet and honeylike, slightly fruity, and just a bit musky—and brings to mind wild plum blossoms. The taste combines mild honey and a pleasant fruitiness, melted snow, and just a hint of honeysuckle. Elderflowers are used to make jellies, syrups, cordials, and fritters. While the fritters are tasty and a rare treat indeed, the delicacy of the bloom is somewhat lost in the heaviness of frying in batter and oil. Infusions such as herbal tea or other beverages, liqueurs, and syrups are the best way to capture the essence of these ethereal blooms. Elderflower liqueur and syrup are very popular in many European countries.

The fragrance of the ripe elderberries, when crushed, is mild. The flavor is more tart than sweet, and suggests a cross between a currant and a grape. Berries should be cooked, because all parts of *Sambucus*—including bark, stems, leaves, and seeds—contain prussic acid, a cyanide-producing component that should not be eaten. Once cooked, the berries are safe to eat and have been used for medicine for cen-

turies; the plant has been referred to through time as "the medicine chest of the people." The berries, which are very high in vitamin C, are an immunostimulant, are used in tinctures, and in cough, cold, and sore throat preparations. Besides medicinal remedies, the berries are lovely in a cup of tea, make a delicious jam or jelly, syrup, shrub, cordial, and vinegar, and are used in desserts from crumbles and tarts to pies and ice cream. Elderberries are often made into a sauce for game and fowl.

Elders are hardy, wild plants often found growing along forest edges, roadsides, ditches, and hedgerows, where the conditions are sunny and slightly moist. We have seen huge colonies of elder along railroad tracks. Eastern elder (*Sambucus canadensis*) is found in the wild in eastern North America from Canada to Texas, and is the species of choice in those regions. Blue elder (*Sambucus nigra* subsp. *cerulea*) is found on the west coast of North America, from southern California to northern Canada. European elder (*Sambucus nigra*) is native to Europe. Some cultivated

Budded flower heads and just-opened elder (*Sambucus canadensis*) flowers

**Just-gathered ripe elderberries
ready for processing**

varieties are now available, with golden, purple, and even fern-leafed foliage, which are handsome additions to the garden. The flowers and dark purple berries of these cultivars are edible.

Red elderberry (*Sambucus racemosa*) produces bright red berries, which are poisonous and should not be consumed.

CULTIVATION AND PROPAGATION

You can grow the species from seed, and you can propagate most elders by cuttings in summer or fall. *Sambucus canadensis* shrubs or trees range in size from 6 to 12 feet, although some may top 20 feet, depending on where they are growing. Susan's elder tree is a native volunteer by the edge of the woods. It attracts all sorts of pollinators, from butterflies to bees and birds.

Once elderflowers appear, they last seven to ten days, which is a small window of time to harvest the blooms for making elderflower cordial, shrub, and elderflower fritters. Cut some flowers to dry, but do not harvest too many flowers, since you will want berries. Gently snip or pull flowers from stems, spread on baking sheets, and put them in the oven with just a pilot light or the oven light on. The flowers should dry in a few hours. Pack dried flowers in glass jars and label, store out of direct sunlight, and use before the next harvest season.

Pay attention once berries are green and fully filled out (green, unripe berries are poisonous), because they soon will be ready to harvest. Once they turn purple-black, gather them before the birds get them (but leave some for the birds). Be sure the berries are fully ripened for making syrup, jellies, cordial, tinctures, or desserts.

Elderberries freeze well. Spread the entire heads (stems with berries) on a tray or baking sheet and put in the freezer. Once frozen, the berries will easily pop off of their stems; do this in a large bowl. Quickly put the frozen berries (in 1- or 2-cup quantities) in freezer bags or lidded containers, label, and freeze up to six months.

You can also make juice from the berries. Cook down freshly harvested or frozen elderberries with just a little water, and let the contents cool. The concentrated juice can be extracted from the berries, then frozen or canned, and will be ready to use in recipes.

Fennel (*Foeniculum vulgare*)
fronds with fennel foliage,
flowers, and dried fennel seed

herbaceous perennial to annual, 6 to 7 feet tall

perennial hardy to zone 7; often naturalized as an annual farther north to zone 4

full sun

keep moist but not constantly wet

well-drained garden loam, average pH 6.6

FENNEL
Foeniculum vulgare

Fennel delights the herb gardener because it not only provides tasty leaves and fruits but also provides food for the vividly striped caterpillar of the swallowtail butterfly. The aroma is sweet and green and aniselike. The flavor of fennel is similar to anise (*Pimpinella anisum*) though more full and earthy, sweet and herbaceous. The fruits (commonly called seeds) of fennel are traditional in Italian sweet sausage. Northern Italians often add the seeds to their tomato sauce, and it is used in biscotti and other baked goods. The aromatic blue-green foliage and crisp stems, particularly the bulblike leaf base, are also sliced and used in a variety of dishes, especially seafood preparations, salads, and vegetables. The blooms can be used as a bright yellow garnish on salads or anywhere that the chopped herb is used.

Bronze fennel (*Foeniculum vulgare* 'Rubrum'), with its unusual dark foliage, is a great garnish, especially when the stems are grilled with meats and vegetables to add a hint of flavor. Try both the showy leaves and flowers of bronze fennel with summer-ripe fresh tomatoes instead of basil for a tasty change.

The essential oil of fennel seeds is used for flavoring foods, confections, and liqueurs such as anisette and absinthe. It is also used in perfume, cosmetics, and pharmaceuticals.

Children love the attractive feathery foliage of bronze fennel. Cut and sprinkled over salads, the leaves look like purplish-black spiderwebs and they smell of licorice candy.

CULTIVATION AND PROPAGATION
Plants should be placed 12 to 18 inches apart, and seedlings will need to be thinned to that distance if sown too close together. Soaking fennel seeds in water for five days prior to sowing increases germination. Additional nitrogen application is recommended for maximum yield.

Some gardeners will find that fennel tends to invade the rest of the garden, but in most gardens, it gently re-sows and does not become a nuisance. Its ability to withstand drought, however, means that it can become an invasive species in some regions. You will often see fennel growing along roadsides in warm, dry areas.

HARVESTING AND PRESERVING
Harvest fennel foliage any time during the season. The many side shoots of fennel complicate the best time to harvest for maximum yield. The highest yields are obtained from two harvests, the first when the umbels reach maturity and another when the umbels are ripened. Fennel foliage and flowers make a delicious herb butter and a zesty vinegar.

For seed, dry the crop under shade for four or five days to preserve the green color, then beat it to release the fruits. Store dried seed in labeled jars out of direct sunlight until the next growing season.

Fenugreek (*Trigonella foenum-graecum*) stems with leaves, long seedpods, and seeds

annual, to 1 foot tall

does not withstand frost

full sun

keep evenly moist

garden loam, average pH 7.3

FENUGREEK
Trigonella foenum-graecum

Fenugreek seed smells a bit woody when crushed, and lends a subtle yet distinctive flavor of maple and celery to food. It is an important ingredient in the cuisines of India and Pakistan, and has been used since the times of the ancient Egyptians, Greeks, and Romans. The herb produces long, narrow seedpods that will yield hard, golden, quadrangular seeds, which when mature are crushed or ground into a powder and used in breads and with meats, poultry, and vegetables. The ground seed is also a staple ingredient in curries, adding both sweet and bitter dimensions. Fenugreek produces a maple syrup–flavored extract that has found its way into the candy, baked goods, pickles, gelatins, puddings, beverages, ice cream, and syrups manufactured in America. Its sprouted seeds are used in salads and on sandwiches, and the leaves are sometimes consumed as a potherb.

Recent medical research suggests that fenugreek seeds may reduce blood sugar in type 2 diabetics and lower blood cholesterol. Fenugreek also has historical interest in the United States because it was a principal ingredient of Lydia E. Pinkham's Vegetable Compound, a popular "women's tonic" of the nineteenth century.

CULTIVATION AND PROPAGATION

Soil for growing fenugreek should drain well and have moderate-to-high fertility. A side dressing of ½ pound of 10-10-10 fertilizer per 100 square feet at first flowering will increase yield. In dry, hot areas, irrigation may be necessary to keep plants from becoming stunted. Early planting is recommended so that the plant can mature before the heat of August.

Fenugreek seed is sometimes slow to germinate, so soak seed in lukewarm water overnight to help it germinate faster. Once soil warms to 50 to 55°F (about the time tomatoes are planted), sow fenugreek seed 2 to 3 inches apart in rows 12 to 18 inches apart. Then cover the seeds with ¼ to ½ inch of soil. A single plant should yield thirty to forty seedpods.

Common diseases that may attack fenugreek plants are root rot, powdery mildew, downy mildew, and leaf spot (*Cercospora traversiana*). Sulfur dust is often recommended by researchers in India to control powdery mildew. Aphids, thrips, and leaf-eating caterpillars may also cause damage.

HARVESTING AND PRESERVING

Seeds ripen four to five weeks after flowering and are harvested when the drying pods become a lighter green and the seeds are mature. Pods should be harvested before they become brittle and shatter (open on their own to scatter seeds on the ground). Plants are often pulled from the ground and taken to another location to separate the pods from the plant and the seeds from the pods. The home gardener may use a screen in a warm room to make drying easier.

The seeds can be separated from the dried pods by placing them in a strong paper bag and pressing it several times with a heavy rolling pin. Then the seeds can be winnowed free from the chaff with a vacuum cleaner: lay the seeds out on newspaper and lower the nozzle slowly until the chaff is picked up, leaving the heavier seeds behind. Store the dried seeds in labeled jars out of direct sunlight until the next growing season.

Artemisia dracunculus 'Sativa'

perennial, 1½
to 2 feet tall
and wide

hardy in
zones 5 to 8

full sun, good
air circulation

can withstand
dry conditions

keep soil
well-drained,
pH 6 to 6.5

FRENCH TARRAGON

Artemisia dracunculus 'Sativa'

The first whiff of tarragon leaves picks up a pleasant anise aroma followed by a combination of green grass or freshly cut hay, with a mere suggestion of mint and licorice. French tarragon is a highly esteemed herb in France and is considered essential in many French dishes.

The rich aniselike flavor of tarragon is sweet, mildly grassy, and a little peppery. When you bite into a leaf, it numbs the tongue slightly, which is caused by the presence of the chemical methyl chavicol.

Tarragon is featured in popular blends of fines herbes along with chervil, chives, and parsley. It is used in sauces, vinaigrettes, and especially with shellfish, seafood, and poultry. The French use tarragon in the most elegant ways, in classic sauces like tartar and béarnaise. It also finds favor in Sienese and Russian cookery. Tarragon adds character to green sauces and is tasty with eggs and cheeses, and often used with chicken, fish,

and grilled meats. Sprinkle fresh, chopped tarragon over simply prepared vegetables, such as peas, asparagus, spinach, cauliflower, beets, and potatoes.

True French tarragon (*Artemisia dracunculus* 'Sativa') is the only choice of tarragon for the kitchen.

In southern regions, Mexican mint marigold (*Tagetes lucida*) is often used as a substitute for French tarragon. It is a perennial in warm climates, and works as a substitute when tarragon is dormant, or where winters are too warm for French tarragon to grow. *Tagetes lucida* has a coarser flavor than true tarragon. Although it has a similar anise flavor, it lacks the subtle basil undertones. The taste is milder in cooked dishes and seems stronger in vinegar.

CULTIVATION AND PROPAGATION
French tarragon (*Artemisia dracunculus* 'Sativa') should be obtained from a trustworthy source. Since it does not produce flowers and seed,

it must be started from a cutting or by root division. If a plant comes from seed, it is most likely Russian tarragon (*A. dracunculus*) and will lack the fragrance and flavor necessary for culinary use. It has gray-green foliage and blue-purple flower spikes, and is a larger, rangy plant than French tarragon, grows 3 to 4 feet tall, and has a bland taste. The true French tarragon is more delicate, is shorter, and has glossy, bright green leaves.

Like rosemary and sage, French tarragon will become a handsome bushy plant. Frequent cutting, especially in summer, and a mulch of sand and gravel will lessen disease problems. All yellow or brown leaves should be removed from the plant as soon as they appear, to deter the spread of fungus.

Tarragon dies back each winter, even in temperate climates. In cold climates, it should be well protected with mulch. We find it slightly finicky, because it doesn't like much heat in summer and won't live where winters are too warm.

We suggest buying rooted cuttings or small plants in the spring and planting them 15 inches apart. Tarragon has a shallow lateral root system and must have good air circulation. Two- and three-year-old plants can be divided easily and transplanted back into the garden or containers. The most important tip regarding tarragon is to give it adequate space. It will not thrive if crowded, so give it good air circulation.

HARVESTING AND PRESERVING

For preserving, make several tarragon cuttings throughout the season. Rinse if necessary. To dry tarragon, place the sprigs on flat baskets or screens in a warm, shady place. The fresh herb has a bright bouquet, whereas we find dried tarragon bland. Small sprigs can be frozen in ziplock plastic bags with reasonable results. Tarragon herb butter is a better option.

The best way to preserve tarragon is in vinegar, which captures and holds its essence. The texture and color of the herb are not the same in vinegar, but the flavor is quite good and more prominent than for the dried herb. Harvest cuttings and rinse if necessary, fill quart jars loosely with the fresh sprigs, and pour in white wine vinegar or rice wine vinegar to cover them, leaving a ½-inch headspace. Place plastic lids on the jars and store in a cool, dark place. In France, jars of tarragon preserved this way are sold in grocery stores and food shops and go for quite a tidy sum. After opening a jar, keep it in the refrigerator. Use the same amount of the preserved herb as fresh for recipes. Use the infused vinegar in salad dressings, marinades, and sauces.

Lepidium sativum 'Wrinkled Crinkled'

annual, 10 to
18 inches tall

does not
tolerate frost

sun to part
shade; part
shade in hot
weather

keep moist

medium loamy
soil enriched
with compost,
pH 6.4

GARDEN CRESS

Lepidium sativum

The leaves of garden cress are curly (it is also called curly cress), and as with most cresses, when rubbed, they smell green and slightly peppery. The leaves are pleasantly peppery hot and tangy in flavor, and so sometimes the plant is called peppergrass or pepperwort. The leaves and flowers are used in green salads, on sandwiches, and combined with grains and pasta. They are good with eggs, and make a tasty addition to deviled egg or egg salad. Although garden cress generally is not cooked, it works well in quickly cooked egg dishes like scrambled eggs or omelets.

This plant has an ancient history. Native to Asia, it spread to Europe and then to North America. Pungent fresh and dried seedpods are also eaten as a garnish or condiment. The seeds can be used to make sprouts, grown in a jar without soil and rinsed daily; the sprouts are ready in 5 to 7 days. The plant's roots are small and woody, though pungent, and can be chopped and used in sauces or salsas.

Lepidium sativum is the garden cress that we cultivate. Cress is an overall name used for many related spicy greens in the mustard family, which vary enormously from field cress and watercress to creasy greens (upland cress).

CULTIVATION AND PROPAGATION

Sow seed and cultivate cress as you would other cool-season herbaceous greens, such as spinach, lettuce, arugula, cilantro, and chervil. Once sown, this fast-growing cress germinates quickly. Small leaves can be harvested in less than 30 days. Cress is a cool-season annual, so treat it like a salad herb: plant it out early in the season in loamy, well-drained soil that has been amended with compost. It can also be grown as a fall crop, after the heat of summer has departed.

HARVESTING AND PRESERVING

Harvest this herb as you would any salad green; gather small leaves early on. The white to pinkish flowers can be eaten. The leaves tend to become tougher, bitter, and hotter once the plant blooms. This is a plant that is best eaten fresh in season; we don't dry or freeze it.

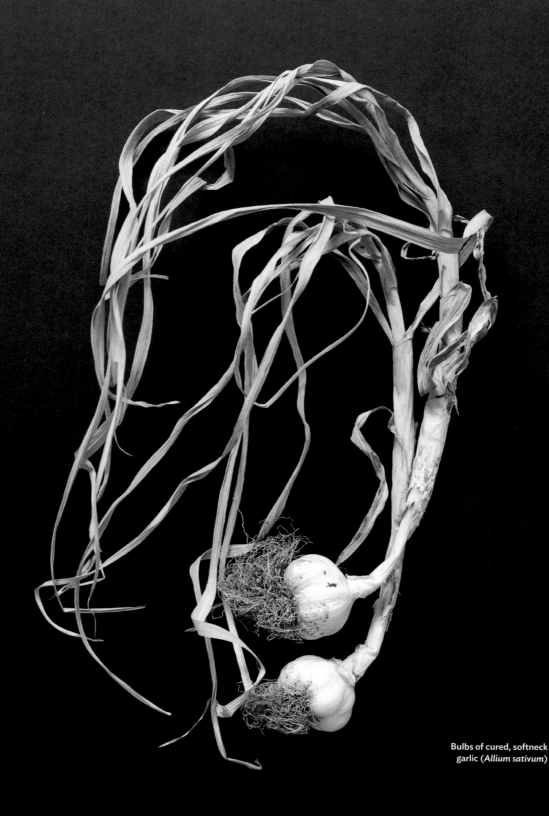

Bulbs of cured, softneck
garlic (*Allium sativum*)

herbaceous
perennial, to 2
feet tall

hardy to
zone 5

full sun

keep moist

well-drained
loam, average
pH 6.3

GARLIC
Allium sativum

Cut fresh garlic has an unmistakable smell: it is acrid, nose-piercing, biting, and pungent from sulfur compounds generated from allicin, the active component that offers many health benefits. Fresh garlic has a burning sensation in the mouth. Cooked or preserved garlic has a reduced, though similar odor and taste. The odor of both fresh and processed garlic is persistent, especially on the hands. If you have never tasted fresh garlic, beware: it may seem like you are having a nasal floss that then deepens to your lungs and penetrates all your pores! Garlic will also influence your mouth odor, so if you find this offensive, chew parsley until you can't stand it anymore, brush your mouth and gargle with mint mouthwashes, or share garlic with all of your family and friends, and enjoy it as we do. This is an herb that we could not live without.

Fresh garlic adds a piquancy to any dish, whether it is tossed in a salad or made into a sauce. Once cooked, garlic becomes less assertive, though that inimitable allium flavor is still there; in long-simmered dishes the garlic becomes muted. Oven-roasting garlic with a drizzle of olive oil at a low temperature transforms the hot and spicy nature to sweet and slightly nutty with warm tones of allium, and the texture becomes soft and creamy—quite spreadable.

We like to mince fresh garlic and use it in salad dressings or serve it straight on crackers with a dairy product, such as goat cheese. We pound it in pestos, salsa verde, skordalia, and aioli, and rub it on crusty, toasted bread to make bruschetta. Diced fresh garlic sautéed in virgin olive oil also is the starting point of so many recipes, from a traditional Italian marinara sauce to a Chinese stir-fry. We rarely make a soup, sauce, gravy, stew, ragout, casserole, or pot of beans without including garlic. We do not use processed garlic, because as seekers of excellent flavor, we want the real thing for culinary and medicinal virtues. Julia Child stated: "Never, never, never use garlic powder." But be wary of old open jars of garlic in olive oil. Garlic and olive oil provide a perfect vehicle for salmonella to develop, so if you use this product, refrigerate it immediately after opening and store no more than one week.

Fresh garlic can also thin blood, so be cautious if you are already on blood thinners. On the plus side, if you have a persistent fungal infection or canker sores, oral fresh garlic can be a major aid combined with other treatments.

Softneck garlics (*Allium sativum* var. *sativum*) are the type of garlic that we generally find at the grocery store. They are often grown commercially because they tend to have more cloves per bulb and they store longer than hardneck garlic (*Allium sativum* var. *ophioscorodon*). While both types of garlic have center stems, hardneck garlic has a stiff center stem, while the softneck stem is more pliable. The softnecks are often braided, while hardnecks are too stiff for braiding. We grow both kinds of garlic and haven't met one we didn't like. We enjoy cultivating the hardnecks for their huge number of cultivar choices, and we find them easier to break apart and peel since most of them have a single set of cloves surrounding the hardneck rather than having the overlapping artichoke heads of the softnecks.

In North America, three garlic cultivars grown extensively in California are 'California Early', 'California Late', and 'Creole' ('American'), which are softneck garlics. Try some of the unusual cultivars for taste and allicin content. 'German Red' and 'Valencia' do well in our Mid-Atlantic zone 7 region, while 'Susanville' thrives in West Coast climates of California and Oregon. An Italian study found that 'Paceco' and 'Campobello di Licata Bianco' had the highest levels of allicin. Over the years, we have grown hundreds of different cultivars ranging in heat from mild to wild. A few we have liked are

Hardneck garlic has a hard, sturdy stem.

popular gourmet item. But serpent garlic requires more management and skill to grow and process. The serpent garlics produce woody flower stalks that produce not fertile flowers, but bulbils (cloves). Underground, around the central woody stalk, a circle of four to fourteen cloves is produced. Peking garlic (*Allium sativum* var. *pekinense*) is similar to serpent garlic and may be correctly classified with it.

CULTIVATION AND PROPAGATION
Growing high-yield crops of good-quality garlic requires more than a casual approach. Proper garlic growing is not for wimps. But if you want to have really good garlic and try unusual cultivars with different tastes, the process is well worth it.

Selections of *Allium sativum* are generally sterile and are propagated from the cloves (the cloves, or bulbils, are often called seed, while the entire bulbs are called sets). Plant (pointed ends up, root ends down) in the fall in full sun, at least four weeks before the ground freezes. Cover with 1 to 2 inches of soil, and space 3 to 6 inches apart with 12 to 32 inches between rows. Plant in well-drained, highly organic loam with a slightly acid pH (6.5 to 6.7). Fall-planted garlic will be ready to harvest the following late spring to early summer, generally 8 to 9 months after planting.

Home gardeners should add 2 to 3 pounds of a common 5-10-5 fertilizer or its equivalent to every 100 square feet of garden area. Alternatively, work in aged horse manure and greensand; distribute 1 pound of 5-10-5 fertilizer or aged horse

softneck, 'Inchelium Red', 'Early Red Italian', 'Italian Late'; and hardneck, 'Chesnok Red', 'German Red', 'Metechi', 'Music', 'Spanish Roja'. We prefer hardnecks because there is more variety in flavor and they are easier to cure, but they do not store as long as softnecks. We do grow softnecks, though, because we like the flavor of some of the cultivars, they last longer than the hardnecks in storage, and we like to make garlic braids.

Hardneck garlic (*Allium sativum* var. *ophioscorodon*) is known as serpent garlic or rocambole, and is also known in French as *rocambole*, in German as *Rocambol*, in Italian as *aglio d'India*, in Russian as *ispansky tschesnok*, and in Chinese as *ta suan, hu suan*, or *hu*. It is referred to as serpent garlic because the garlic scapes "snake" around in coils and different directions as they grow. The semiwild taste and easily removed skins make serpent garlic a

manure and greensand along a 50-foot row as a side dressing. The largest cloves will produce the largest bulbs, so cull out the smallest cloves. Mulch lightly with straw for winter protection, increased yields, and weed control. Studies done in a cold-winter region show that black plastic mulch produced greater marketable weights and bulb diameters than bare soil–wheat straw mulch treatment. Garlic cloves may also be planted in spring six weeks before the last frost, but the resulting bulbs will not be as large as those sown in autumn.

Just like for onions, temperature and day length are extremely important in growing garlic. Garlic requires temperatures below 40°F for six to eight weeks to vernalize (provide cold for maturation) the plant. Once treated with cold temperatures, the plant initiates bulbing when the day length reaches approximately thirteen hours and soil temperatures are above 60°F. Prolonged temperatures below 32°F cause rough-shaped bulbs and small axillary cloves. Temperatures above 80°F speed up bulb formation with favorable day length. Warm temperatures continuously above 60°F and days with fewer than twelve hours of daylight prevent bulbs from forming.

Keep plants evenly moist during the growing season, using a mulch if possible. Irrigation should be adequate to moisten the soil to a depth of 12 to 18 inches for proper bulb development. While moisture is critical as the bulb develops from late May until July, withhold additional water two to three weeks before harvest. Vegetative growth is greatest around 61°F in short days, while bulbs are formed and enlarged in long days with temperatures above 68°F.

Early in the spring, when garlic leaves are green and plants are 8 to 12 inches high, we thin some of the new plants in order to enjoy green garlic, which is a gourmet's delight to cook with. Later in the season, the plants send up their flower stalks, which are called scapes. Remove the flowering stalks when they are 6 to 9 inches tall above the foliage, to assure that growth energy goes to the bulb. Garlic scapes can be finely chopped and used for salads and garlic butter or briefly sautéed in stir-fries.

Reduction in yield may indicate the presence of viruses, particularly onion yellow dwarf virus— look for virus-free stock. The most damaging pest in commercially grown garlic in America is the stem and bulb nematode (*Ditylenchus dipsaci*), followed by onion thrips (*Thrips tabaci*).

HARVESTING AND PRESERVING
In late spring to early summer (eight to nine months after your cloves were planted), the bulbs are ready to harvest when the leaves turn yellow to brown, weaken, and fall over. As a second test of harvest readiness, inspect the leaves at soil level near the bulb. They turn from a succulent, fleshy texture to a dry, papery sheath at harvest time.

Once the bulbs are dug up, or lifted, peel off one or two of the outer leaves to expose the clean bulb and trim off the roots. The bulbs need to be cured before storing: during this step, the outer and inner membranes need to dry so the bulbs will store well. If you wish to braid the tops, leave them on and do so when they are somewhat dry but still pliable. Dry in a shady place with a relative humidity of 60 to 70 percent and temperatures of 60 to 70°F; allow one or two weeks for drying. Chicken-wire racks or old screens work well for drying. Finish curing at 80 to 100°F for four to six weeks or until the papery skin changes from pure white to off white and becomes crisp.

Storing garlic for long periods of time at 39°F and above and at humidities greater than 70 percent will lead to high losses from sprouting and mold, respectively. Optimum storage conditions for garlic are eight to ten days at 68 to 86°F, followed by temperature reduction to 32°F and maintenance at 32°F ± 0.9°F and relative humidity of 65 to 70 percent with permanent air circulation. Under these conditions, storage life is 130 to 220 days, depending on cultivar type and cultivation practices. In general, 2.2 pounds of planted garlic yields 11 to 15 pounds harvested. Yields reflect the garlic variety used, soil quality, moisture, nutrition, weed competition, and planting density.

Susan stores her garlic in mesh bags in the coldroom of her basement (low about 50°F in winter and high about 65°F in summer), which is out of direct light. Four, 50-foot rows of garlic harvested in July generally lasts her through February, maybe March, when the green garlic is just coming up.

Matricaria recutita

| annual, 3 inches to 2 feet tall | seedlings can withstand frost | full sun | keep moist but not constantly wet | well-drained garden soil, average pH 6.7 |

GERMAN CHAMOMILE

Matricaria recutita

The essential oil from German chamomile flowers has been used in nonalcoholic beverages, alcoholic beverages, ice cream and ices, candy, baked goods, and chewing gum, although the most popular use of the dried flowers is in teas or tisanes (herbal teas). The aroma of German chamomile tea is like daisies and fresh hay with tinges of apple and perhaps a whiff of sweetgrass. The flavor echoes the fragrance and, although there is a pleasant sweetness, is slightly bitter. Besides having no caffeine, German chamomile tea also has health benefits. Research has shown that German chamomile reduces inflammation, allergies, and muscle spasms, and is effective against certain fungi and bacteria.

German chamomile (*Matricaria recutita*), also called Hungarian chamomile, is widely confused with Roman chamomile (*Chamaemelum nobile*) and the two have been used almost interchangeably. However, Roman chamomile is a low, ground-hugging perennial while German chamomile is an upright annual, and the essential oils are also vastly different. Consuming Roman chamomile sometimes induces allergic responses in ragweed-sensitive individuals, but these responses are rare for German chamomile.

A large number of German chamomile seed lines have been developed, especially by the Hungarians. Some specialty catalogs carry these, but the straight species is what we usually grow.

CULTIVATION AND PROPAGATION

German chamomile grows best in a light, sandy loam with abundant moisture. Additional fertilizers should have a ratio of one part nitrogen to two parts potassium because potassium advances flowering. The surface of the soil should be firm to ensure good contact with the seeds, in furrows 2 to 4 inches high with plants in rows 4 to 32 inches apart.

Early autumn seeding is best in areas with regular autumn rain, late-autumn seeding is best in areas with early frost and little snowfall, and spring seeding is best in areas with spring rain. Spring sowings produce a higher content of essential oils, and so we normally seed our German chamomile in spring. Seeds germinate at 43 to 45°F within seven to ten days after seeding.

Leaf rosettes form thirty to forty days after germination and flowers quickly follow. Optimal temperature for flowering is 66 to 68°F. At 82 to 90°F, the flowering time is shortened.

HARVESTING AND PRESERVING

Under optimal conditions, German chamomile plants flower two to three times per year. Regeneration of flowers after cutting requires ten to twenty days, depending on weather conditions. The highest essential oil content is found in fully developed flowers approximately one week after beginning of flowering. Flowers may be dried with forced hot air or in an oven with a pilot light or oven light on. Store the dried blooms in a dark glass jar, label, keep out of direct sunlight, and use before the next season's harvest.

Chenopodium bonus-henricus

perennial, 15 to 24 inches tall   hardy in zones 3 to 9   semishade to full sun   keep moist but not wet   enriched loamy soil, average pH 6.7

GOOD KING HENRY

Chenopodium bonus-henricus

This European potherb was brought to America by the colonists. The leaves of good King Henry are somewhat like spinach, smelling green and herbaceous. The flavor is also similar to spinach but a bit more bitter, with mineral elements, and somewhat chalky. The leaves taste best in early spring and in the fall. The arrow-shaped leaves are not harvested from first-year plants, and shoots shouldn't be harvested until plants are in their third year.

Eat leaves fresh in salads or in green sauces in small amounts since they contain saponins (compounds characterized by their foaming ability). They are more often cooked (the saponins are broken down when cooked) for sauces and soups, and are used in pasta, grain, and egg dishes, and casseroles.

We grow the straight species (*Chenopodium bonus-henricus*).

CULTIVATION AND PROPAGATION

Direct sow the seeds in fall, or purchase a few plants to transplant; the seeds are a bit difficult to germinate. Do not move the plants once they are established. Good King Henry likes an enriched soil in dappled shade, although it will grow in full sun.

HARVESTING AND PRESERVING

Once plants are well established, you can harvest the tender shoots when they are 5 to 6 inches tall and use them like asparagus. Snip leaves from the outer perimeter of the plant to encourage center growth. Wash them well to make sure they are free of grit. Eat tender leaves in salads and cook older leaves. Leaves can be blanched, drained, and frozen like spinach and then used in cooked dishes. The shoots from older plants are often harvested like asparagus, and are considered a gourmet delight.

Branches of hibiscus (*Hibiscus sabdariffa*) with mature leaves and red calyces (sepals)

tender perennial, to 10 feet tall	hardy to zone 9; cannot withstand frost	full sun	keep evenly moist	fertile, sandy soil

HIBISCUS

Hibiscus sabdariffa

The red calyces (sepals) of this hibiscus are the main reason to grow this plant. Unless crushed or broken open, they don't have much odor, and then the aroma is mild, rather like sour citrus. The flavor of hibiscus is best described as lemony, acid, and rhubarblike. Hibiscus tea is a tasty alternative to beverages high in caffeine and has been documented to lower blood pressure. The tea, which is popular worldwide, is made with the brewed dried calyces of the flowers and flavored with orange and lime juices, grated orange peel, grated ginger, and sugar.

All parts of hibiscus (also known as roselle or sorrel) are edible, though the fleshy red calyces are the most popular. Not only do they impart a deep red color, but they also are rich in pectin, which facilitates the setting of jellies and jams. They are used for teas, wine, juice, syrup, gelatin, puddings, cakes, and ice cream. Nowadays, flowers packed in syrup are available to add to champagne or cocktails and they make a ruby-red cordial. Eat the young leaves and tender stems raw in salads or cooked as greens or added to curries. Use the roasted seeds in soups and stews or as a coffee substitute.

The straight species is the only one generally available for purchase. In the Caribbean, cultivars are grown, such as 'Local Tall', 'Dwarf Early Red', 'Rico', 'Victor', and 'Archer' ('White Sorrel').

CULTIVATION AND PROPAGATION

Hibiscus is easily grown from seed. Since it is native to India and Malaysia and only hardy to zone 9, it is best grown in large, deep pots to allow full maturity and seed production in more northerly zones. If grown in a container and brought into a cool greenhouse for the winter, it does not get as tall, perhaps about 4 feet and nearly that wide, though it can still produce quite a bit of fruit.

HARVESTING AND PRESERVING

Hibiscus is harvested to use fresh or dried. As days become shorter, smaller flowers appear at intervals up the stem, withering by midday. Once the seeds begin to form, large red calyces form around the seedpods and gradually grow crisp and juicy. These can be used fresh, or dried on baking sheets in an oven with a pilot light or oven light on. Once completely dried, pack them into jars, label, and store out of direct light. When the calyces are preserved in syrup, the mixture turns a bright ruby-red color. Process the syrup in canning jars; the syrup can also be made into a cordial. Or freeze the syrup; be sure to leave over an inch or more of headspace, since freezing will expand the liquid. Frozen syrup keeps for up to a year.

Humulus lupulus

| perennial vine, to 33 feet long | hardy to zone 5 | full sun | keep moist but not constantly wet | deep sandy loam soil, average pH 6.5 |

HOPS

Humulus lupulus

Hops are used to flavor beer. The flower heads (cones) of these prolific vines provide a unique bitter taste that is not offered by any other ingredient, and the aroma is a spicy, herbaceous odor. Depending on the cultivar used, sometimes the smell, and especially the taste, reveals citrus notes or intense bitterness.

With a change in federal law in the U.S., home brewing of specialty beers has become a current craze to replace home brewing of wines. The home brewer may buy dried hops at specialty shops, but more and more home brewers who also garden are raising their own hops, especially organically. Beer is prepared by fermenting malt (soaked and germinated grain, typically barley) and then flavoring the brew with a plant full of bitter resins, typically hops.

German beer makers have used hops for hundreds of years, certainly since the ninth century. Beer may have been hopped before that time, but the earliest record of hopped beer dates from 822. During the Middle Ages, beer often accompanied every meal, and hop cultivation was widespread throughout Europe. But until hops arrived in England toward the close of the fifteenth century, bitter plants like ale-hoof (gill-over-the-ground, *Glechoma hederacea*) were used to flavor fermented malt. Henry VII and Henry VIII of England liked their beer without hops and therefore prohibited the use of hops.

Hops were introduced by Europeans in North America in the seventeenth century. European hops have become naturalized (along with Japanese hops, *Humulus japonicus*) in vacant lots, fencerows, and old house sites from Canada to New Mexico. The first commercial crop of hops in the United States was established in New York in 1808. Today, the Yakima Valley in Washington state produces about 75 percent of the hops grown in the United States.

Numerous hops cultivars are available. While they can look somewhat similar, they taste different. Among the more commonly available ones for the home gardener is 'Cascade', which has a distinct fragrance and is used to give flavor to American light lagers. Other cultivars now available in specialty fruit catalogs include 'Centennial' (with floral and citrus notes), 'Nugget' (with acute bitterness), and 'Tettnang'

(with a mild aroma). Golden hops (*Humulus lupulus* 'Aureus') is a showy plant in the garden.

CULTIVATION AND PROPAGATION

Hops are perennial dioecious (sexes on different plants) vines to 33 feet long. Male vines bear male flowers in loose axillary clusters, while female vines bear flowers that are conelike at maturity. Only the female flowers are used to flavor beer. Leaves are bright to dark green, and heart-shaped with three to five deep lobes. The whole plant is rich in bitter resins but that feature is concentrated in the female flowering cones. Seedless hops, produced by preventing pollination, are considered more desirable by brewers; their weight is 30 percent less than seeded hops, but seedless hops are more shatter resistant.

Hops are adapted to a wide range of climates. In areas where rainfall is lacking, irrigation may be required. Deep, sandy loam in full sun produces the best hop harvests. Feed plants levels of phosphorous and potassium similar to those required for corn. A soil test is necessary before any recommendations can be made,

These mature hops are growing up
and over the wire trellis, showing their
vining habit and cones.

and your county agricultural agent
can provide interpretations of the
results.

Since nitrogen is removed with
the harvested portion of hops every
year, organic fertilizers of 2 to 5 percent nitrogen are recommended.
Hops are propagated by the runners
that arise from the crown just below
the soil surface. In May, the runners
are cut into 6- to 8-inch-long
pieces, each bearing at least two
sets of buds. Cuttings are planted
directly in hills, two to four cuttings
per hill, with the buds pointed up
and covered by ¼ to 1 inch of soil,
with a spacing of approximately 8
by 8 feet.

In colonial times, hops were
often grown on single tall poles
about 12 feet in height. Hops are
best grown on an overhead trellis.
When the vines are about 2 feet
long, two to six vigorous vines per
hill are selected and trained up
a wire trellis. When the vines are

securely attached to the wires, the lowest 4 feet of leaves and lateral branches are carefully removed to help prevent diseases such as downy mildew and insect pests such as spider mites. Suckers rising from the base early in the season are continually removed to promote the growth of selected vines, but the hardiness of the crown is fostered by allowing the suckers to persist later in the season.

Weed control is usually by early mechanical cultivation 6 to 10 inches deep to incorporate surface organic matter, followed by shallow cultivation 2 to 4 inches deep later in the season. Late-season cultivation inhibits growth and leads to early ripening.

HARVESTING AND PRESERVING

In North America's Pacific Northwest, hops are harvested from mid-August to mid-September; plants are prime for picking for only five to ten days, and delayed harvesting causes shattering of the cones and discoloration.

Home gardeners should gauge harvest readiness to when the cones grow slightly papery and give off a pronounced odor; brown spots indicate overmaturity. To dry and store hops, a food dehydrator can be used, but do not exceed 140°F. After drying, move the hops to a cooling room for a week to allow them to "even up." Any storage and transport should be below 40°F; home brewers may prefer to refrigerate or freeze the cones. Store dried hops in labeled jars, out of direct sunlight, in a cool place for six months; for longer storage, keep the hops in the refrigerator or freezer.

Horseradish (*Armoracia rusticana*)
leaves and small roots

hardy perennial,
24 to 36 inches tall

hardy to
zone 5

full sun

keep moist but
not wet

loamy, well-
drained soil,
pH 6 to 6.5

HORSERADISH
Armoracia rusticana

Primarily grown for its pungent root, horseradish also offers the gardener the bonus of early, small tender leaves and the white flowers, which can be added to salads, sandwiches, soups, and butters. The leaves have a pleasant green, herby flavor with just a touch of pungency and the blooms are mildly spicy.

When freshly dug, the root has a nose-tingling aroma. In the kitchen, once cleaned and then chopped or grated, the root's main active component, allyl isothiocynate (mustard oil), is released, and if inhaled directly, can take your breath away and may bring tears to your eyes. The taste of freshly grated horseradish root is equally as incendiary as the aroma, so use caution when processing, and use in small quantities.

The assertive flavor of grated horseradish root enhances all types of dishes from cocktails to dessert. An essential ingredient to a proper Bloody Mary, horseradish adds a kick to this popular drink or to plain tomato juice. It enlivens salads, soups, and sauces, and is often added to mayonnaise and mustard to make them more piquant. Use horseradish-laced mayonnaise in coleslaw and potato salads, on sandwiches, with seafood, and as a dipping sauce for artichokes.

A popular use of horseradish, commercially or homemade, is in cocktail sauce. Prepared by combining ketchup and grated prepared horseradish, sometimes with a squeeze of lemon juice, this zesty condiment is favored for every type of fresh seafood including shrimp, clams, oysters, and mussels and with breaded or battered fried fish. Freshly grated horseradish mixed with cream or vinegar is an excellent pungent accompaniment to raw oysters, clams, roast meats (often served with roast beef), fish, and smoked fish.

When cooked, horseradish root changes from hot to rather earthy, sweet, and nutty, although a slight pungency remains. Enjoy it baked in all sorts of vegetable casseroles with root vegetables, especially carrots, beets, winter squashes, and the brassicas (like Brussel sprouts, broccoli, cabbage).

We grow *Armoracia rusticana* plants that are passed-along roots or divided crowns from other gardeners; most catalogs don't offer cultivars. A standard in the industry is 'Maliner Kren', often referred to as common horseradish. Cultivars 'Big Top Western', 'Bohemian', and 'Sass' are grown because the root is highly resistant to many diseases.

CULTIVATION AND PROPAGATION
Horseradish prefers cooler weather; fall is the season for the greatest growth and the time to use the

Dig mature horseradish roots in the fall of the first year; second-year roots can become tough and pithy.

fresh roots. Horseradish is easy to cultivate. In early spring, dig or till the earth 18 to 24 inches deep, working in well-rotted manure or compost. Young root cuttings should be fairly straight, 6 to 8 inches long and about ½ inch across. Purchased roots come trimmed with a sloping cut on the bottom end; plant with this end down. Make holes in the soil about 12 inches deep and at least 18 inches apart, place a root in each hole, and cover with well-tilled soil.

Horseradish will grow in almost any sunny location (heavy soils tend to promote forked roots), and it will thrive in enriched, well-drained soil that is kept weeded. Roots left in the garden for more than a year tend to be pithy and more prone to disease. We dig horseradish roots every year, store them, and then plant root sections in early spring. Generally, plants do not flower the first year; they flower in the spring of the second season.

HARVESTING AND PRESERVING

Harvest early small leaves to eat fresh or dried. The best-tasting and most tender roots come from first-year plants. Roots can be left in the garden year-round and dug as needed, or they can be dug in late fall and kept in the refrigerator or in a cold root cellar, so they are available to be grated as needed. Once the root is dug, it must be refrigerated; heat is the enemy of horseradish roots and will cause them to quickly lose their potency. Freshly grated horseradish turns brown after grating and tends to lose its pungency after sitting, so grate the root right before using it unless you make it into a sauce or preserve it with vinegar. Fresh horseradish is hotter and more pungent than commercially prepared; substitute 4 teaspoons of prepared horseradish for 1 tablespoon of freshly grated horseradish.

To preserve horseradish root, peel away the tough, brown outer skin. Grate the root or process in a food processor or blender. Take precautions to ensure adequate ventilation in the kitchen, and when you remove the top of the processor, step back for a few minutes to avoid inhaling the fumes. Let the roots sit for about 10 minutes, because processing immediately with vinegar will lessen the potency of the prepared horseradish.

To process, mix ½ cup white vinegar (use white wine vinegar or rice vinegar; apple cider vinegar will work, but the color is a bit darker) with every 2 cups freshly grated horseradish. Several brands of commercially prepared horseradish contain a little soybean oil or lemon juice, and some added salt. To make sure that the mixture is well moistened but not too liquid, stir in a little more vinegar or water if necessary. Pack into sterilized jars, seal, and refrigerate. Use in six months since it will lose its pungency in storage.

Hyssopus officinalis

perennial, to 2
feet tall

hardy to
zone 6

full sun

keep moist;
can withstand
drought

well-drained
or rocky loam,
average pH 6.7

HYSSOP

Hyssopus officinalis

We find it somewhat curious that hyssop is planted in so many herb gardens today despite the stinky skunklike odor it develops on hot summer days. While hyssop provides attractive blue, pink, or white flowers in the herb garden, its continued cultivation is more traditional than useful. In the Middle Ages and the Renaissance, hyssop was employed in cooking and was used with fruits and in salads, soups, and stews. But our ancestors also bathed less frequently and used musk and civet as flavorings and personal fragrances, so the skunky odor was not as unappealing as today.

Hyssop is an ingredient in the herb liqueur chartreuse. Hyssop oil and extract have been employed in sauces, condiments, and canned foods as well as liqueurs to provide a minty aroma and slightly bitter taste with hints of green herbs. Yet, the pinocamphone and isopino-camphone in hyssop oil can cause convulsions. Above 0.002 ounce per pound, ingestion of hyssop oil causes convulsions; above 0.020 ounce per pound, it can be fatal. For a person weighing 150 pounds, those two amounts would be 0.31 ounce and 3 ounces, respectively. Therefore, we are reluctant to recommend hyssop for foods despite its GRAS status. Hyssop, however, is an excellent bee plant, and the resulting honey is curiously minty.

Hyssop typically has blue flowers; 'Rosea' has pink blossoms, and 'Alba' has white ones. Massed hyssop is very effective in the garden, and it makes a good border plant, because it looks similar to a green-leaved lavender with spikes of flowers.

CULTIVATION AND PROPAGATION

Hyssop requires full sun and well-drained, gravelly or rocky soil. Hyssop can be easily grown from seed, but most gardeners prefer to buy young plants from herb nurseries. Trim hyssop back sharply in the early spring and after flowering— the first time to prevent the plants from becoming woody and leggy, and later to maintain trim, compact plants. Under favorable conditions, hyssop readily reseeds itself.

HARVESTING AND PRESERVING

Despite the odor and our cautions on excessive ingestion, hyssop can create a wonderful potpourri of summer memories when combined with sweet woodruff. The result is reminiscent of new-mown hay fields with a slight whisper of animal pungency. Harvest and dry hyssop for potpourri when the plant is flowering.

Juniper (*Juniperus communis*)
branch and berries

prostrate shrubs or trees, to 49 feet tall	hardy to zone 5	full sun	keep moist but not constantly wet; can withstand drought	well-drained soil, pH adaptable from acid to alkaline

JUNIPER

Juniperus communis

Juniper, also called common juniper, is a cone-bearing tree, not a flowering plant; it does not bear fruits. The fleshy cones, or juniper berries, resemble small blueberries and ripen in the fall. They are used to flavor items such as gin, liqueurs, and game, like goose, venison, and wild boar, as well as poultry stuffing, beef stews, and pâtés. Juniper berries' taste is aromatic and quite bitter, and resinous—a bit like turpentine; the berries do not have an odor unless they are crushed and then they smell piney, slightly sweet, and resinous, with a subtle hint of head-clearing eucalyptus. In Germany, juniper berries are used to flavor sauerkraut and a conserve called *Latwerge* eaten with cold meats. The spicy, resinous flavor goes well with parsley, thyme, fennel, marjoram, bay, and other herbs, as well as garlic, spices, wine, brandy, and port. Juniper berries vary in strength, and the ones from Italian hillsides are considered stronger than those that grow in Great Britain.

The genus *Juniperus* includes both male and female plants, and only the female plants bear the fleshy cones called juniper berries.

Approximately sixty named cultivars of juniper are available in the trade. Many cultivars are male, and sometimes females do not bear cones under cultivation. The only named cultivar that reliably bears cones seems to be 'Suecica'.

CULTIVATION AND PROPAGATION

Grow juniper in full sun and moist but well-drained garden loam. Junipers can withstand mild drought. Juniper plants, especially the named cultivars, are propagated by cuttings taken in late fall and wintered over in a cold frame or cool greenhouse. The home gardener will have the most success by simply sowing seeds cleaned of the fleshy coating in fall in the garden and then waiting for spring. Or purchase young plants if you want a head start.

Juniperus communis seems to be relatively resistant to disease, but sometimes it is affected by phomopsis twig blight. This fungus is especially active during weather in which the evaporation rate is low, especially during hot, humid summers or cold, wet springs, or when overhead irrigation is employed. So water your junipers from below.

HARVESTING AND PRESERVING

Juniper berries can be harvested any time after they acquire a waxy coating and assume a bluish color. Harvest time varies widely depending on moisture, winter temperatures, and other factors. Berries can be used fresh or dried. Pick them and remove any stems. To dry, spread them in a baking pan and place them in the oven with a pilot light or the light on for overnight and up to twenty-four hours. Check for dryness by crushing a berry; it should no longer be sticky inside. Store dried juniper berries in a labeled, glass jar out of direct sunlight until next year's harvest.

Citrus hystrix

tender spiny tree, 6 to 25 feet tall

 hardy to zone 9

 full sun

keep moist but not constantly wet

well-drained soil

KAFFIR LIME
Citrus hystrix

The odor of the crushed kaffir lime leaves is citronella with a slight floral aroma. In Thailand, the leaves are used in curries, especially in combination with coconut milk. They provide a unique citrusy taste to *tom-yam* soup, a Thai delicacy. The fresh kaffir lime fruit is so sour it cannot be eaten alone, although the juice, and occasionally the zest, is used in food products to provide a lemon-lime flavor.

The term "kaffir" has been used in the English language as far back as at least 1888. It means "infidel" in Arabic, and was applied by Arab slavers to the inhabitants of the east coast of Africa. So the term could be viewed as offensive. Some now refer to the plant by the Thai name, *makrut* (pronounced ma-gruud). Kaffir lime (*Citrus hystrix*) is heavily armed; *hystrix* means "porcupine," which no doubt refers to the numerous spines on the plant's branches.

CULTIVATION AND PROPAGATION
Kaffir lime can be grown from seeds, but most gardeners purchase young plants from herb nurseries. It is easily grown in pots. Since the tree is not hardy above zone 9, in cooler areas it should be overwintered preferably in a cool greenhouse.

HARVESTING AND PRESERVING
Harvest leaves fresh anytime. Rather than just plucking a leaf or two from the tree, snip a branch or stem tip and then pull the leaves as needed from the cutting. For most recipes, the leaves are torn into small pieces or finely shredded; if used whole, remove them from the dish before serving. The leaves can be dried or frozen, though they will lose some of their bouquet when preserved. Place dried leaves in a labeled jar and store out of direct light for three to six months. Place whole, fresh leaves in a small freezer container, label, and place in freezer for up to six months. Some recipes call for kaffir lime zest; grate it into a small container and freeze any leftovers for up to three months.

Chenopodium album

LAMB'S QUARTERS

Chenopodium album

The smell of lamb's quarters is similar to spinach. And while the flavor is green and spinachlike, lamb's quarters sometimes has a slight metallic taste, probably from the nutritious minerals the plant contains. *Chenopodium album* is often referred to as wild spinach. It is a relative of spinach and can be substituted for spinach in most recipes.

Leaves of this potherb can be gathered and used fresh in salads, sandwiches, and salsa verde. The small flower buds are tender and tasty, and harvesting them will help the plant produce new growth. The leaves and flowers can be wilted for cooked greens, and cooked in soups, sauces, casseroles, eggs, quiches, and spanakopita. Use them on their own or combined with other greens. Leaves are best when the plants are young and the weather is cool. As the weather warms and the plants start to flower, the leaves can become a bit tougher and bitter.

While we gather the species wild from our gardens, we cultivate 'Magenta Spreen' for its handsome appearance with fuchsia-pink splashes on its leaves. It can get very tall if conditions are right—we've seen it reach 10 feet.

CULTIVATION AND PROPAGATION
Lamb's quarters can be propagated by seed. If you live in a temperate or warm climate, once it is in your garden, it will volunteer for years.

HARVESTING AND PRESERVING
Cut plants back and harvest tips to encourage bushy growth and prevent seeds from forming. When there is an abundance of lamb's quarters to be had, gather them and bring them indoors to process them. Remove leaves from stems, and put them into a bowl with cold water to keep them from wilting until they are ready to use. It is always surprising how much they wilt down when you steam them. To process for storing, blanch and freeze them in freezer containers for three to six months.

This cultivar, 'Magenta Spreen', is very colorful.

Lavandula angustifolia

LAVENDER

Lavandula species

Culinarily, cultivars of lavender (*Lavandula angustifolia*) have more floral fragrance and taste, whereas the lavandins (*L. ×intermedia*) are stronger tasting, with a bit more eucalyptus and camphor to their aroma and flavor. The smell of fresh lavender flowers is light and clean, though assertively floral and sweet.

The leaves are not edible, so use only the tiny flower blooms, which taste strongly of a floral perfume. The fresh or dried flowers are used to flavor chocolates and other desserts often containing fruit or cream, such as cookies, teacakes, custards, and ice cream. Innovative chefs today are using the dried flowers in an herbes de Provence blend (recipes vary, but can include savory, rosemary, thyme, oregano, basil, marjoram, bay, parsley, tarragon, or fennel) to flavor meats, fish, pasta and pizza, egg and cheese dishes, and vegetables.

The most economically important lavender has been common lavender (*Lavandula angustifolia*). This plant typically lives at high altitudes and the floral oil is widely used in finer perfumes. Spike or spike lavender (*L. latifolia*) is usually grown at low altitudes, and the floral oil is usually used for everyday items such as soap. Lavandin (*L. ×intermedia*) is a hybrid of common lavender and spike lavender and has been increasingly substituted for both.

Lavender flowers and oil have been used in bath products since prior to Tudor times. Common lavender oil is colorless or pale yellow with a sweet, floral-herbaceous odor and a pleasant, balsamic-woody undertone. The oil evaporates quickly. It blends well with clove, oakmoss, patchouli, rosemary, clary sage, and pine-needle oils, as well as bergamot and other citrus oils. Lavender and lavandin oils are also used in commercial moth repellents.

Lavender is an essential ingredient for many potpourris, and in the herb garden, roses and lavenders just seem to be made for each other. Lavenders and lavandins make attractive edging plants, with their blooms draping over the walkways. They attract butterflies as well as bees.

The numerous cultivars of common lavender and lavandin vary in flower color, height, vigor, and scent, and more seem to be introduced every year. For the maximum amount of production and flowering over a long period of time, we plant both common lavender and lavandin cultivars. The lavandins seem to survive the longest in our garden, sometimes up to ten years, while the lavenders inevitably succumb to fungus or heat in two to three years. And so, we are constantly experimenting with new cultivars. 'Royal Velvet', for example, has lovely dark flowers and is uniquely

A lavender field is a spectacular sight.

not shatter prone, so even though it dies out, we constantly replace it. 'Tucker's Early Purple' is a common lavender with an extended growth season. Our real standby, though, is 'Grosso' lavandin (named after M. Pierre Grosso), sometimes sold as 'Fat Spike'.

CULTIVATION AND PROPAGATION

Lavender must have full sun, air circulation, and good soil drainage to produce sturdy plants and maximum fragrance. Light-colored mulches such as sand or gravel will also help produce sturdier plants more resistant to sudden wilts. Lavenders grown in shade or with dark-colored mulches in any climate with consistent cloud cover inevitably succumb to sudden wilts, grow spindly, and give poor fragrance. Mulching with oyster shells has been found beneficial in many climates. Granite and other rock dust, sand, and marble or limestone chips are also beneficial as a light top dressing. Soil pH is best near neutral; around pH 7.1 is recommended.

'Grosso' lavandin

Lavender will reseed in the garden unassisted if growing conditions are excellent. Seed propagation is not recommended for home gardeners. Lavender roots easily with late spring and early summer cuttings treated with rooting hormone and planted in 1 part perlite to 1 part baked cat litter (clay frit) in 50 percent shade. Layerings are very easy to do any time of the year: merely scrape the bark off a long stem near the base, apply rooting hormone, bend the stem down, and cover with soil, and peg the stem down with an upside-down V bent from a wire coat hanger.

HARVESTING AND PRESERVING
Lavender flowers produce maximum oil yield when about half of the blossoms are open. Harvest by cutting, and hang or spread on screening for a few days until dried. Since most lavender is prone to shattering, it is best to strip off the blossoms and save them separately, using the leftover stems as fire starters. Lavender flowers may also be used fresh or dried for cooking, but use them sparingly, because they are very perfumy and a little goes a long way. Store dried flowers in labeled jars out of direct sunlight for up to a year.

Apium graveolens var. secalinum

LEAF CELERY

Apium graveolens var. *secalinum*

Leaf celery has a more intense aroma than conventional celery, and is somewhat similar to lovage in that feature. Also known as Chinese celery, it has an intense flavor that is encapsulated in its older English name, smallage or smellage. The flavor of leaf celery also is much stronger, more assertive than that of conventional celery; it tastes very green, somewhat pungent, and slightly bitter.

Microgreens of leaf celery can add additional flavor to salads, but mature leaf celery is more often cooked as a potherb. It is used traditionally in Asian stir-fries, and is also good in soups and stews. Use it as you would use lovage leaves—or anywhere you might use celery—but in smaller amounts because its strong flavor can overpower a dish. Add to stocks, casseroles, and grain dishes in small amounts. It is also sometimes used in rural Greek kitchens for adding a piquant celery flavor.

Seeds are readily obtainable from catalogs that sell specialized herb seeds or Asian vegetable seeds; there, it is sometimes called cutting celery. We like 'White Queen', which has a flavor and aroma that is stronger than Western celery. The long, white stems are much smaller than conventional celery, but the leaves are a must for Chinese food dishes. Alternatively, choose 'Kintsai' (dark green) or 'Nan Ling' (light green). 'Kintsai' makes a good microgreen, while 'Nan Ling' has a pungent flavor necessary for Asian stir-fries. 'Amsterdam' has been around for years and is a hardy, dark green cultivar.

If you want to try cooking with leaf celery before sowing your own seeds, you will commonly find it fresh in markets specializing in Asian vegetables.

CULTIVATION AND PROPAGATION

Leaf celery grows best in the cooler temperatures of spring and fall. Sow seeds directly in the garden in early spring or late summer, about the same time that you might put out brassica crops like cabbage and broccoli. This is another herb that does well under a floating row cover, which will extend the fall season until it freezes.

HARVESTING AND PRESERVING

Harvest leaf celery fresh, just as you would parsley, cutting the outer stalks. Seedlings also make good microgreens for salads. Typically, as leaf celery matures, the flavor intensifies. Leaf celery is more perishable than conventional celery. Harvest, rinse off the dirt, and wrap in paper towels in plastic bags to store it for a few days in the refrigerator. Leaf celery is best used fresh; we do not dry or freeze it.

Melissa officinalis

herbaceous
perennial, to 3
feet tall

hardy to
zone 5

full sun

keep moist but not
constantly wet

well-drained
garden loam,
average pH 6.6

LEMON BALM

Melissa officinalis

Lemon balm is sweetly scented of lemons tempered by a citronellalike aroma. The flavor is mild and sweet, full of lemon notes and a hint of honey. The genus name is derived from the Greek *melissa*, or bee, presumably because honeybees are attracted to the flowers. The leaves and tiny flowers can be used in all sorts of dishes from appetizers to desserts. And it is a lemony addition to beverages, syrups, puddings and custards, scones and cakes; it is also good in sauces and vinaigrettes with vegetables, chicken, and fish.

Lemon balm, or simply balm, was once a major medicinal herb. The Swiss-born alchemist and physician Paracelsus (1493–1541) used it to prepare his elixir vitae, *primum ens melissae*, which he claimed would regenerate the strength of man and render him nearly immortal. Lemon balm has been employed in tisanes, wines, and cordials, and we still find it in liqueurs. It has also been used in eau de cologne, such as Arquebusade, Eau de Berlin, Eau des Carmes, and Hungary water.

We grow the straight species. A virus-infected form, known as golden balm or 'Aurea', is sometimes grown, though it should be avoided because the virus is Tulip Virus X (TVX), which has not yet been detected in the United States in tulips.

CULTIVATION AND PROPAGATION

Lemon balm is easy to grow from seed—almost too easy. If allowed to reseed, it will be with you forever. Start seeds early for transplanting or sow them directly in the garden. Layerings and cuttings are also possible. Lemon balm grows in any reasonably moist garden loam at pH 5 to 7.5, but can be problematic because of the copious seedlings that spread.

HARVESTING AND PRESERVING

Leaves of lemon balm may be used fresh, but are also easily dried over screens and then stored in sealed containers in a cool, dark cupboard. With summer abundance, make an aromatic herbal paste or syrup to preserve, so you will have this bright lemony herb to brighten recipes during the cold days of winter.

Lemongrass (*Cymbopogon citrates*),
showing succulent leaf bases

herbaceous
tender
perennial, 2 to
3 feet tall

cannot
withstand
frost, zone 10

full sun

keep moist but not
constantly wet

well-drained
sandy soil,
average pH 6.0

LEMONGRASS
Cymbopogon citratus

At the base of lemongrass's many fibrous leaves, you will find a pale, succulent core that resembles a scallion. This core is sliced into Southeast Asian dishes to impart a pungent lemon flavor with a whisper of citronella. The mildly lemon-scented leaves are also used in broths, teas, and potpourris.

We grow the straight species. While usually called lemongrass in the American and European herb trade, the commercial common name for *Cymbopogon citratus* is West Indian lemongrass to differentiate it from East Indian lemongrass (*C. flexuosus*) and Jammu lemongrass (*C. pendulus*), which are two species raised for essential oil and normally not found in the kitchen (although they have a similar lemony odor).

CULTIVATION AND PROPAGATION
A single pot of lemongrass will be enough for most home cooks. The potted plant should be overwintered indoors or in the greenhouse. If your local nurseries do not sell lemongrass, check the Asian food markets for lemongrass pieces with stems. Place the unrooted pieces in pots of moistened, sterile potting soil and cover with a polyethylene bag for about two weeks, or until roots appear. Then gradually remove the bag. Lemongrass, once rooted and placed in optimum conditions, will grow rapidly and will need to be repotted within a few months. Lemongrass is shallow rooted and cannot withstand dry soil.

HARVESTING AND PRESERVING
Home gardeners harvest fresh lemongrass leaves a few stems at a time by cutting at the base just below the white core as needed. Finely chop the fresh herb to use in your recipe. It makes a delicate lemon syrup. We do not dry or freeze lemongrass.

Aloysia citriodora

tender perennial
shrub, to 8 feet
tall

hardy to
zone 8

full sun

keep moist but not
constantly wet

well-drained,
friable soil,
near neutral
pH (pH 7.0)

LEMON VERBENA

Aloysia citriodora

Lemon verbena was very popular with Victorian ladies, who tucked sprigs into hankies or rubbed the herb on their necks for its refreshing scent.

Lemon verbena, sometimes simply called verbena in popular literature, is considered among the best lemon-scented herbs. It has a strong lemon bouquet combining sweet floral lemon with that of lemon oil. The flavor of lemon verbena is intensely lemon, even more so than true lemons, and reminds us of candied lemon drops.

The leaves are prized for tea and used in lemonade and alcoholic beverages, cordials, and syrups. The liquid extract has GRAS status. Leaves can be chopped and added to vinaigrettes, grain salads, and fruit salads, and added to desserts such as cakes, cookies, muffins, scones, pies, custards, ice cream, and sorbets. Fresh leaves or flowers are used to decorate all sorts of confections from cakes and pies to puddings; they also candy well. Put a few leaves into your next crème brûlée custard or glasses of iced tea. Leaves or oil of lemon verbena also add a superb lemon fragrance to potpourri and sachets.

We grow the species, which is native to Argentina. Lemon verbena has no commercially available cultivars.

CULTIVATION AND PROPAGATION
Lemon verbena prefers near-neutral garden loam and full sun if grown outdoors. To grow in pots, use a friable, porous soil; a peat and perlite mixture with water-soluble fertilizer works well. In a cool greenhouse during the winter, lemon verbena often drops its leaves and appears dead, but leaves typically reappear when the temperature and day length increase. During this time, watering can be reduced, but the soil should be kept slightly moist. Plants remain evergreen when grown during the winter with supplemental light to extend the day to twelve hours, and continue to grow and then produce flowers in the spring. Prune plants to maintain a bushy appearance.

Lemon verbena is marginally hardy at zone 8; there, it should be protected from excessive frost and wind. Plant it along a south wall. For added winter protection, also cut it back and mulch it with straw. Most gardeners, however, treat lemon verbena as a tender perennial and grow it as a potted plant that can be wintered in the house or in a cool greenhouse.

Lemon verbena is best propagated by cuttings from new growth, although it may also be grown from layerings or seeds (in cooler climates, seeds do not always fully ripen). It is highly susceptible to spider mites and white flies, particularly under hot, dry conditions.

HARVESTING AND PRESERVING
Lemon verbena leaves may be used fresh or dried. They make a delightful syrup. Extracts and tinctures of verbena are also used in the formulation of liqueurs. They can also be made into an aromatic paste for baked goods. Lemon verbena sugar is easily made by layering a generous handful of leaves in a pint jar of sugar.

Levisticum officinale

herbaceous perennial, to 6 feet tall

hardy to zone 5

full sun

keep moist but not constantly wet

soil rich in organic matter, average pH 6.5

LOVAGE
Levisticum officinale

Lovage smells and tastes like a strong, concentrated celery leaf. If you find celery hard to grow, lovage is an easily cultivated plant that is a good substitute. Use lovage wherever celery is desired: soups, stews, salads, casseroles, and stuffings. But use about a third to half as much lovage as celery to compensate for the more concentrated flavor. The leaf stalks of lovage were once blanched like celery by piling soil around the base. The large flowering stems can be candied, while the tender young stems are good in salads. The seeds (actually fruits) have been used as an alternative to celery seed (fruits). The essential oil is used in the formulation of sauces, bouillons, preserves, and condiments.

We grow the straight species.

CULTIVATION AND PROPAGATION

You can grow lovage easily from seeds planted in early spring in rich, moist garden soil with good drainage and partial shade where summers are hot and steamy.

Given the proper nourishment and moisture, lovage can be a giant plant with flowering stalks towering to over 6 feet. Lovage responds to rotted manure and other organic applications when deeply dug into the soil. Mulch well to conserve moisture.

HARVESTING AND PRESERVING

One lovage plant usually produces more leaves than a single household can use. Plants are harvested beginning the second year. Seedlings started indoors and transplanted in the garden will produce yearlings larger than giant Italian parsley that can be harvested the first year. Older plants can be cut back to 1 foot tall in mid-season before flowers appear; they will regrow to produce more leaves before frost. When older leaves turn yellow, simply clip them off; more will replace them later.

Use fresh leaves and stems judiciously. Though not quite as tasty as fresh, you can dry lovage leaves, stems, and seeds in a dehydrator or in an oven with the light on or with a pilot light. Store dried lovage in labeled glass jars until the next harvest season.

Malva neglecta

annual but can
winter over in
mild climates, 15
to 24 inches tall

hardy to
about zone 5

prefers sun,
will tolerate
some shade

keep moist but
not wet

fertile, well-
drained soil,
pH 6.0 to 6.5

MALVA
Malva neglecta

Both the fragrance and flavor of the leaves and flowers of malva are mild and slightly herbaceous—like a mild leaf lettuce—with a touch of sweetness. Harvest leaves at any time, and remove the stems or just leave a very short bit attached to the leaf, since they can be tough and chewy. Leaves and flowers can be eaten fresh in salads, in sandwiches, and as garnishes. Although the leaves can be eaten alone, they have tiny hairs, so they are best combined with other salad greens.

Leaves can be cooked as a potherb and used as a wilted green, or added to soups, stews, sauces, and casseroles. Once cooked, the leaves, and also the little green buds (which have a bit more vegetal, per-haps slightly nutty flavor, are sort of crunchy like peas, and can be eaten raw) release their mucilaginous properties and become slimy like okra (they are kin) and will act as a thickener. Use them just like okra in a gumbo, soup, stew, or gravy with meat. In fact, they have so much mucilage (like *Althaea officinalis,* which marshmallows used to be made from) that wild foods expert John Kallas (in *Edible Wild Plants*) describes in great detail how to make confections from the "mal-low peas," such as mallow foam, meringues, whipped cream, and mallowmallows.

We grow the species, *Malva neglecta,* which is referred to as common mallow or the rather odd name "cheeseweed" or "cheese flower" because the little green fruits (or buds) look like tiny cheeses. It is native to and grows wild across most of North America. The annual dwarf or low mallow (*M. rotundifolia*) and the biennial, sometimes called common or high mallow (*M. sylvestris*), are both edible mallows. The former is small and native to the United States, while the latter grows 15 to 36 inches tall and is native to Europe.

CULTIVATION AND PROPAGATION
If you don't have malva in your yard, it can be propagated from seed. Once you have malva plants, they will reseed, often with abandon. Although the plants will do better in fertile, well-drained soil, with adequate water they are often found on roadsides, in fields, and in vacant lots, so they can tolerate dry conditions. They grow in full sun but will tolerate some shade. Cut the plant back and prune tips to encourage growth.

HARVESTING AND PRESERVING
Harvest small leaves early in the season and cut back tender tips, which will cause the plant to bush out and give you more leaves to harvest. Both leaves and flowers wilt quickly, so putting them in a bowl of cool water will keep them fresh while the rest of the leaves are stemmed and prepared. The leaf stems can be tough and stringy, so test them for tenderness. The little green buds can be plucked from the plants and eaten raw or cooked. All parts of this plant—leaves, flowers, and fruits—are best eaten fresh as soon after harvesting as possible.

Lippia graveolens

tender perennial
shrub, 3 to 9 feet
tall

hardy to
zone 9

full sun

keep moist but not
constantly wet

well-drained
soil, pH
average 6.0

MEXICAN OREGANO

Lippia graveolens

Mexican oregano has the scent of European oregano with thyme and eucalyptus undertones and a slight floral hint. If you want to make authentic Mexican cuisine, you can substitute European oregano and most people will not be able to taste the difference. But smelling them side by side, they are easily distinguished. Use the leaves in any dishes where oregano would be used—to flavor tomatoes, salsa, sauces, soups, vegetables, pasta, and cheese dishes.

Mexican oregano exists in at least two different forms in the commercial herb trade: one scented of oregano, the other of eucalyptus. Let your nose be your guide when purchasing Mexican oregano.

CULTIVATION AND PROPAGATION

Mexican oregano makes a fine pot plant that can be trained into a tight shrub. If you live in a cool climate, overwinter the plant in its container in a cool greenhouse. You can propagate it easily by cuttings, and seeds are also easy to germinate. Beware, however, that the resulting plants from seeds will sometimes smell of eucalyptus and not oregano, so don't propagate from seed if you want the guarantee of true oregano taste. Instead, buy a plant or make a root cutting from one that you can smell and taste and are sure about.

HARVESTING AND PRESERVING

Harvest leaves as needed. The leaves are easily dried on screens. Mexican oregano can be pruned hard to flush out more leaves, but don't do this more than twice in one season or you may weaken the plant. Store dried leaves in a labeled jar out of direct sunlight until the next growing season. Try using Mexican oregano in an herb butter or to make an herb vinegar.

Tagetes lucida

herbaceous tender perennial, 2 to 3 feet tall

 marginally hardy to zone 7b; hardy to zone 8

 full sun

💧 keep moist but not constantly wet

 light loamy soil, pH 6.1 to 7.8

MEXICAN TARRAGON

Tagetes lucida

Annual marigolds (*Tagetes* species) have been popular for so long with the general public that they have become a landscape cliché in many regions of the world. These familiar, bright flowers in yellows and oranges are mostly the product of selection from the African marigold (*T. erecta*) and the French marigold (*T. patula*). Their pungent foliage and flowers do not endear them to many gardeners.

Mexican tarragon (also called sweet marigold, sweet mace, and Mexican mint marigold) has an entirely different aroma, superficially similar to French tarragon (*Artemisia dracunculus* 'Sativa') though without the full, warm herbaceous smell of that classic culinary herb. The yellow-orange flowers of Mexican tarragon, unlike the flamboyant blooms of its bedding plant cousins, are small enough to be overlooked when they appear in late fall. In warm climates with high rainfall or high summer humidity, where French tarragon is difficult or impossible to grow because of its susceptibility to diseases, Mexican tarragon is often grown as a substitute.

While the essential oils of African and French marigolds (and Mexican marigold, *T. minuta*) have GRAS status, Mexican tarragon unfortunately lacks this critical legal classification. Yet, it is still found in supermarkets, where it is sometimes sold as winter tarragon or Texas tarragon, or mistakenly as French tarragon.

Mexican tarragon, under the Nahuantl names *yahutli* or *tumuts·li*, is an ingredient in an herbal mixture smoked by Huichal Indians in Mexico. In many parts of Latin America today, sweet marigold is used to brew a tea and in salsas.

We grow the straight species (*Tagetes lucida*). A few selected forms are gradually appearing in the herbal marketplace.

CULTIVATION AND PROPAGATION

Mexican tarragon is easily propagated from cuttings, and branches near the base often have adventitious roots (roots not formed from other roots, for example, stems) already formed that can be broken off and planted. Seed is difficult to find and often slow to germinate. Plants may be grown in pots, where a soil-free growing medium works well, or in the garden with good, friable, well-drained soil in full sun.

We grow Mexican tarragon in large pots with other tender herbs and bring them indoors for the winter to ensure plants for next year. While French tarragon droops under summer heat, Mexican tarragon luxuriates in high temperatures. Keep the moisture constant, though, to prevent wilting from water stress.

HARVESTING AND PRESERVING

Harvest leaves as needed for recipes calling for tarragon, such as béarnaise sauce. Leaves can be used fresh or dried, and they make a tasty vinegar. Although dried leaves do not have quite the same scent as fresh, they still retain some flavor. Store dried leaves in labeled jars out of direct sunlight and use before the next harvest season.

Claytonia perfoliata

annual, 4 to 15 inches tall

hardy, cold tolerant, though will perish with severe frost

sun to part shade

keep moist but not wet

well-drained, sandy loam soil, pH 6.5 to 7.0

MINER'S LETTUCE

Claytonia perfoliata

The aroma and taste of these pretty green leaves with small white or pink blooms is mild and green, sort of spinachlike. It appears in sunny spots in early spring and is found in shady places when the weather gets warmer. It was given the moniker "miner's lettuce" by California gold rush miners because it is one of the first wild, green edibles growing in the spring after a long, cold winter without fresh vegetables, and they ate it for vitamin C to avoid getting scurvy.

Eat miner's lettuce fresh in salads, and it is a tasty garnish for sandwiches. This potherb can be steamed on its own or with other greens as a hot dish. We grow the species, *Claytonia perfoliata*.

CULTIVATION AND PROPAGATION

This plant is native to the northwest coast of North America. Start it from seed for early planting in the garden, broadcast or in rows. The plant form is unusual and intriguing in appearance. The first leaves form a basal rosette, then a stem is sent up and the next leaves are rounded and grow to surround the stem. Then the flower stem grows up from that leaf, which makes the flower look like it is in a saucer.

Often, reseeded plants are more vigorous than the initial planting, so allow it to reseed in the garden for the following year.

Miner's lettuce is a cool-weather plant and enjoys the spring, or it can be planted in late summer for a fall-to-winter crop, if wintered over in a hoop house or greenhouse.

HARVESTING AND PRESERVING

To ensure continuous leaf production, cut the plant back about 1 inch above the soil level. It will sprout again and grow more leaves even with continuous harvests. Foliage and flowers are best eaten fresh.

Mentha spicata

herbaceous
perennials, from
procumbent to 3
feet tall

/// hardy in
zones 5 to 10

full sun to part
shade

keep moist but
not wet

well-drained
loam, average
pH 6.2 to 6.9

MINT
Mentha species

If there is only one mint plant in your garden, then it has to be spearmint (*Mentha spicata*). There are many mint species grown around the globe, yet spearmint is grown on all of the continents, with the exception of the North and South Poles. While the sweetness of spearmint can be used in almost any dish, the intense peppery, menthol flavor of peppermint is usually reserved for desserts and chocolate, where a big impact is desired.

Since red-stemmed double-mint combines the characteristics of spearmint and peppermint, it works well where a bright mint flavor is called for. Although there is no mint flavor to orange mint, its flavor suggests Earl Grey tea, so it is perfect for desserts, baked goods, fruit dishes, chocolate, and as a beverage. All these mints, fresh or dried, make lovely herbal teas. Mint plants have square stems, a feature of the mint family of herbs.

Spearmint

There are many spearmints on the market, but you can't go wrong with the cultivar *Mentha spicata* 'Kentucky Colonel'. The value of this plant was recognized by the Spanish invaders in the New World. Wherever they went in the sixteenth century, they took what we now call 'Kentucky Colonel' with them from Guatemala to New

Mexico to the Philippines. Mary Peddie, an herb grower in Kentucky, went down to the ditch near her farm, grabbed the local "ditch mint," and introduced it to the world as 'Kentucky Colonel'. Mary recognized that 'Kentucky Colonel' has large, pale green, wrinkled leaves that crush well with ice and bourbon. 'Kentucky Colonel' has that unique fragrance that you expect of spearmint, clean and sticking to the nasal passages. It has a fresh, sweet mint aroma, and the taste is cool, clean, and sweet. The flavor of 'Kentucky Colonel' reminds us of those sugary spearmint-flavored, green gummy candies in the shape of a leaf that we loved when we were children.

We enjoy spearmint on a hot summer day by placing a few sprigs of fresh 'Kentucky Colonel' in a large pitcher of ice water, lemonade, or iced tea. In any Middle Eastern dish, from tabouli to tzatziki dressing, this spearmint just has no match. As the name implies, it makes a tasty contribution to alcoholic drinks, from mojitos to the traditional mint julep, and it is a perfect flavoring for cakes, cookies, and ice cream.

For a very similar flavor, we recommend Egyptian or Bowles mint (*Mentha* ×*villosa* nothovar. *alopecuroides*). The large, ovate, wrinkled leaves are similar to 'Kentucky

'Kentucky Colonel' spearmint

'Madalene Hill' has a distinctive inflorescence.

Red-stemmed doublemint 'Madalene Hill' has the flavor of both spearmint and peppermint.

Colonel' but with a fuzziness that seems to help release the heady spearmint aroma. This may be sometimes sold as apple mint, but that moniker is better applied to the true apple mint or pineapple mint (*M. suaveolens*). Alternatively, if you can find it, Scotch spearmint (*M. ×gracilis*) has narrow leaves but with a guaranteed aroma of spearmint; this selection is also cultivated for spearmint oil.

Doublemint and peppermint

Mentha ×gracilis 'Madalene Hill' is the only true doublemint commercially available, combining the flavors of spearmint and peppermint in one plant. It is also sometimes sold as red-stem apple mint. It brings Wrigley's Doublemint Gum to mind. While we have true peppermint in our garden, the sharpness of its cool flavor limits its use to items like peppermint candies, chocolate brownies, and mint chip ice cream. 'Madalene Hill' is more versatile, since it combines the sweetness of spearmint and the coolness of peppermint, and so its use extends beyond desserts and is especially appreciated in both alcoholic and nonalcoholic drinks.

If you want to grow true peppermint and mix it with a spearmint instead, then we recommend 'Mitcham', 'Blue Balsam ', or 'Chocolate' (which, by the way, has no chocolate flavor but has a sharp coolness that one might associate with chocolate).

Orange mint

We usually grow orange or bergamot mint (*Mentha aquatica* var. *citrata*) in our garden for potpourri (combined with rose petals, rose geranium, and lavender), and use it mostly in desserts and beverages. Sometimes called the "eau de cologne" mint, American lavender, or perfume mint, orange mint is elegant floating in finger bowls with lemon slices at a dinner with greasy finger foods. While orange mint has notes of lavender and Earl Grey tea, its citrus flavor is bright, and there is no hint of mint whatsoever in the taste. Orange mint works well with the stone fruits of summer—peaches, nectarines, plums, apricots, and cherries—whether it is macerated with them for fruit salad, baked in pies or cobblers or crisps, or made into jam or preserves. It is also delicious when combined with chocolate, especially in bittersweet chocolate truffles.

CULTIVATION AND PROPAGATION

For most people, the problem is not how to cultivate mint but, rather, how to control the plants. Mints are like stray cats: you take them in, feed them a little, provide some conditions to their liking, and they are yours forever—usually.

While some mints will often set seeds, many, such as true peppermint, are sterile hybrids. As a rule, unless you are interested in generating new types of mints (or just want surprises), don't bother with propagation by seeds. Even in those mints that do set seed, the total appearance, from hairiness to leaf shape to odor, will not come true from seed.

Abundant long, thin stems, called stolons, grow from the base of the plant, either just above the soil level or just below. To propagate, merely snap off some stolons, cover with about 1 inch of soil (with the delicate tips poking their noses just above the soil), and water. Mint is also among the few herbs that will quickly form roots in a glass of water. Mint will gradually form a large colony from the stolons, typically with the center of the colony becoming less and less dense and forming lots of young plants on the periphery. If you have too many plants, share them with friends.

HARVESTING AND PRESERVING

Mint leaves are excellent fresh and also dry well. Harvest mint at the time of flowering by simply cutting the stems near the base and hanging them to dry. Dried leaves may be stored whole, in sealed jars until the next harvest. Try to avoid crushing the leaves and pack them whole, because bruising releases essential oils and flavor is lost. We also preserve our mints by making them into syrups and aromatic herbal pastes and freezing them.

'Mitcham' is a true, peppery, peppermint.

We like orange mint though it does not have a minty fragrance or flavor.

Mioga ginger (*Zingiber mioga*) leaves, rhizomes, and inflorescence

herbaceous tender perennial, 3 to 10 feet high

 marginally hardy to zone 7

 part shade to full sun

🜄 keep moist but not constantly wet

✧ well-drained organic soil

MIOGA GINGER
Zingiber mioga

Mioga (or myoga) ginger grows to 2 to 3 feet in the average garden, and up to 10 feet under optimum conditions. It has fragrant rhizomes and bamboolike leaves, but the choice culinary portions are the young buds and the ghostlike, fleshy inflorescences that appear at the base of the leaves in the fall. Gingery yet floral, the pale yellow flower clusters are usually pickled and then sliced for soups, stir-fries, and sour dishes. The young leaves and sheaths can be finely chopped and used as a garnish for soup and raw fish. The young shoots are also blanched and used in soups, tempura, and as a spice for bean curd. Mioga ginger does not have GRAS status, although it has been used for millennia in Japan with no reported ill effects.

We grow the straight species (*Zingiber mioga*). Some specialty catalogs also list the beautiful variegated form with yellow flowers, 'Dancing Crane'. Both provide a tropical element in the garden.

CULTIVATION AND PROPAGATION
Most species in the family Zingiberaceae are not hardy except in tropical climates. But mioga ginger is hardy to at least zone 7. Provide the plant with good, humusy soil and part shade to full sun. Propagation is via the abundant rhizomes, which will quickly form a dense, slowly spreading colony (but not to the point of being weedy). A 4- to 6-inch layer of sawdust can provide a substrate to help you locate and pick the buds. If you live in a cool climate, grow the plant in a pot and overwinter it in a cool greenhouse.

HARVESTING AND PRESERVING
Harvest the flower buds in the autumn of the second year. They can be used fresh or pickled in salted rice vinegar and sake. Use shoots and young leaves fresh.

Cryptotaenia japonica

perennial, about 12 inches tall (in flower)

 hardy to at least zone 6

 part sun to light shade

 keep moist but not constantly wet

 soil rich in organic matter

MITSUBA
Cryptotaenia japonica

Mitsuba looks like a flat, broad Italian parsley and tastes of a mix of chervil, celery, and parsley. Sometimes called Japanese parsley, mitsuba has been used for centuries in Japan as a fresh topping for vegetables. The aroma is not pronounced unless the leaves are chopped, and then it is decidedly green and herbaceous, suggesting parsley with a hint of celery. It is believed to have a stimulating effect on the appetite. Mitsuba can also be used as a potherb.

In Japan, there are named cultivars such as 'Yanagawa 1 goh' and 'Kanto-masurmori', but these are not readily available elsewhere. Form *atropurpurea* (or murasaki-mitsuba) has dark purple leaves.

CULTIVATION AND PROPAGATION
Give mitsuba moist, well-drained humusy soil in a shady section of the herb garden. This short-lived perennial has small white flowers. It readily reseeds and may become weedy. It is very similar to honewort (*Cryptotaenia canadensis*), which is found in piedmont forests in eastern North America and has also been used as a chervil substitute, though it is not as delicate in flavor.

HARVESTING AND PRESERVING
Use mitsuba leaves fresh as a substitute for chervil or parsley. As with most salad greens, use the leaves fresh and do not dry them.

Monarda didyma

| annual or perennial, to 47 inches tall | hardy to zone 4 | full sun to part shade | keep moist but not constantly wet | well-drained garden loam, neutral pH 6.8 to 7 |

MONARDA
Monarda species

Monarda, also known as bee balm or bergamot, is a native American herb named after a Spanish physician and botanist, N. Monardez, of Seville. Its bristly, colorful ornamental flowers have a shaggy-headed appearance. All species attract hummingbirds and bees and are good honey plants. The twelve species of *Monarda* offer a wide assortment of fragrances and flavors—from lemon to thyme to oregano to rose—produced on annual or perennial plants. The leaves of all monardas offer great relief when rubbed on bee or wasp stings, and thereby the apt common name, bee balm.

Monarda cultivars with red flowers tend to have a tealike aroma and flavor, suggesting Earl Grey tea and rose geranium. The leaves are more herbaceous, while the flowers are sweeter like honeysuckle. Leaves and flowers can be used for sweet dishes—in syrups and beverages, with summer fruits—and baked in scones and tea breads. The lemony forms, although rare, are delightful in tea and in fruit salads. The more common thyme- and oregano-scented types can be used as substitutes for thyme and oregano, and generally their blooms are shades of purple, pink, and white. Use the leaves and flowers of these savory monardas wherever you would use oregano. The flowers are fun and tasty scattered over pasta and vegetable salads, grain salads, and pizza. Before using monarda, smell and taste the flowers and foliage so that you know if they belong in a savory dish or a dessert because they can be quite different in flavor.

Monarda species do not have GRAS status but they lack any

'Cambridge Scarlet' monarda

Wild monarda (*Monarda fistulosa*) has
a pungent flavor similar to oregano.

potentially poisonous or harmful
chemical components and have
been used for millennia by Native
Americans.

While we love the bright red
blooms of 'Cambridge Scarlet',
most selections of *Monarda* are
prone to powdery mildew. So
choose mildew-resistant cultivars,
particularly 'Colrain Red', 'Marshall's
Delight', 'Purple Mildew Resistant',
'Raspberry Wine', 'Rose Queen',
'Rosy Purple', 'Violet Queen', and
Monarda fistulosa f. *albescens*.

CULTIVATION AND PROPAGATION

You can generally cultivate monarda in moist, well-drained garden loam in full sun to part shade, depending on the species. Hybrids with red blooms, derived from *Monarda didyma*, can grow in sun or some shade, but prefer shade, deep humusy soil, and plenty of moisture. Hybrids that have light and lavender floral shades, derived from *M. fistulosa*, prefer well-drained, gravelly soil in full sun.

HARVESTING AND PRESERVING

Harvest the leaves fresh as you need them. Use the red flowers in beverages and syrups, and use the purple- and pink-flowered cultivars with an oregano flavor in herb butters and cream cheese. The leaves and flowers are easily dried by hanging or laying over screens. The dried flower heads, sometimes tinged with reds and purples, also make beautiful dried flowers. Dried leaves or flowers can be stored in labeled jars out of direct sunlight until the next harvest season.

Brassica species

annual, 1 to 3 feet tall	withstands frost; will brown on edges with prolonged freezing weather	full sun	keep moist	well-drained loam, average pH 6.2

MUSTARD
Brassica species

The genus *Brassica* gives us many agriculturally important crops, including cabbage, broccoli, cauliflower, kale, and Brussels sprouts. The leafy mustards are derived primarily from two species, *B. juncea* and *B. rapa*. They have little fragrance whole, but when you crush the leaves, they release that biting aroma of mustard.

By themselves, the fresh leafy mustards can be almost too pungent. We most often enjoy the piquant taste of mustards raw in salads, mixed with blander lettuces. The leaves can also be used as a potherb, wilted on their own or with other greens, or roughly chopped and added to soups. Visitors to our gardens will frequently find us grazing the tops of our leafy mustards as we garden.

Of the leafy mustards, our top choices are the reddish 'Scarlet Frills' (*Brassica juncea*) and the bright green 'Mizuna' (*B. rapa*). Both offer a frilly, pungent addition to salads.

'Scarlet Frills' also has a golden green version, 'Golden Frills'. They are delightful garden plants, for their colorful foliage as well as their flavor. For a flat-leaved version of 'Scarlet Frills', 'Red Giant' produces a large amount of salad herb and is slower to bolt, while flat-leaved 'Garnet Giant' is probably the darkest available for baby leaf mustard. 'Suehlihung No. 2' is similar in taste to 'Mizuna'.

CULTIVATION AND PROPAGATION

Mustards are native to cooler regions of Europe and perform best in the cool weather of spring and fall. They are also an excellent crop for a sparsely heated greenhouse or a cold frame that might otherwise go unused in the cooler months. The growing season can be extended by using a floating row cover.

The leafy mustards have weedy characteristics, so they are among the easiest vegetables or herbs to grow; both species are already naturalized in many regions. We like to grow leafy mustards in large plastic tubs with the other greens that constitute a mesclun mixture.

Sow from early spring, as soon as the ground can be worked, and again in late summer. For ease of harvesting, sow thickly in bunches rather than rows. Sow seeds ¼ to ½ inch deep in a 2-inch-wide band, about 15 seeds per foot in rows 18 to 24 inches apart. For tender baby-leaf greens, sow about 60 seeds per foot.

HARVESTING AND PRESERVING

Cut leafy mustards when they reach full size (about 12 inches). Harvest baby-leaf greens as entire plants when they reach 3 to 6 inches tall. We eat our mustard greens fresh. But if you have an abundance, you can blanch, drain, and freeze them in freezer containers for up to six months.

'Scarlet Frills' mustard

Green 'Mizuna'

Myrtus communis 'Microphylla'

large shrub or
small tree, to
16 feet tall

hardy to
zone 9

full sun

keep moist but not
constantly wet

well-drained
garden loam,
average pH 6.8

MYRTLE
Myrtus communis

In his massive book, *The Food of Italy*, Waverly Root wrote, "Sardinia's favorite flavoring is myrtle, a preference which may well go back to the Stone Age." On this western Italian island, myrtle wood is used for the fires to spit-cook whole animals, and myrtle stems and leaves are used to line holes dug in the ground for pit cooking, a Sardinian method that imparts what Root says is an "exquisitely delicate flavor" to meats, especially whole pig. After the Sardinians boil a chicken and remove it from the pot, they cover it with myrtle leaves and put a plate over the bird while it cools; this dish is called *gallina col mirto* and is eaten cold the next day.

The flavor of myrtle, sometimes called Greek myrtle, is close to that of Grecian bay, for which myrtle is often used as a substitute. The aroma brings bay to mind, though it is sweeter and slightly more floral. The essential oil of Greek myrtle, similar in odor to Greek bay, is considered GRAS only in alcoholic beverages. It is also used in perfumes (the oil is sometimes known as *eau d'anges*, or angels' water) and is excellent in potpourri.

For culinary uses, the broad-leaved cultivars, usually unmarked as to name, are preferred. Many selections of myrtle lend themselves to easily trained handsome topiaries, especially the cultivar 'Microphylla', also called Greek myrtle, which has tiny leaves.

CULTIVATION AND PROPAGATION
Greek myrtle is not hardy above zone 9, so it is best grown in a pot and then moved in the winter to a cool greenhouse. Use a friable potting soil and place in full sun. While Greek myrtle may be propagated by seed, it is most commonly propagated by cuttings. The cultivars we've specified can only be propagated by cuttings.

HARVESTING AND PRESERVING
Harvest leaves or flowers fresh as needed. Dry branches easily by hanging, and dry leaves spread on screens. Although when dried, myrtle leaves lose some of their aroma and flavor, they can be stored in labeled jars out of direct sunlight until the next harvest.

Variegated nasturtium (*Tropaeolum majus* 'Alaska') leaves, flowers, and dried seed

annual, dwarf bushy cultivars, 8 to 18 inches tall; climbers, 6 to 10 feet tall

 hardy in frost-free locations

 full sun; can tolerate some shade, which produces more leaves, less flowers

 keep moist but not wet; will tolerate some drought

friable, porous garden loam, average pH 6.5

NASTURTIUM
Tropaeolum majus

The name nasturtium combines the Latin *nasus* for "nose" and *tortus* for "twisted," describing how our nose twists or wrinkles when we inhale the nasturtium's spicy scent. Related to some cresses, nasturtiums add a botanical piquancy to seasonal dishes. You can use both the leaves and flowers to add a pleasant hint of heat and pungency (which dissipates when cooked). The foliage lends a peppery, cress-like taste to salads, sandwiches, and green sauces. Use the leaves chopped as a topping for pizza, and shredded and tossed with pasta, rice, couscous, or chicken salad.

The flowers have a similar pepperiness, though they are a bit milder with a hint of floral scent. They make showy containers for dips or spreads, as well as for cold dishes like egg salad, chicken salad, or vegetable salad. They are slightly fragile when filled, so place them on a slice of bread or vegetable to pick

them up easily. Whole blooms can be used in salads or as garnishes. Nasturtium-flavored vinegar is pretty in color and interesting in flavor. Cut flowers and leaves into chiffonade (thin ribbons) and blend with butter, or toss with pasta, vegetables, or fish.

The species is a vine or mounding annual. The vining forms can easily grow 8 to 10 feet long. You can grow them along a fence or up a trellis for support, or you can do as Monet did, and just let them trail across paths, spill over walls, or hang over the edges of containers. Some of our favorite "nasties" are *Tropaeolum majus* 'Alaska' (brightly colored flowers with variegated foliage) and 'Amazon Jewel' (fire-cracker colors, and a prolific climber); and the bicolor cultivars like 'Peach Melba' (pale creamy yellow with orange splotches), 'Empress of India' (brilliant orange-red blooms against blue-green foliage, a knockout),

The bicolored 'Peach Melba' nasturtium has yellow and orange blooms.

'Empress of India' reigns supreme with her scarlet flowers against blue-green foliage.

and 'Whirlybird' (semidouble flowers in many shades with medium green leaves).

CULTIVATION AND PROPAGATION

Nasturtiums start easily from seed in average soil and full sun. Sow seeds in early spring, about the same time as early greens. Poke the bumpy, round seeds into the cold earth along the edges of the kitchen bed or anywhere you want showy mounds, 8 to 12 inches apart. Use them for borders in flower beds, to spill over the edges of the raised kitchen garden bed, plant them in rows between the lettuce and peas in the vegetable garden, and cultivate them in containers as well as hanging baskets. Once they have germinated, keep them well watered and free of weeds. Over-fertilization results in considerable leaf growth with fewer flowers.

HARVESTING AND PRESERVING

For the leaves, harvest them and remove stems, wash, and use like lettuce. Harvest leaves regularly to keep them bushy. Pick the flowers with long stems and put in a glass of water until ready for preparation. Rinse blooms gently and shake or pat dry. Pull the flower from the stem and use whole or gently tear into separate petals. Eat the leaves and flowers fresh, or use them to make vinegar or herb butter.

The unopened buds, marinated in wine or vinegar, make an unusual refrigerator pickle. Green seeds are harvested and pickled and used as a substitute for capers.

'Whirlybird' nasturtium comes in an assortment of colors.

Atriplex hortensis 'Triple Purple'

| annual, 2 to 6 feet tall (if not harvested) | hardy, though not frost tolerant | sun; some shade in hot climates | keep moist but not wet | fertile, well-drained soil, about pH 7.0 |

ORACH
Atriplex hortensis

Also called mountain spinach, orach (or orache) is a tasty salad green. The leaves do not have much odor: they smell like a salad green, slightly herbaceous. The taste is like a mild spinach, with pronounced flavors of red beets and minerals. Fresh, the green- or ruby-colored orach leaves are used in salads and on sandwiches. When cooked as a potherb, leaves wilt quickly and are best combined with other greens.

Atriplex hortensis is the common green-leaved orach found most often. We love the ruby-red color of A. hortensis var. rubra, sometimes sold as A. hortensis 'Ruby'.

CULTIVATION AND PROPAGATION
Orach is easily grown from seed sown directly in the garden in fertile, well-drained soil 8 to 10 inches apart. The richer the soil, the bigger and juicier the leaves. Plants tend to get tall and leggy if not harvested regularly; keep them cut back so the plants get bushy and provide more leaves. Once the weather gets hot, orach will bolt, so keep plants cut

back to prevent this. But bolting will be inevitable, so do a spring planting and a late summer planting for fall harvests. This potherb does better in cooler weather, but it will produce in summer if it is watered. In very hot weather and bright sun, the red leaves sometimes get scorched, so place them accordingly.

At the end of the season, allow a few plants to set seed, and gather them just before ripening. If allowed to seed in the garden, there will be many volunteers for years to come.

HARVESTING AND PRESERVING
Harvest the leaves regularly to encourage more leaf production. Eat them fresh, when in season. Orach does not dry or freeze well.

Origanum vulgare subsp. *hirtum* 'Greek'

herbaceous
perennial, to 3
feet tall

hardy to
zone 6

full sun

keep moist to
somewhat dry

well-drained
gravelly loam,
average pH 6.7

OREGANO

Origanum vulgare subsp. *hirtum*

The taste and scent of oregano are particularly evocative of the Mediterranean region. They bring back memories of the local cuisines and of the rocky hillsides covered with sweet and savory scents and sparkling flowers. Confusion exists about what constitutes oregano, so it's good to remember that oregano is a flavor from more than one species. Cooks throughout the world use oregano-scented plants in such concoctions as za'atar (a spice mixture of salt, sesame seeds, sumac fruits, and oregano-scented thymes) of Syria to the pizza created at your local pizzeria (flavored with Greek or Turkish oregano) and the chili of Tex-Mex restaurants (sometimes flavored with Mexican oregano). What really defines

"oregano" is a chemical, carvacrol, which has a harsh, nose-prickling, creosotelike odor similar to thyme (thyme is scented with thymol, a related phenol). With the presence of carvacrol, you can be sure that there will be a pungency in taste—a hot bite to the tongue.

Confusion also exists regarding the subspecies of *Origanum vulgare*. *Origanum vulgare* subsp. *vulgare* is called wild marjoram in English, *origan vulgaire* or *marjolaine sauvage* in French, and *Wilder Majoran* in German. This plant bears pretty pink flowers with purple bracts but is useless as a condiment. But wild marjoram is often sold as oregano, so buyer beware.

Origanum vulgare subsp. *hirtum* is Greek or Turkish oregano, and the

Italian oregano is a cross between a spicy oregano and sweet marjoram.

'Hot and Spicy' oregano

characteristic odor and pungent savory flavor make it relatively easy for any gardener to identify. In addition, the flowers of Greek or Turkish oregano are white (not pink, as in wild marjoram) and the bracts are green (not rosy as in wild marjoram).

The so-called Italian oregano in American herb markets (*Origanum* ×*majoricum*), sometimes sold as Sicilian oregano, is a cross between *O. vulgare* subsp. *hirtum* and *O. majorana* (sweet marjoram) and therefore has a bit of pungency tempered by the sweetness of marjoram. It is used to create many dishes in Italy, from tomato sauce and marinades to minestrone, and is cooked with vegetables and beans. It is one of Susan's favorites in the kitchen both fresh and dried.

To be sure that you are getting the real, pungent oregano plant and not its wimpy cousin, wild marjoram, purchase the cultivar known as 'Hot and Spicy'. Plants labeled "Greek" are also usually the real thing. Ultimately, you will need to let your nose be your guide; the foliage should smell strong and pungent. Then taste a leaf; it should be hot on the tongue. The same goes for "Italian oregano": when you rub and smell the leaf, it should have a big bouquet, both pungent and sweet.

CULTIVATION AND PROPAGATION

Grow oregano in well-drained loam in full sun. The addition of a light top dressing of gravel or sand will result in more stout growth that is resistant to disease. For oregano with a full, robust flavor, set out plants in full, blaring sun and give them plenty of room with good air circulation. Oregano is particularly subject to sudden wilts caused by *Fusarium oxysporum* and *F. solani fungi*, which tend to strike in shady, moist, crowded conditions.

HARVESTING AND PRESERVING

The flavor of oregano is most intense in the flowers. Harvest plants when about half the flowers have opened. Use leaves and flowers fresh or dried. Oregano dries quite nicely; dry by hanging for several days. Then strip off both leaves and flowers, and store in labeled jars out of direct sunlight until next season's harvest.

Porophyllum ruderale
subsp. *macrocephalum*

annual, 3 to 6 feet tall	very sensitive to frost	full sun	keep moist but not constantly wet	well-drained, garden loam

PAPALOQUELITE
Porophyllum ruderale subsp. *macrocephalum*

Papaloquelite has been used in Mexico as the equivalent of today's cilantro (originally native to China) since well before Columbus. Branches of papaloquelite are still kept today in glasses of water on the tables of cafes and bars in Mexico, and the leaves are torn fresh and sprinkled on beans or eaten with tortillas and garlic. The egg-shaped leaves impart a strong, unique, cilantro–green pepper–cucumber flavor, a bit stronger in flavor than cilantro and slightly resinous. Cilantro haters call it "buzzard's breath," but it makes a really authentic salsa, so just ignore them. Despite its consumption for perhaps millennia in Latin America, papaloquelite has no GRAS status (probably because no one has petitioned for it).

In South America, the leaves of the subspecies (*Porophyllum ruderale* subsp. *ruderale*) are used in foods under the name *quinquiña* (in Bolivia) or *cravo de urubu* ("black vulture's marigold" in Brazil). Occasionally, Mexican markets and some herb nurseries in Texas and Mexico will also offer related species, such as *P. coloratum* or *P. tagetoides* (called *pipicha* in Mexico); these have narrow leaves with a similar flavor.

CULTIVATION AND PROPAGATION
Each marigoldlike plant may grow to 6 feet tall and provide plenty of foliage, but the rayless flowers are rarely produced in the northern areas before frost. If you grow this outside of southern Texas and Mexico, grow it in pots so that you can gather the dandelionlike fruits with their tiny, bristly parachutes.

HARVESTING AND PRESERVING
Harvest leaves of papaloquelite fresh as needed. Like cilantro, these just don't retain their flavor well if dried. During harvest season, when the herb is ready at the same time as chiles and tomatoes, be sure to make a batch or two of salsa with papaloquelite and preserve it in canning jars or freeze it for up to six months.

Petroselinum crispum
var. *neapolitanum*

biennial, to 27
inches tall

can withstand
frost

full sun

keep moist but not
constantly wet

well-drained
garden loam,
average pH 6.2

PARSLEY

Petroselinum crispum

Parsley is an herb that many people recognize quickly. But it may be among the most misunderstood plants in the herb garden. Parsley is often used as a green garnish, especially on restaurant dinner plates, and sometimes it just gets thrown away, which is a shame because the leaves are quite high in vitamins A, B1, B2, and C, as well as niacin, calcium, and iron.

The smell and taste of this vibrant herb are pleasantly green and herbaceous. Throughout the world, parsley plays a starring role in a variety of prepared foods. It is used fresh in salads and sauces or added toward the end of cooking to just about any savory dish. Parsley is the main ingredient in salsa verde, as well as in the Italian *gremolata* (a simple blend of chopped parsley, garlic, and lemon zest) and can be used as an alternative or supplement to basil pesto. Parsley is a key ingredient in many herbal blends because it combines well with just about all herbs, supporting their flavors—sometimes tempering a strong-flavored herb, or complementing a milder one. The

clean, delicate flavor also acts as a breath freshener.

The bright green, fernlike leaves provide a delightful accent in the sunny herb garden and make an excellent edging plant. Three types of parsley are grown in the United States: common (curled-leaf, var. *crispum*), plain (flat-leaved, or Italian, var. *neapolitanum*), and Hamburg or turnip-rooted (var. *tuberosum*). The first two are used in sauces, stews, soups, prepared meat products, and condiments, while the latter's large, edible root is considered a vegetable.

Flat-leaved parsley

All parsleys taste green and herbaceous, a bit grassy with just a hint of sweetness and tanginess (think mild spinach or strong green leaf lettuce) and a mineral aftertaste. Many cooks maintain that Italian flat-leaved parsley has a more pronounced flavor. In reality, this perception is related more to texture than chemistry: the curly leaved parsleys are fluffy and airy, dispersing the parsley flavor into a cotton-candy type of delivery

Petroselinum crispum var. *crispum* is a
curly leaved parsley.

vehicle. Flat-leaf types include
'Perfection', 'Plain', and 'Plain Italian
Dark Green'.

In Italy, the cultivar called 'Catalogno', with its long, thick stems and
large, dark, flat, green leaves, is considered to be the true Italian parsley,
while other flat-leaved parsley
selections are regarded as "comune"
(common or ordinary). In the United
States, 'Catalogno' is rarely available.
It is usually listed as 'Giant Italian',
and is superior in flavor and yield to
other flat-leaved parsleys.

Curly-leaved parsley
Curly-leaved cultivars include many
very similar ones, so take your pick:
'Afro', 'Banquet', 'Bravour', 'Curlina',
'Dark Moss Colored', 'Decorator',
'Deep Green', 'Envy', 'Evergreen',
'Ferro', 'Forest Green', 'Improved
Market Gardener', 'Moss Curled',
'Paramount', 'Perfection', and
'Sherwood'.

CULTIVATION AND PROPAGATION

Seeds (really fruits) have slow, irregular germination, with 10 and 28 days needed for the first and last germination, respectively. Parsley's slow, erratic germination has given rise to the fanciful tale that the seed has to go to Hell nine times and back before it will germinate. Germination can be enhanced by soaking the seeds in aerated water for three days at 77°F, draining, rinsing, and then sowing ¼ inch deep in a fine seed bed.

Seed started indoors and transplanted into pots has a more rapid and uniform germination without special treatment, probably because of constant moisture levels and warm soil temperatures. Parsley presents no problems as a transplant as long as it is properly hardened off before it is planted in the garden. A floating row cover will prolong fall harvest.

In other aspects, parsley should be treated as a leafy green vegetable and grown in rich, moist soil with good drainage and a pH of 5.3 to 7.3.

HARVESTING AND PRESERVING

Although parsley is a biennial, it occasionally blooms the first year, which reduces yields. Parsley subjected to thirty days of temperatures below 40°F will flower. Parsley in its second year is usually useless as an herb because the leaves turn bitter after the flower stems rise from the center of the plant in early spring. When grown for its foliage, parsley is considered an annual.

Parsley may be harvested by hand continuously throughout the year as a culinary green. The outer leaves should be clipped 1 to 3 inches above the crown. Up to three sowings of seeds may be possible in some areas for harvests April to December, and the home gardener will find that a cold frame will provide fresh parsley all winter. Since dried parsley loses much of its flavor, use parsley fresh from the garden, or buy it fresh since it is readily available in supermarkets throughout the year. Keep some parsley butter on hand in the freezer for spontaneous use.

Dried black and white peppercorns
(*Piper nigrum*) and fresh leaves

PEPPER

Piper species

Black pepper (*Piper nigrum*) plants are tropical vines. The genus *Piper*, derived from the ancient Latin name, includes more than 1,000 species of vines, shrubs, and small trees. The best-known species are *P. nigrum*, black pepper; *P. cubeba*, cubeb; and *P. betle*, the betel leaf or pan. The fruits, or berries, from these plants have a pungent, spicy aroma—in fact, it's downright nose-tingling. The taste is quite warming and pungent, hot to the tongue, with some spice, and can be slightly acrid. Black pepper (*Piper nigrum*) is the pepper most often used internationally. Its popular piquant flavor is used in everything, including soups and stews, sauces, casseroles, vegetables, pickles, seafood to steaks, and game.

The dried fruits, referred to as peppercorns, are best ground fresh as needed. Once ground or powdered, pepper rapidly loses its pungency, so a good-quality peppermill is an important tool for a cook. The fruits and leaves of many other species are also used for seasoning; many have heart-shaped leaves. All *Piper* species have an inflorescence of tiny white flowers on a fleshy spike. All are tropical greenhouse plants not hardy above zone 9.

Black pepper vines grow up a support or host tree, and they need semishade. On a trip to Costa Rica, Susan saw a spice plantation of black pepper plants. They had hung palm fronds as shade cover over the vining plants, which were covered with stems of hanging fruits in the green stage. Outside of the tropics or subtropics, you need a greenhouse to cultivate the plants, which are handsome with heart-shaped leaves.

Piper auritum, sometimes called makulan, is the only Central American *Piper* species in general cultivation in the United States, but it is often confused with *P. sanctum* (known as *hoja santa, hierba santa,* or *acuyo*). The bases of the leaves of *P. auritum* are unequal and overlapping, so they have an earlike appearance (which is the meaning of the species name). The large, velvety, heart-shaped leaves, studded with crystal-like glands, have a wonderful sassafras odor from which derives the alternate common name, root beer plant. The stems have swollen nodes and become quite woody; they are frequently used as canes or walking sticks.

Crushed makulan leaves are used by natives in Panama to attract fish during the dry season, and so the fish taste like this sassafras-scented herb after feeding regularly on the leaf. In Veracruz, the leaves are ground with garlic, chiles, and roasted tomatoes to make a sauce for fish; the leaves are sautéed with shrimp and roasted peppers. The large leaves are also used to line fish or chicken casseroles that are laced with spicy chile sauces. In the southwestern United States, the leaves are wrapped around pork tamales before cooking.

Because of the known liver toxicity and carcinogenicity of the chemical safrole, the main component of the plant's essential oil, and because the U.S. Food and Drug Administration has prohibited safrole in foods since 1960, *Piper*

auritum is not recommended for consumption in the U.S. (see sassafras for a discussion of safrole).

Piper lolot, or *lá lốt* in Vietnamese, is one of a number of herbs that reached the shores of the United States with refugees who fled Vietnam at the end of the war in 1975. The glossy heart-shaped leaves of *P. lolot* are used by the Vietnamese to impart a delicate herbal, black pepper–like flavor to roast beef or to a type of shish kabob. To use the leaves for such dishes, first dip them in boiling water to keep them from burning, and then wrap them around small pieces of beef, secure with a toothpick, place on a skewer, and barbecue.

CULTIVATION AND PROPAGATION
Black pepper, makulan, and *lá lốt*
should be grown in rich, well-
drained soil in dappled afternoon
shade. Provide ample moisture.
We recommend growing the plants
in large pots, since these plants
must be moved indoors north of
zone 9 in winter. They can be easily
wintered over in a greenhouse or on
sunny windowsill. Makulan and *lá
lốt* can be purchased from specialty
food stores; neither has GRAS status.

HARVESTING AND PRESERVING
Leaves should be harvested fresh
and used immediately. If you are
fortunate enough to have a black
pepper vine produce fruits, harvest
the fruits when they are green and
pickle them green or dry them until
they turn brown and wrinkled. Store
dried black peppercorns in labeled
glass jars for up to a year.

Perilla frutescens

annual, to 39
inches tall

seedlings cannot
withstand frost

full sun

keep moist but not
constantly wet

friable garden
loam, average
pH 6.1

PERILLA

Perilla frutescens

In Japan, different forms of perilla, or beefsteak plant, are given different names: *e-goma*, *remon-egoma*, *tora-no-o-jiso*, *chirimen-jiso*, or *shiso*. The purple-red leaves of perilla are used to color apricots, gingers, and tubers of Jerusalem artichokes. When used this way, the leaves are salted or pickled to remove the water-soluble cyanogenic glycosides (sugar-bound hydrocyanic acid), which reduces their harshness. The aromatic foliage, whether green or reddish purple, is somewhat anise-scented and smells and tastes flowery sweet though herbaceous with a hint of bitterness after the sweet perfume. It is used in salads, to flavor bean curd, sushi, and sashimi, or as a garnish for tempura. The flower spikes are used in soups or fried, while the seedlings are used to flavor raw fish.

We cannot recommend most forms of perilla (*Perilla frutescens*) for culinary applications. It has no GRAS status, and many forms are rich in perilla ketone, a chemical shown to be a potent lung toxin. However, forms of *P. frutescens* high in perillaldehyde, providing a strong cuminlike odor and flavor, are popular in Japan as *aojiso* for suppressing the sardine odor of *niboshi* soup stock. A Vietnamese cultivar called 'Tia To' (sometimes sold as "cumin-scented") has no toxic perilla ketone and also has the cumin scent and flavor. Although this cultivar was recommended for GRAS status by the Flavor Extracts Manufacturers' Association in 1978, its full safety remains unestablished. If you cannot find seeds of 'Tia To', the cultivar is easily rooted from cuttings sold as fresh herbs at Asian grocery stores. 'Tia To' is unique in color, purple-red on top, and green on the bottom, unlike the typical forms, which are purple-red throughout.

CULTIVATION AND PROPAGATION

Culturing perilla is almost too easy: it requires friable garden loam in full sun. The herb generously reseeds and becomes a weed that can spread throughout the garden. 'Tia To' usually does not bloom until very late in the fall or early winter, so it rarely has time to produce seeds. Aside from being the safest perilla plant to consume, it has the fewest horticultural bad habits.

HARVESTING AND PRESERVING

Harvest seedlings, leaves, and flower spikes as needed. *Perilla* does not dry well and is best used fresh. The leaves are often pickled.

The leaves of this plantain
(*Plantago lanceolata*) show how
heavily veined plantain leaves are.

tough perennial, with flower spike 8 to 12 inches tall

hardy to zone 5; not frost tender

sun to shade

keep moist but can endure dry conditions

well-drained soil, average pH 6.2

PLANTAIN
Plantago species

Broadleaf or common plantain (*Plantago major*) was brought to the United States from Eurasia and became naturalized very quickly, where it encountered a similar native species, *P. rugelii*, blackseed plantain. *Plantago coronopus*, buck's horn plantain, came later from Eurasia and also became naturalized in some sections of North America. The Native Americans gave broadleaf plantain the name "white man's foot" or "Englishman's foot," referring to wherever an Englishman stepped, a plantain grew in his footsteps. Known best for its many medicinal virtues, these potherbs were also cooked and eaten as a vegetable. Many of the *Plantago* species are edible potherbs; we prefer *P. major* and *P. coronopus* culinarily.

The leaves of these plantains have very little aroma and flavor—they are bland, mildly herbaceous, perhaps vaguely suggesting minerals and spinach. And they do leave a bit of the chalky mouth feel that spinach has. Since the leaves contain tannins, they are slightly astringent. Leaves are best early in the season when they are very young, eaten raw when small, otherwise they get stringy and tough. Cook them to make them more tender: blanch them in boiling water for about 1 minute, drain, and cook them again—boil, steam, or sauté until tender, and dress them with olive oil or butter, perhaps some garlic, salt, and freshly ground pepper. They are best combined with other, more lively tasting greens. Chopped, they can be added to soups, sauces, and casseroles. Immature flower spikes are edible: they can be eaten raw or steamed.

Variants of the naturalized broadleaved plantain can be found in lawns and fields, and along roadsides worldwide; blackseed plantain seems to be confined, for the most part, to the United States. The selected cultivar, *Plantago coronopus* 'Minutina', is a good selection to grow for winter salads.

CULTIVATION AND PROPAGATION
These plantains are very adaptable, green plants that grow close to the ground. The leaves are ribbed, grow in basal rosettes, and can be oval, lance-shaped, or nearly round. The size of the leaves and the height of the flower stalk vary depending on growing conditions. They can grow in sun or part to full shade, and although they prefer well-drained soil, they will survive in clay, sand, or loam. The plants are self-fertile; they spread by seed, and most likely you will never have to plant them.

HARVESTING AND PRESERVING
Do not harvest plantain from any landscape that has been sprayed or fertilized with chemicals. To harvest, gather up the leaves of the rosette in your hand and cut across the bottom of the plant above the ground. Leaves can be gritty on the undersides, so be sure to wash them and spin dry; remove the lower tough stem. For culinary purposes, harvest fresh leaves when they are young. For medicinal use, leaves can be gathered throughout the season. Seed stalks can be harvested and dried, and then the seeds can be saved for planting, or they can be ground and used as a nutty-tasting flour.

Dried poppy (*Papaver somniferum*)
seedpods and seeds

POPPY

Papaver somniferum

Papaver somniferum is the poppy that produces opium, but it also is the only source of edible poppy seed and poppy seed oil. Today, most poppy seed is imported from the Netherlands and Australia; the slate-blue Dutch poppy seed is standard. The tiny, crunchy seeds have an aroma and taste that are slightly earthy and nutty, with the seedlike flavor being a bit reminiscent of sesame. Lightly toasting or baking the seeds will enhance the nutty flavor. The whole seeds are commonly used in poppy seed dressing and on dinner rolls, while the crushed seeds, mixed with sugar and other ingredients, are used as filling in pastries.

The seed oil is considered GRAS. The pressed oil is used in artists' paints, salad oil, soap, and other commercial products.

Because of the potential abuse of the opium-yielding sap of this plant's seedpods, cultivation in many countries has been prohibited since the early twentieth century. Opium poppies were once widely cultivated for their beautiful, shaggy, pink blossoms and pale gray-blue-green foliage, and sometimes they persist in old cottage gardens. Since growing your own poppies of this species is illegal, we have omitted directions on cultivation.

Relatively recent tests have shown commercial poppy seed to contain small amounts of morphine and codeine. Perhaps those warm poppy seed milkshakes that are sometimes given to German and Eastern European children to soothe them into slumber have a real effect!

For long storage, keep poppy seed in the freezer since they can go rancid because of their high oil content.

Portulaca oleracea

PURSLANE
Portulaca oleracea

Purslane, also sometimes referred to as "pusley," is a succulent that has been cultivated for thousands of years in China and India, and is grown and sold today in many European markets by the kilo for those who enjoy this potherb. The succulent leaves of the plant do not exude much aroma, but the taste is tart and lemony from the oxalic acid, somewhat mild and herbaceous, and the texture is both crunchy and mucilaginous. The leaves, stems, and small yellow flowers are all edible. The plant contains lots of minerals and vitamins, and has the highest amount of omega-3s of any plant in the vegetable kingdom. The fat stems and leaves, as well as the flower buds, can be eaten raw as a salad; added to other salad greens or vegetable salads like cucumbers, grain, or pasta salads; or used in tzatziki or salsa. Purslane is a traditional ingredient of *fattoush*, a well-known Middle Eastern salad.

The leaves and stems can be cooked like greens in boiling water, or sautéed and wilted with olive oil and garlic like they do in Greece, Italy, and France. It is great in stir-fries. When cooked, it loses some of its tartness, and its mucilaginous texture can be used to thicken soups, gumbos, and sauces. Some cultures used to pickle the stems, and Native Americans gathered the seed and ground it for flour.

We grow the species, *Portulaca oleracea*, without even planting it—it is a welcome naturalized weed in our gardens. It has green, paddle-shaped leaves and stems with a red-purple tinge. We prefer a few cultivars with larger leaves and upright growth, such as golden purslane ('Goldberg'), which has golden-green leaves and orange stems, and 'Gruner Red', which has succulent green leaves and pink, upright stems.

CULTIVATION AND PROPAGATION
Purslane does not like cold weather, so don't sow it outdoors until the soil is warm and the daytime temperature is about 80°F and nights have warmed up, because it is prone to damping off (dying from fungal attacks) if sown too early. Seed can be sown indoors for an early start, or wait and sow seed in the garden in late spring or early summer. It will grow rapidly if planted in a sunny location in rich, well-drained soil. Keep harvesting the tip ends or whole stems to encourage new growth throughout the season.

Being a succulent, purslane holds water in its stems and leaves. Once acclimated, it is fairly resistant to drought, but lack of water will slow down and stunt growth. It prefers open space and hot sun to crowding and shade.

Purslane's main pest in the garden is slugs, who love to munch on this crunchy plant, so beware and maintain slug patrol, especially when weather is wet.

HARVESTING AND PRESERVING
When harvesting during the season, cut center leaves and tip ends to encourage growth; use the new smaller growth for salads. If harvesting a lot, cut the plant back to 1 to 2 inches above the ground, making sure to leave at least a full set of lower leaves so the plant can make new growth. The larger, older leaves and stems are better cooked. Leaves and stems wilt quickly, so wash in cold water and refrigerate if not using right away.

Allow the plants to flower and set seed near the end of the growing season, if you want to save seed for next year. Purslane is best used fresh, soon after harvest. It does not freeze or dry well, though stems and leaves are tasty when pickled in vinegar.

Limnophila chinensis
subsp. *aromatica*

annual to
short-lived
perennial, to
20 inches tall

hardy to
zone 9

full sun

keep wet;
standing water
preferred

friable garden
loam

RAU NGÔ

Limnophila chinensis subsp. *aromatica*

The scent of rau ngô's leafy branches is like lemon, though subtler and more floral. The taste is minimal. Rau ngô is an essential ingredient for several Vietnamese sweet-and-sour dishes, particularly a traditional soup made with tamarind and cantaloupe. Despite millennia of use, rau ngô has no GRAS status. Only the straight species is available.

CULTIVATION AND PROPAGATION

If you cannot find rau ngô plants at a nursery, simply root cuttings from plants purchased at an Asian grocery. Rau ngô prefers mud and a film of standing water in full sun. In the following spring, just buy another plant or two from your favorite Asian grocery.

HARVESTING AND PRESERVING

Harvest whole plants as needed. Rau ngô does not dry well and is best used fresh.

Persicaria odorata

herbaceous perennial, to 6 inches tall

marginally hardy to zone 7

full sun

keep wet; standing water preferred

garden loam

RAU RĂM

Persicaria odorata

Rau răm, often pronounced "zow-zam," is widely sold in the United States as Vietnamese coriander. The odor of the leafy branches is that of cilantro with a hint of lemon. The taste is similar, though a bit more pungent and bitter. Rau răm is used by the Vietnamese to garnish meat dishes, especially fowl, and is also eaten with duck eggs. The herb is also an ingredient in a Vietnamese pickled dish resembling sauerkraut. Rau răm has no GRAS status despite millennia of use. Only the straight species is available.

CULTIVATION AND PROPAGATION

If you cannot find rau răm plants at a nursery, simply root cuttings from plants you purchased at an Asian grocery. Rau răm grows best in mud and a film of standing water in full sun.

HARVESTING AND PRESERVING

Harvest whole plants as needed. Rau răm does not dry well and is best used fresh.

Persea borbonia

tree, to 66 feet tall

hardy to zone 7

full sun

keep moist but not constantly wet

light loamy soil, slightly acid pH preferred

RED BAY
Persea borbonia

The mildly spicy leaves of red bay (*Persea borbonia*) are used on the southeastern coast of North America as a substitute for Greek bay or laurel (*Laurus nobilis*). Red bay looks, smells, and tastes similar to Greek bay, although the bouquet is not nearly as big or intense. It is more green grass–scented with some spice and is slightly sour or acrid. It smells and tastes similar to wheat grass juice. The flavor is green first, than a bit sour, followed with some of the spice of bay laurel and a hint of balsam. Use as you would use *Laurus nobilis*.

Only the straight species is available. A closely related species, swamp bay (*Persea palustris*), occurs as far north in North America as southern Delaware and also bears spicy leaves with fuzzy, brown undersides. Neither red bay nor swamp bay is considered GRAS, despite no harmful chemistry and millennia of use by Native Americans.

CULTIVATION AND PROPAGATION
While leaves are commonly gathered from the wild, you can easily cultivate the tree from zone 7 and warmer in sandy to rich, moist soil and full to part sun. This attractive evergreen is nearly pest-free and deserves to be more widely known.

HARVESTING AND PRESERVING
Harvest leaves as you would bay leaves (*Laurus nobilis*). Use them fresh or dry them. Store dried leaves in labeled jars out of direct sunlight for six months.

Chamaemelum nobile

| perennial, to 12 inches tall | hardy to zone 5 partial to full | sun | keep moist but not constantly wet | garden loam, average pH 7.0 |

ROMAN CHAMOMILE

Chamaemelum nobile

Roman chamomile may be every herb gardener's favorite plant to simply walk on. A barefoot sunrise meander through a patch of chamomile, when crushed, on a dewy summer morning may bring to the body a soft tranquility and to the nose a fruity aroma reminiscent of bananas and apples. The scent has been described as sweet herbaceous, somewhat fruity-warm and tea leaflike with nuances of green apples, while the taste has fruity, herbaceous characteristics along with a mild bitterness.

Chamomile flowers are most famous for their use as a calming tea. They can be used to make syrups, a popular ingredient in today's cocktails, cordials, used with fruit, and in desserts from cakes and cookies to puddings and pies.

Ingestion of raw leafy branches of Roman chamomile as tea, bee-pollen, and even honey can induce various allergic reactions in susceptible individuals (particularly those who are ragweed-sensitive).

At least two different cultivars are available: 'Flore Pleno' has double white flowers rising to about 3 inches; we gather these flowers for the kitchen. 'Treneague' generally does not flower, making it ideal for lawns or as a delightfully scented nonflowering ground cover.

CULTIVATION AND PROPAGATION

The cultivar 'Flore Pleno' will typically grow best for the home gardener. Roman chamomile prefers cool, moist summers. Under the best circumstances, the home gardener should be happy to allow Roman chamomile simply to ramble cottage-garden style through the moist, humusy border along walking stones.

HARVESTING AND PRESERVING

Harvest flowers from late July to early August, and then dry them. Spread them on baskets or screens and dry them out of direct sunlight in a place with good air circulation, or use a dehydrator. If you are in a humid climate, spread the flowers on baking sheets and place in an oven with just a pilot light or turn on the oven light and leave for 24 to 48 hours or until completely dried. Store the dried blooms in labeled jars out of direct sunlight and use before the next harvest season.

Rosa rugosa 'Fru Dagmar Hastrup' hips

shrub, 2 to 6
feet tall

most selections
hardy to zone 6

full sun

keep moist but not
constantly wet

friable garden
loam, pH 5.5
to 6.5

ROSE
Rosa species

Roses have enthralled humans for their beauty of form and scent through the ages. Today, we use rose petals for perfumes, cosmetics, and even salads, while the fruits, known as hips, are high in vitamin C. Roses have long symbolized romance. We find special pleasure and meaning in being able to grow, touch, and inhale the fragrance of the same rose that grandmother grew in West Virginia or Napoleon's Josephine grew at Malmaison.

The fragrance of rose flowers is unique unto itself—light, floral, and rosy, an ethereal perfume. The blossoms' aroma can vary from a strong perfume to a mild apple aroma or no scent at all. The more intensely scented roses tend to taste like their fragrance, and usually the more aromatic the rose is, the more flavor it has. The flavors also vary from flowery to subtle perfume or sour and downright bitter. So taste the petals before using them in a recipe.

The flavor of roses suits desserts particularly well, especially pastries, cakes, and custards. Petals, rose water, and rose syrup are often used in Middle Eastern cooking in beverages, desserts, butter, with grain dishes, and even meat and fowl. Rose also blends well with egg dishes in a supporting context of herbal flavors.

Rose hips taste lemony and tomatolike, tart and sweet. Rose hip jelly is especially good on toast, scones, and other savories served at breakfast, especially in conjunction with a good English tea. They make a delightful syrup with honey.

With about 100 species and several hundred hybrids to choose from, it is difficult for the novice gardener to decide on just a few roses to plant. For flowers to use in the kitchen, we prefer the old-fashioned roses: the damask (*Rosa damascena*), the rugosa (*R. rugosa*), and the apothecary's *R. gallica* 'Officinalis', and their hybrids.

With even more petals than and a fragrance similar to the apothecary's rose, the gallica hybrid 'Charles de Mills' is without equal.

Rosa rugosa 'Hansa'

'Celsiana', a damask hybrid, yields abundant pale pink blossoms, while 'Hansa', a rugosa hybrid with dark pink flowers, mimics the scent of the commercial rose attar (waxy essential oil) from Bulgaria. For maximum rose hip (fruit) production, we prefer the species *Rosa canina*, the dog rose, along with the single selections of *R. rugosa*.

CULTIVATION AND PROPAGATION

Most roses do best in deep, fertile, moist, well-drained soils with a pH of 5.5 to 6.5. A position that provides full sun and good air circulation helps reduce disease and insects. The choice of species or cultivar (as well as your climate) will dictate spacing. We prefer own-root roses (roses grown on their own roots, not grafted). Some gardeners prefer fall planting to give the roots extra time to establish themselves, but in zone 7 and north, some winters will be so cold that the fall-planted roses will not survive.

Do not fertilize newly planted roses; wait four to six weeks for the plants to become established. Authorities agree that roses are heavy feeders, but they do not seem to agree on the type of fertilizer or the rate. We recommend yearly feedings of about a cupful of 5-10-5 fertilizer per established rose bush, sprinkled in a circle around the base, supplemented with monthly feedings of fish emulsion, manure tea, or other organic sources of nutrients for maximum growth.

Many heritage (old-fashioned) roses are easily propagated by cuttings. Those that don't root easily from cuttings, such as the roses with heavy *R. gallica* ancestry, produce suckers, which are easily transplanted. Many people swear by using pencil-sized cuttings that are still green taken in the fall, though we have had good success with "heel" cuttings of blooming stalks: just grab a recently bloomed branch and tear down, pulling off a "heel" of mixed tissue. Taking cuttings at the time of flowering also guarantees proper identification. The cleanliness, temperature, and humidity of the rooting process are of primary importance; rooting medium that suffers from fungi contamination, high temperatures, or low humidity guarantees failure.

HARVESTING AND PRESERVING

Do not expect typical blossoms or fruits of a species or cultivar until the second year after planting. The blooms of the first year are smaller and sparser than are typical.

You'll need to be sure to harvest organic flowers for culinary use—those that have not been sprayed with pesticides. Harvest flowers at the peak of flowering and either use immediately in recipes for beverages, syrups, and jellies, or air-dry slowly, and when completely dry, pack in tightly sealed jars. Fruits are best after a hard frost, when they soften up and become somewhat mushy. At this point, they are easily processed into syrups, jams, and jellies, and they can also be slowly dried for teas.

Rosmarinus officinalis

tender perennial
shrub, to 6 feet
tall

hardy to
zones 7 or 8

full sun

keep moist but not
constantly wet

light loamy
soil, average
pH 6.8

ROSEMARY

Rosmarinus officinalis

Rosemary has long symbolized remembrance, and for good reason. After we work with rosemary plants or even brush against them, the invigorating, piney fragrance clings to wool, hair, and skin. The fragrance evokes images of fresh-roasted lamb on skewers of rosemary branches prepared over a campfire on a gravelly beach, with the Mediterranean Sea breaking in the background.

Rosemary scents can be varied, but good culinary rosemary is deeply resinous, scented of pine with nuances of eucalyptus. The strong taste echoes the aroma, with pine, green resin, and sometimes just a hint of bitterness. Rosemary is used in kitchens throughout the Mediterranean region, especially in France, Italy, and Spain. Rosemary goes well with fatty foods—many meats, from chicken to pork to beef, and also cheeses. It is excellent with seafood, and pairs well with many vegetables, especially grilled potatoes. Rosemary branches, left over from stripping the leaves, also make great skewers for grilling. A bit of caution for those who have not cooked with rosemary before: use sparingly at first until you are

used to the flavor and its intensity, then gradually try recipes with more rosemary.

Sometimes, a few whole sprigs of rosemary can be added to a dish, perhaps laid in the bottom of a roasting pan for potatoes, chicken, or a roast. The foliage on rosemary is tough and needlelike, so use the whole sprigs for flavoring, and remove them before serving, or finely mince the rosemary leaves before adding them to a recipe.

Many cultivars of rosemary are available, but we prefer those that do not smell of camphor but have the aroma of pine with nuances of eucalyptus and lemon. 'Shady Acres' is particularly tasty and low in camphor. 'Tuscan Blue' is a handsome specimen with blue flowers, and the camphor content is very low. Flowers on different cultivars range from lavender, blue, to deep purple, and even white and pink, while growth can be upright or sprawling.

Although needles vary in thickness, most upright rosemary bushes look similar except for the blooms. If in doubt, reject any rosemary with an overpowering scent of camphor and steer toward those with a piney-eucalyptus aroma. For example, 'Arp' is routinely hardy to zone 7, but it contains 19 percent camphor in its essential oil.

CULTIVATION AND PROPAGATION

Rosemary is difficult to grow from seed because of low seed viability and slow growth, and named cultivars do not remain true to type when seed-grown. Cuttings root readily in water, in a variety of aggregates, or in a combination of sphagnum peat moss and perlite.

Rosemary in pots is especially sensitive to overwatering; the soil must dry slightly between watering, though not to the point where the plant wilts. Overwatered rosemary develops brown leaf tips, an indication that some roots may have begun to rot. Clay pots will allow the soil to dry faster, a condition that lessens root-rot problems during periods of low light in winter. Pot-grown plants may become root-bound quickly (yellowing of lower leaves at the base of the plant is an early warning of this stress) and should be repotted during periods of rapid growth—generally spring and summer. If planted directly into the garden, rosemary may be fertilized once in the season with a granular 5-10-5 or 10-10-10 fertilizer during active growth.

Rosemary may be pruned severely to shape the plants or to keep them from interfering with nearby herbs. Pruning is also a good method of maintaining airflow around and through rosemary plants, an important cultural feature that helps prevent foliar diseases that cause wilt. If you grow rosemary in a cool climate, grow in pots and bring indoors for the winter.

Rosemary is subject to attacks

from spider mites, mealy bugs, whiteflies, and thrips, as well as attacks by fungi and stem galls. Organic mulches near the base of the plant often hold water and moisture near low-lying foliage, which provides a home and pathway for water-borne fungi and bacteria. Mulches of pea gravel, ground oyster shells, or sand, which dry rapidly and radiate drying heat into the interior of dense rosemary plants, help to lessen diseases.

HARVESTING AND PRESERVING
Harvest plants fresh as needed. The flowers are edible too, and can only be used fresh. Rosemary may be easily dried by hanging or by placing the leaves on screens, and storing them in labeled jars out of direct sunlight until next season's harvest.

Dried "threads," or stigmas, of
saffron crocus (*Crocus sativus*)

cormous
perennial, to 6
inches tall

hardy to at
least zone 6

full sun

keep well-
drained

basic garden
loam, average
pH 6.9

SAFFRON

Crocus sativus

Saffron flowers with precious stigmas.

Ounce for ounce, saffron is the most expensive herb or spice in the world, with natural vanilla second. Saffron, the stigmas of *Crocus sativus* flowers, has an unusual, intensely sweet, somewhat spicy, flowery-soapy aroma with a slightly fatty-herbaceous undertone. In the kitchen, saffron imparts a distinct, floral perfume and mildly pungent taste that is slightly bitter (similar to blackstrap molasses in the most minute amount), and an exotic richness to a wide array of dishes, as well as a bright, orangish yellow color.

Many cultures consider saffron's inimitable bouquet and taste essential, for both color and flavor, in the best-loved, traditional dishes. It is especially paired with all types of seafood, as well as rice, pasta, grains, and breads. It is added to Spanish paella, a seafood and rice casserole; Italian risotto, a rice dish; Provençal bouillabaisse, a fish stew; Russian *kulich* or Easter bread; Pennsylvania Dutch *bot boi*, or chicken noodle stew; and Swedish *lussekatter*, or Saint Lucia's cakes. Saffron also is used to color cheeses and liqueurs such as Fernet-Branca.

CULTIVATION AND PROPAGATION

In Spain, saffron planting traditionally begins during the feasts of Saint John and Saint Peter at the end of June. Corms are planted 5 to 7 inches deep, 6 to 8 inches apart, and 4 inches between rows, in well-drained, loose, sandy, or calcareous soil that has been well dressed with rotted manure before planting. Blossoms are fewer when corms are planted at shallower depths. The corm lies dormant from about May to September, then autumn rain causes blossom production.

The home gardener can plant a few dozen saffron corms and gather enough stigmas to make a few culinary creations. It is fun to see how the plants grow and experience why the stigmas are so prized. Every three years, dig up the corms, separate them (each corm produces four to ten daughter corms each season), select for size and health, and transplant to avoid disease and crowding.

HARVESTING AND PRESERVING

Gather the crocus flowers in the morning. Spread the flowers on a table, and split the crocus blossom down the stem. With your fingers, remove the three-part stigma, which is the only edible part of the plant. Place the fresh saffron stigmas onto a fine-meshed screen and dry over gentle heat or in the oven with just the pilot or oven light on. The final product will be dry to the touch, with its distinctive flavor intact. Saffron should be stored in tightly sealed glass jars out of direct light, at a relative humidity not exceeding 57 percent.

Salvia officinalis

shrub, 2 to 3
feet tall

hardy to zone 6;
pineapple sage
hardy to zone 9

full sun

keep moist but not
constantly wet

well-drained
garden loam,
average pH 6.4

SAGE
Salvia species

Sage, or more properly common or garden sage (*Salvia officinalis*), has a unique assertive, warm-spicy herbaceous note of camphor and eucalyptus. This feature is evident in both the bouquet and the taste along with a musky characteristic and just a bare suggestion of lemon as the endnote. Slightly bitter and resinous, sage is particularly associated with sausage and poultry stuffing and is widely used in flavoring condiments, meats, beans and stews, cheeses, grain and pasta dishes, root vegetables, sauces, liqueurs, and bitters. Fresh sage leaves are especially attractive when pressed onto turkey, chicken, and ravioli. The flowers can be used as a savory garnish on grain dishes, pasta, or pizza. Use sage in small quantities at first, since it has a strong flavor.

Pineapple sage (*Salvia elegans*) is a vigorous, strongly stemmed plant with red-tinged green leaves scented of pineapples, providing the common name. Think of the cream-colored Lifesaver in the Five Fruit Flavors roll that you ate as a kid—this is what *S. elegans* smells and tastes like. It is pleasantly fruity and sweet in aroma and taste, and does not have the camphor or muskiness of *S. officinalis*. *Salvia rutilans* is a name sometimes applied to pineapple sage and is synonymous with *S. elegans*. Pollinators, particularly hummingbirds, are attracted to pineapple sage.

The young shoots of pineapple sage have been used to flavor drinks, and its fresh leaves and scarlet-red flowers have been used as garnishes for desserts despite the plant's lack of GRAS status. But no poisonous components are known in pineapple sage. In the kitchen, we use the showy flowers, leaves, or the syrup made from them to echo the pineapple flavor in pineapple sorbet, piña coladas, and pineapple upside-down cake.

Garden sage
'Berggarten' (mountain garden) is the best aromatic plant and strongest tasting of the numerous cultivars of garden sage. It has large, rounded leaves, few flowers, and a fragrance that matches the imported Dalmatian sage (the commercial dried sage that is most often encountered by cooks). We also like the diminutive-leaved 'Nana', since the small, whole leaves can be used in cooking. We enjoy the garden aesthetics of 'Purpurascens', which has lovely leaves tinted lavender and gray-green, and 'Woodcote Farm', which has foliage in mottled shades of sage green, although these are not quite as big in flavor.

'Berggarten' has more rounded leaves than the other sages and a more robust flavor.

The diminutive leaves of 'Nana' make it a good choice for cultivating in containers.

221

The bright green leaves of *Salvia elegans* are sweet and scented of pineapple.

Pineapple sage

For pineapple sage (*Salvia elegans*), we grow the straight species. 'Honeydew Melon' is an attractive selection with a melonlike scent, scarlet flowers, and lime-green foliage. We also like to use fruit-scented sage (*S. dorisiana*), which is sometimes called peach sage because of its large, bright green, peach-scented leaves and fuchsia flowers often used to line cooking pans for peach cobbler to enhance flavor. Hands down, peach sage is the herb that kids will always choose to use in scones; it's often called tutti-frutti sage. The flavor and fragrance of the leaves and flowers of all the fruit-scented sages are best captured in baked goods, ice cream, sorbets, and infusions. They are good in tea, fresh, or dried.

CULTIVATION AND PROPAGATION

The home gardener will usually be satisfied with one or two large plants of 'Berggarten' garden sage.

The variegated leaves of 'Woodcote Farm' are subtle shades of gray-green.

'Purpurascens' brings a striking purple hue to the herb garden.

Bright red blooms of pineapple sage appear late in the season.

Pinch the growing tips of any of the culinary salvias regularly throughout the first summer to create many branches. Also cut back the plant about one-third before new growth starts in the second year. Give a side dressing of fertilizer six to eight weeks after planting. When plants are established, fertilize in spring when growth starts and again about the first week in June.

Named cultivars of garden sage are easily propagated from cuttings 1½ to 2 inches long dipped in root hormone. If taken in late fall to early winter, the cuttings will establish ample roots in the greenhouse for transplanting in the garden by spring. Take cuttings from new growth of nonflowering stems, preferably from the base of the plant if available.

Both pineapple sage and fruit-scented sage can be grown in the garden and treated as annuals. We prefer to grow them in large pots so we can enjoy them into winter and the next year.

HARVESTING AND PRESERVING

Harvest fresh leaves of culinary sage as needed. Only fresh garden sage leaves, not dried, can be sautéed for the popular garnish for pasta. Sages are easily dried by hanging or by placing the leaves on screens, and storing the dry leaves in sealed, labeled jars out of direct sunlight until the next harvest. The flowers of *Salvia officinalis* and *S. elegans* sages are edible, too. They can be used fresh as a garnish or in an herb butter. Use *S. officinalis* blooms in savory dishes and *S. elegans* in desserts, syrups, and beverages. The red blooms of pineapple sage and the fuchsia-colored flowers of fruity sage can be dried for tea.

Common garden sage in bloom

Sanguisorba minor

short-lived herbaceous perennial, to about 18 inches tall

 hardy to zone 5

 part to full sun

 keep moist but not constantly wet

 well-drained garden loam, average pH 6.8

SALAD BURNET

Sanguisorba minor

Salad burnet is one of those herbs that can shine in the garden as well as in the kitchen. Considered a landscape plant, it has unusual accordionlike, bright-green leaves, which are somewhat lacy and ferny in appearance, providing texture and contrast in the herb garden. In the kitchen, salad burnet's light cucumber-flavored leaves are useful in several ways. In France and England, the leaves are used for dressings, salads, soups, and sauces—wherever a light cucumber flavor is needed. The decorative leaves make it especially useful as a garnish for pâtés and aspics, and folded into a butter spread for a cucumber sandwich. Its serrated leaves are often used to echo the flavor of the cucumber and citrus slices in the traditional Pimm's Cup, a refreshing summer cocktail. Most often, salad burnet is used fresh rather than cooked and makes a good alternative to decorative sprigs of parsley for many dishes. Only the straight species is available.

CULTIVATION AND PROPAGATION

You can easily grow salad burnet from seeds planted in fall or spring. It will freely reseed, and the reseeded plants are often healthier than the original plants. Provide light, well-drained organic soil with good moisture retention in full sun.

HARVESTING AND PRESERVING

Start cutting one-year-old plants in early spring through early summer. The plant grows to 12 to 18 inches tall when flowering, but normally exists as a tight rosette of leaves. Flowers are minute and green in small, tight heads, and the fuchsia-red stigmas are often visible. To keep the plants vigorous and to limit self-seeding, cut the flowers as they appear. They are good to eat but can become fibrous if cut too late. Leaves are best fresh because they lose much of their flavor when dried. Salad burnet leaves make mild-flavored though tasty herb vinegar or herb butter.

Long taproot, outer bark of the root,
leaves, and twigs of the sassafras tree
(*Sassafras albidum*)

| tree, to 66 feet tall | hardy to zone 5 | full sun | keep moist but not constantly wet | well-drained soil rich in organic matter |

SASSAFRAS

Sassafras albidum

Sassafras has been a tree of many uses. Aromatic tea from the root bark, mixed with milk and sugar, was once consumed in England as a beverage called *saloop*. The root bark was used to brew root beer, and root beer is the best description of the odor and taste of the roots— pleasantly sweet, spicy, and woody.

The chief constituent of the roots, safrole, has been prohibited by the U.S. Food and Drug Administration (FDA) since 1960 in foods because it is metabolized as a liver toxin and carcinogen. Yet, sassafras root tea, which is made by stripping the outer bark from the freshly dug root and brewing a hot infusion, is still sold (the FDA does not have enough time and money to police every farmers' market), and its many adherents claim that it is a blood purifier. The FDA does approve safrole-free extracts of sassafras at 10 to 290 ppm (parts per million), while the leaves, known as *filé*, are GRAS at 30,000 ppm. Artificial sassafras oil is safrole-free and relatively safe.

The odor and taste of the leaves is like lemons and fat—slightly tart and resinous, with a tealike tannin. Dried and powdered, the leaves are known commercially as filé or gumbo filé (from the Choctaw *kombo ashish*), used in Cajun cooking, sometimes mixed with other herbs and spices, as a thickener and flavoring in soups and stews. Add the filé at the last few minutes of cooking or else a stringy mass will result (the French *filé* means thread). Fortunately safrole is either absent or only present in trace levels in sassafras leaves, which also have a history of safety backed by centuries of use in the kitchen.

Only the straight species is available.

CULTIVATION AND PROPAGATION
Sassafras roots and leaves are usually gathered from the wild. If you cultivate sassafras in your garden, start it from seed or transplant seedlings very early before the taproot develops; transplanting later is difficult.

HARVESTING AND PRESERVING
An identifying characteristic of sassafras is its variously shaped leaves, which are egg-shaped or two- to three-lobed ("mitten-shaped"). The leaves should be dried and powdered for later use. Store filé in a labeled glass jar out of sunlight until the next harvest.

Satureja montana

annual or perennial, 12 to 18 inches tall

perennial hardy to zone 6

full sun

keep moist but not constantly wet

light loamy soil, average pH 6.8

SAVORY

Satureja species

Savory lets you know its flavor just by its name. Its pungent, thyme- and oreganolike taste goes well with stuffings, sausages, stews, and meats, as well as vegetable dishes, especially beans. In Germany, it is known as *Bohnenkraut* (bean herb), and its flavor complements both fresh and dried beans. Savory is among the main herbs in the traditional French blend herbes de Provence, which is used to flavor everything from game and pasta to eggs and cheese dishes. The oregano odor in savory is more muted, not as harsh, as in Greek oregano, though its spice can be hot on the tongue.

The annual, summer savory (*Satureja hortensis*), is the preferred savory for culinary purposes in most cuisines. For the average palate, it is milder with hints of citrus, though it still has a bite. Summer savory is used commercially in the formulation of vermouths and bitters, sauces, soups, and prepared meats. The perennial, winter savory (*S. montana*), is quite pungent, with a somewhat harsher oregano-thyme-eucalyptus aroma and taste, and the leaves are thicker and tougher than those of the annual.

Most seed catalogs only list the annual, summer savory. Specialized herb nurseries often carry the perennial, winter savory. Both are only commonly available as the straight species, although there is a creeping winter savory and a lemon-scented savory.

CULTIVATION AND PROPAGATION
Sow the seeds of annual summer savory in spring and they will germinate in two to three weeks. Seeds older than one year quickly

Summer savory (*Satureja hortensis*) is easily grown from seed.

lose their viability. Light is necessary for germination, so sow the seeds shallowly. For best growth and development, thin plants to about 6 inches apart. This 15- to 18-inch-tall herb has narrow, bright green leaves with light pink flowers. Summer savory grows rapidly. Harvest young, tender shoot tips when the plant reaches 6 inches in height, to slow flower production and encourage branching. Otherwise, summer savory has a tendency to get leggy and flop over.

Winter savory, a perennial, is more commonly grown from young nursery plants set in spring, but seeding is also possible, and the directions are identical to those for summer savory. Whereas summer savory is easily grown in the vegetable garden, long-term growing conditions of winter savory are similar to those of other semiwoody plants of the Mediterranean (think hot sun and dry conditions), like lavender, oregano, sage, and thyme, and all benefit from a gravelly or sandy, light-colored soil with good drainage.

HARVESTING AND PRESERVING

As the season progresses, harvest summer savory regularly to retard flowering. Before the first autumn freeze, cut the entire plant for drying. Freezing may also preserve the fresh leaves. Winter savory can be cut back by about one-third, like most other perennial plants. The thin, needlelike leaves dry fairly quickly. Store the dried leaves of either savory in a labeled jar out of direct sunlight until next season's harvest. Savory-infused vinegar, a pantry staple, is a perfect condiment for dressing green beans and three-bean salad, as well as taco salad and other Mexican dishes.

Given the right conditions, winter savory (*Satureja montana*) can get quite bushy and woody.

This oak-leaved *Pelargonium* has a piney scent.

❧	///	☀	💧	⋮⋮
tender perennial shrub, 1 to 30 feet tall	hardy to zone 9	full sun	keep moist but not constantly wet; can withstand drought	light, loamy soil, pH 6 to 6.5

SCENTED GERANIUM
Pelargonium species

Name a delectable fragrance—rose, lemon, orange, lime, strawberry, peppermint, nutmeg, spice, apple, apricot, coconut, filbert, ginger— and there's a scented geranium to match. With such a palette of flavors, it is difficult to select just a few favorites, but here we are focusing on those with culinary uses. Most of the scented geraniums taste like they smell. But since some are a bit bitter or astringent, be sure to taste a leaf before using it in a recipe. Also, since many of the leaves can be fibrous or tough, remove the tough stems and chop the leaves finely, or make an infusion with the leaves and then discard them.

While commonly called scented geraniums, they are often confused by the novice gardener with the hardy *Geranium* species, or cranesbills, and the hardy *Erodium* species, or heronsbills. Scented geraniums are selections of the genus *Pelargonium* (thus our nickname "pellies"), especially those native to South

Africa. They are tender plants that must be cultivated in pots and brought indoors over winter.

Our first choice of the scented geranium most frequently used in cooking is the cultivar 'Graveolens', sometimes called 'Old Fashioned Rose' geranium. It is often sold as *Pelargonium graveolens*, which it closely resembles but is not in common cultivation. The fragrance is definitely roselike but with lemony undertones and touches of lavender and a somewhat green leafy-rose. It is tasty in pastries and baked goods (with the whole leaf baked on top or diced and incorporated within) and also in teas. Rose geranium scones smeared with blackberry jam and piled with clotted cream are delicious and impressive. Black tea with cloves and rose geranium leaves is quite a delightful alternative to usual tea, either hot or cold. 'Rober's Lemon Rose', with its asymmetrical leaves, combines the aroma and flavor of roses and lemon that is a

Rose-scented geraniums are the most popular pelargoniums.

Pelargonium citronellum 'Mabel Grey' has a dynamite lemon fragrance and flavor.

favorite of Susan's and is very tasty in baked goods and tea, and with poached fruits.

Our second choice from this plethora of flavors would be the lemon-leaf pellies, either *Pelargonium citronellum* 'Mabel Grey', with its large, jagged leaves, or the smaller leaved *P. crispum*, or selections like 'Variegated Prince Rupert'. These leaves have an intensely sweet, lemon perfume and flavor, so they make excellent syrups, infusions for custards, puddings and dessert sauces, or cake decorations. And the smaller leaves can simply be floated in punches or macerated in fruit salads. If you still recall the day when they served fingerbowls with greasy finger foods such as duck, then you may be interested in the tiny-leaved lemony version called 'Fingerbowl'.

CULTIVATION AND PROPAGATION

Scented geraniums do best in full sun in near-neutral garden loam in places with relatively cool, dry summers. Most scented geraniums flower best in late winter to early spring after a cool but not freezing winter. Because most species are not hardy below freezing, they are best raised as potted plants and overwintered indoors or in a cool greenhouse. Cuttings may be easily rooted in late summer to carry over through the winter.

Propagation by cuttings is important for preserving the unique characteristics of individual cultivars, which are often complex hybrids. While many geranium cultivars root easily and quickly in water, this is not usually recommended. More traditional rooting methods use vigorous basal side-shoots ripped off in a downward tug that produces a "heel" cutting, for best results. Some gardeners claim that cuttings root most easily after hardening (drying) a few hours, but this is not required for most scented selections. Some scenteds refuse to root unless basal cuttings or extra watering is used.

HARVESTING AND PRESERVING

As the season progresses, scented geranium leaves and flowers may be harvested fresh. The leaves may also be dried for teas, but they tend to lose their color and bouquet when dried. Pellies make a lovely jelly (pellie jelly). Even better ways to capture their essence are to make a syrup or scented geranium sugar—both are easy to make and are quite flavorful—which you can use in baked goods and teas, and to poach fruit.

Black and white seeds and the fuzzy
seedpods of sesame (*Sesame indicum*)

annual, to 4
feet tall

cannot withstand
frost

full sun

keep moist but not
constantly wet

well-drained
garden loam,
near neutral pH

SESAME
Sesamum indicum

Sesame, also known as *gingelly*, *jingili*, or *benné* (formerly *Sesamum orientale*), is cultivated for its oil and its edible seeds. The seeds have 45 to 63 percent oil and 25 percent protein. India and China are currently the world's largest producers of sesame. The United States also produces sesame; its cultivation is centered around Paris, Texas.

The white or pale rose-colored flowers are followed by black or white seeds, which are about the size of dill seeds, and smell and taste nutty, somewhat sweet, and oily. The crunchy seeds are commonly used to flavor breads, and the oil is used in baking. Sesame seeds are often sprinkled on hamburger buns or rolls before they are baked and are among the fast food industry's most used herbs. They are used around the world in dishes from stir-fries to confections. Sesame seeds are ground to make a sesame seed butter or paste known as tahini, which is very popular in eastern European and Middle Eastern cuisines. Benné seed cookies are a popular sweet in the southern U.S. states.

Sesame seeds are eaten raw or toasted. To achieve the best flavor, toast at 375 to 400°F for a few minutes until lightly browned on the edges; watch carefully and do not overcook or they will taste burnt and acrid. Roasting brings out the nuttiness in the seeds. Sesame seeds are considered GRAS, although some people have demonstrated a life-threatening allergy to sesame seeds.

CULTIVATION AND PROPAGATION

Sesame can require 90 to 120 or even 150 frost-free days. The home gardener can start transplants earlier to speed the process, but take care to disturb roots as little as possible when transplanting. Sesame should not be planted before the soil reaches 70°F. Because of slow early growth, sesame is a poor competitor against weeds. Select areas with low weeds and cultivate shallowly so you don't injure the surface roots. Daytime temperatures of 77 to 80°F are optimal for cultivation.

Sesame has an extensive root system and is very drought tolerant, but it requires adequate moisture for germination and early growth. Rainfall late in the season prolongs growth but will increase seed loss from shattering.

The best soils for sesame growth are well-drained, fertile soils of medium texture and neutral pH. Increased levels of nitrogen result in increased protein and decreased oil content, while potassium demonstrates a similar, though smaller response; phosphorous alone has no effect on protein or oil content.

HARVESTING AND PRESERVING

As the seedpods ripen, the long pockets split and release the seeds ("open sesame"). Because of shattering problems, the discovery of nonshattering sesame in 1943 was an innovation toward the development of high yielding, shatter-resistant varieties that could be mechanically harvested (and they also make a fun, impromptu musical rattle).

Remove the seeds from the pods, dry them thoroughly, and store them in labeled jars, out of direct light. For longer storage, put them in the freezer; because of their high oil content, they can turn rancid. We like to make gomashio, a tasty Japanese condiment for sprinkling on vegetables and grains, by grinding toasted sesame seeds with sea salt and sometimes with seaweed flakes.

Chrysanthemum coronarium

hardy annual, 24 to 48 inches tall with bloom stalk

can withstand some frost

sun; semishade in hot climates

keep moist but not wet

well-drained soil, average pH 6.5

SHUNGIKU

Chrysanthemum coronarium

While not often grown and used in North America or the United Kingdom, this herb is native to the Mediterranean (where it is called the crown daisy) and is very popular in Asian cooking. Like most chrysanthemums, the leaves of *Chrysanthemum coronarium* are aromatic and have a sort of musky smell with a hint of mint, somewhat reminiscent of the florist's chrysanthemum. Small leaves taste herbaceous, slightly bitter, with a suggestion of mint. Sometimes referred to as chop suey greens, small leaves are used in salads, and both leaves and flowers are used in soups, Asian hotpots, tempura, and stir-fries, wilted or steamed; cook them only briefly.

Allow the pretty white or yellow flowers to bloom later in the season—pull the petals from the center disk, since it is very bitter tasting—and sprinkle them as a tasty salad garnish. For some fun, try rolling the petals in springrolls or sushi. There is a Japanese pickle called *kikumi*, which uses the petals soaked in sake and soy sauce along with pickled apricots or peaches.

We grow the species, *Chrysanthemum coronarium*.

CULTIVATION AND PROPAGATION

Shungiku prefers cool weather, so it does best in spring and fall, although it will grow and bloom through the summer if given some light shade. Sow this annual from seed in the garden in early spring or late summer for a fall crop. Space seeds 2 to 4 inches apart in rows 15 to 18 inches apart in fertile, well-drained soil. Thin the seedlings to 6 to 8 inches apart and eat them. To keep the leaves small and tasty, the plant should be cut back rather than allowed to flower; it is a rapid grower. Later in the season, the yellow flowers are pretty and tasty, but the leaves become more bitter. Tall plants tend to get leggy and flop over.

HARVESTING AND PRESERVING

Harvest from the plants regularly during the growing season to keep the leaves new, tender, and less bitter and to prevent flower stalks from forming. Gather the fresh leaves just before using, since they tend to wilt quickly. While both the leaves and flowers are best used fresh, the flowers may be dried. Gather them and pull the petals from the bitter disk. Dry the petals in an oven with a pilot light or with the oven light on, and once dried, store them in a glass jar out of sunlight until the next season's harvest. Dried petals are rehydrated in warm water and can be added to soups and stir-fries.

Rumex acetosa

hardy perennial; garden sorrel 20 to 50 inches tall; French sorrel 8 to 20 inches tall

hardy to zone 3

full sun to light shade

keep moist but not wet

prefers rich, loamy soil, slightly acid pH 6.5

SORREL
Rumex species

Sorrel's culinary laurels rest on the French classics: sorrel soup and sorrel sauce. Renaissance herbalist John Gerard complimented sorrel when he said, "It is the best of sauces not only in virtue, but in pleasantness of taste." Leaves smell herbaceous and perhaps with a hint of lemon. The flavor is indeed sour with a lemony zest, providing a clear, tart accent to any recipe. This feature comes from the presence of oxalic acid. Therefore, do not eat sorrel in large quantities or too often, especially those individuals subject to kidney stones. Sorrel is considered a spring tonic by the French and is a welcome harbinger of spring—among the first green herbs to appear in the garden.

When small, this tender-leaved potherb is used in salads, especially in England; its lively taste is best combined with other salad greens. If leaves are large, remove the tough center ribs and tear the leaves into bite-sized pieces. Salads contain-

ing sorrel will require less lemon juice or vinegar, or none at all, in the dressing. Sorrel is also tasty in egg dishes; with potatoes, beets, or other vegetables; and in sauces or mayonnaise. It is a perfect addition to salsa verde. Sorrel sauce is often paired with seafood—for all types of fish, or scallops—and also is a tasty accompaniment to poultry. To retain the bright green color in soups and sauces, cook it briefly or blanch for about a minute and then shock it in cold water.

We cultivate both garden sorrel (*Rumex acetosa*) and French sorrel (*Rumex scutatus*). Garden sorrel has arrow-shaped leaves and is sometimes called broad-leaf or common sorrel, and, mistakenly, French sorrel. French sorrel's leaves are more shield-shaped, and it is sometimes referred to as buckler-leaf sorrel.

Blood sorrel (*Rumex sanguineus*) is a fairly recent addition to gardens. It has very ornamental foliage—green with dark red veining—and

Common garden sorrel has
elongated leaves.

prefers some shade. The leaves are
not very tasty, although they can be
added to salads when they are very
small. Sometimes called red sorrel,
it is an attractive and colorful plant
in the herb garden.

CULTIVATION AND PROPAGATION

You can grow sorrel easily from
seed or propagate it by root division
in spring or fall. Both *Rumex acetosa*
and *R. scutatus* are hardy perennials, somewhat frost resistant. They
prefer rich, well-drained soil and
full sun, though they will grow in
partial shade. Sorrel tends to look
a bit weedy. The leaves appear
on tall stems in dense clusters,
sending up a flower spike with tiny
greenish flowers, which form small,
yellow-brown seeds. Cut back
flower stalks continually so leaves

can be harvested throughout the season. Sorrel does not like hot weather; the leaves become more bitter tasting and may die back if it is very hot and humid. But the plant will put out new growth in the fall and grow new leaves until a killing frost. In temperate climates, the herb may stay green all winter, though growth is limited.

HARVESTING AND PRESERVING

Harvest leaves when they are small and tender to use in salads. Once leaves get larger, use them in cooked dishes or with other foods; remove the center rib if it is stringy or tough. Sorrel is best eaten freshly picked. It has thin leaves and does not freeze or dry well. Some cooks blanch it and freeze it like spinach.

The leaves of young French sorrel (*Rumex scutatus*) are shorter and wider than those of garden sorrel (*R. acetosa*).

Sonchus oleraceus

hardy annual, 12 to 60 inches tall

 can withstand mild frost

sun

 keep moist but not wet

fertile, well-drained soil, pH 6.5 to 7.0

SOW THISTLE
Sonchus oleraceus

This weed is sometimes called common or smooth sow thistle. Originally hailing from Europe and Asia, it has naturalized in temperate zones around the globe. Leaves smell slightly herbaceous; they are green tasting and have a bitterness, though they are milder than dandelion greens. The leaves, which are most tender and less bitter in spring, can be harvested when small and eaten in salads, on sandwiches, or cooked as a potherb like any green. Once cooked, they lose some of their bitter flavor.

The leaves and flowers might first appear similar to dandelion, and leaves of both plants do have a bitter taste in common. But on closer inspection, there are many differences. *Sonchus oleraceus* does have toothed leaves that grow in a basal rosette, like dandelion, though when it sends up a stem, it forms more leaves that wrap around the stem, and it eventually sends up a flower stalk. In contrast, a dandelion sends up a single stem that forms a single flower. Sow thistle flower stalks can have more than a few yellow flowers blooming at one time, along with unopened buds, spent flower buds, and white, fuzzy seed heads—similar to, though smaller than, dandelion. The unopened buds as well as the stem tips can be eaten. If the stem tips are harvested with tender leaves,

6 to 8 inches in length, they can be blanched or steamed and eaten like asparagus, a wild delicacy.

We look for the species *Sonchus oleraceus,* with its smooth, hairless leaves. There are many species in this genus. Two edibles are *S. arvensis,* the perennial, field sow thistle, which is somewhat hairy; and *S. asper,* spiny-leaved sow thistle, which has prickly leaf edges that must be trimmed. Both can be cooked to make them more palatable.

CULTIVATION AND PROPAGATION
Annual sow thistle can be started from seed; it is dispersed naturally by its floating seeds and also by birds. If the conditions are good, the seed can germinate spring, summer, or fall—it will do so more quickly if the soil is moist or wet, rather than dry. It is often found growing in any disturbed garden soil, fields, and roadsides. It prefers sunny locations with loamy soil and adequate moisture, though it can tolerate wet areas. Foliage lasts longer on spring plants; summer and fall plants tend to send up a flower stalk sooner.

HARVESTING AND PRESERVING
As with most wild weeds, sow thistle is best harvested and eaten in season. All of the sow thistles exude a milky latex, which will stain things brown, so when harvesting, cut the leaves and stems with sharp scissors and put them in a plastic bag so they don't get their sap everywhere. Try to use them as soon as possible. Cut them just before use and put them in cold water to wash away the milky sap. Spin dry just before cooking.

Harvest unopened flower buds (which look like short, fat, striated cylinders—sort of like tiny drums) and pickle in vinegar. Spent flower buds that hang on to the plant after flowering are sort of vase-shaped; these are bitter, so if you aren't sure if you will like their taste, just try them.

Leaves, stem, and fruits of
spicebush (*Lindera benzoin*)

deciduous shrub, 6 to 15 feet tall

 hardy to zone 5

 full to part shade

 keep constantly moist

 soil rich in organic matter, slightly acid

SPICEBUSH

Lindera benzoin

Spicebush has an appealing fragrance and a history of use as a spice. All parts of the plant—leaves, stems, bark, and fruit—have a strong, distinctive spicy smell and taste. The fragrant leaves, with a grassy-eucalyptus to woody-floral scent, turn a brilliant gold in the fall, a striking contrast to the red fruits. The fruits are similar in flavor to the leaves, though more pungent— slightly peppery and bitter—and are best used in small amounts.

Spicebush is also an admirable garden plant, but unfortunately, it is rarely cultivated and is only found at wildflower and specialty shrub nurseries. When grown in home gardens, the herb performs admirably as a handsome deciduous shrub. Susan has hundreds of them as an understory plant in her woods, which is above a creek. They are thriving natives in this natural habitat, and are among the first trees to leaf out in spring. This native plant ought to be reconsidered by the nursery trade for its beauty and fragrance.

Spicebush is also known as Benjamin bush, feverbush, or wild allspice. The fruits of spicebush (this species has male and female plants) have been dried and powdered and used as a substitute for allspice or pepper in soups and stews, while the leaves and bark produce a spicy, lemony tea. An herbal vinegar from the twigs and fruits was once used to preserve beets. Unfortunately, spicebush has no GRAS status, despite centuries of use and apparently no harmful chemistry. Dried leaves of spicebush are fragrant ingredients in potpourri.

Only the straight species is available, but be sure to obtain male and female plants if fruit is desired.

CULTIVATION AND PROPAGATION

Spicebush is a native plant typically found in damp woods and along stream banks. While it will tolerate a variety of climates, soils, and exposures, it prefers a humusy soil with constant moisture in part shade.

HARVESTING AND PRESERVING

Harvest the leaves during summer before they turn yellow in the fall; use fresh or dry them. The red fruits are generally only available in the fall (harvest some before the birds get them all). Use them fresh or dry them. You want to remove the seed, and it is easier to remove the seed while they are fresh than when they are dried. Use a sharp knife to slit the fruit and pop the seed out. The fruits will turn a brown color when dried; once completely dried, store them in a labeled jar out of sunlight until next season's harvest.

Stevia rebaudiana

shrubby
perennial, 18 to
28 inches tall

hardy to
zone 9

full sun

keep moist but not
constantly wet

well-drained
garden loam

STEVIA
Stevia rebaudiana

The leaves of stevia (*Stevia rebaudiana*) have been known to the Guarani Indians of Paraguay as "sweet herb," and used for centuries as a sweetener for traditional bitter drinks such as *maté*. Stevioside, the active sweet component, is 100 to 300 times more sweet than sucrose, and is noncaloric, anticariogenic (inhibits tooth decay), and nonfermentable; it does not darken upon cooking and is highly stable when exposed to both acids and heat. Stevioside has a detectable taste at a threshold of 0.002 percent, though large amounts taste bitter.

Stevioside is commonly used as a sweetener in Japan, China, Korea, Israel, Brazil, and Paraguay. In Japan, stevia extract and stevioside are used to sweeten Japanese-style pickles, dried seafoods, fish, meat pastes, soy sauce, and bean paste products, as well as fruit-flavored drinks and other beverages, and dessert items such as ice cream and chewing gum. In North America, stevia has been used as a natural sweetener for years.

Stevioside is passed through the human digestive system apparently unaltered and does not appear to be harmful. No allergic reactions have been reported. Stevia may actually be beneficial for your health. A number of studies have focused on its antidiabetic activity in both rats and humans. A study in China found that stevia should be considered as a supplemental therapy for patients with hypertension. Stevia may also be anticarcinogenic and antibacterial.

Only the straight species is available, either from seed or small rooted cuttings. There seems to be some variability in vigor and ability to flower among seed strains.

CULTIVATION AND PROPAGATION
Stevia is easily cultivated in pots or good garden loam in full sun. This species is normally found in moist to wet areas, and it does not tolerate drought well. Seeds may set after flowering in late fall to early winter, but these inevitably fail to germinate. Propagation is best from cuttings during active growth in summer.

HARVESTING AND PRESERVING
Leaves can be used fresh, infused to sweeten tea or other beverages. Dry leaves during the growing season and before a frost. Harvest leaves on a sunny, dry day, and then rapidly dry them to a moisture content of 15 to 20 percent in a low oven (110 to 158°F). Leaves should be kept dry and stored in labeled jars out of direct sun until the next growing season. Crumble or crush dried leaves as needed.

Urtica dioica

hardy
herbaceous
perennial, 4 to
7 feet tall

hardy in
zones 5 to 10

sun or light
shade

keep moist

nitrogen-rich
soil, pH 5.6
to 8.5

STINGING NETTLE

Urtica dioica

While the prickles of stinging nettle (or common nettle) may seem a deterrent, it is well worth the effort to cultivate this plant for its virtues, both culinary and medicinal. You will need to wear protective gloves to harvest and prepare them in the kitchen, and tongs come in handy.

There is very little aroma to nettle leaves. When crushed, they give forth a light smell that is herbaceous and slightly sweet. Nettles have an appealing mild flavor. They taste a bit green and mineral-like, slightly sweet, not strong but with a hint of bitterness. A cup of nettle tea is a wonderful spring tonic: it detoxifies and promotes kidney function, helping the body cleanse itself of waste. The leaves contain vitamins A, C, and many of the Bs, beta-carotene, calcium, iron, phosphorous, and potassium, as well as a good amount of chlorophyll. This nutritious potherb has long been regarded to strengthen the immune system, renew and tone body tissue, and nourish and purify the blood. Make room for stinging nettle at the edge of your garden or the outskirts of the yard.

Nettle has deeply veined, hairy, oval, toothed leaves. The leaves are covered with bristly hairs, which cause the sting. You will know if you brush up against any part of this plant! The stinging hairs are hollow and contain formic acid and histamine, which create the stinging sensation. The sting stays with you for hours, but the pain can be somewhat relieved if the area is rubbed with jewelweed or dock leaves. We all learn to handle nettles with respect. Even the pale green-yellow flowers can sting.

Nettles should be cooked before ingestion. They can be enjoyed as an infusion, are good wilted, in soups and casseroles, tossed with pasta, used in green sauce, and delicious in spanakopita or any dish where you might use spinach. Cook them on their own or with other greens, and use them as you would any wilted green. They are delicious with garlic and olive oil.

The common, everyday nettle that we find in the wild (*Urtica dioica*) is the one to gather or cultivate.

CULTIVATION AND PROPAGATION

Wild stinging nettles characteristically grow in waste areas at the woods' edge and near compost piles, especially in the vicinity of a stream or water source since they like damp areas. They spread on a creeping rootstock and can tend to be invasive. They can be kept under control by removing dormant rhizomes. The plants can be sown from seed, or divided, which is best done in spring before much leaf growth. If you are introducing them into your garden, place them in an out-of-the-way spot of the garden, and warn friends and family about their stinging nature.

HARVESTING AND PRESERVING

So how does one deal with fresh nettles? Handle them very carefully with gloves and protective clothing. Do not harvest nettles wearing flipflops and shorts. To ensure a few harvests, cut young nettle stems back almost to the ground in the spring, again a time or two, and just as flowering begins to encourage another round of growth. Older leaves contain gritty calcium oxalate, are bitter, and should be avoided.

In the kitchen, wearing gloves, rinse and dry the foliage in a salad spinner or bowl of cold water and pat dry, then remove the leaves from the large stems. The leaves can be steamed or wilted to be eaten or used in recipes, or laid out on screens or baskets or hung in small bundles to be dried. Once the nettles are cooked or dried, there is no stinging sensation. Pack dried leaves in labeled jars and store out of sunlight until next season's harvest.

Myrrhis odorata

| herbaceous perennial, to 6 feet tall when flowering | hardy to zone 5 | part to full shade | keep constantly moist but not wet | humusy soil, pH 6.6 |

SWEET CICELY

Myrrhis odorata

The genus *Myrrhis* has only one species and its generic name is derived from the Greek *myrrha*, meaning fragrant. Sweet cicely, also called garden myrrh, sweet-scented myrrh, or fern-leaved chervil, has a long history of being cultivated for its sweet, anise-scented foliage, seeds (really fruits), and roots. The flavor is also sweet, tasting of anise with a green herbal note. It flavors liqueurs such as Chartreuse, spiced wines, iced tea, baked goods, and salads, but it does not have GRAS despite millennia of use and no reported harmful chemistry.

Sweet cicely is a winter-hardy herb that is a perfect landscape specimen for that shady nook that challenges every gardener. The plant's delicate, fernlike green leaves provide a soft, informal touch to any planting scheme. The small white flowers sparkle in umbelliferous clusters in late spring and early summer and are followed by green then brown fruits that stick to your socks if you brush against them.

The straight species is available as seeds or young seedlings.

CULTIVATION AND PROPAGATION
Sweet cicely is among the few strongly scented herbs that thrive in shade and a humusy, moist soil. The plant cannot withstand hot, humid climates. It enjoys the cooler summers of the mountains and the upper latitudes of North America and Europe.

Gardeners often find it difficult to germinate seeds of sweet cicely. Use these two methods to get sweet cicely seeds to germinate. In the first method, scatter the fresh, ripe seeds where you want them to grow and let nature take its course. In the second method, thirty to forty days after flowering, splinterlike seeds will fall from the plant. Separate them from the seed head and mix them with damp peat moss in a plastic bag, then place the bag in the refrigerator (not freezer). The seeds will begin to germinate, and when seedlings form, they can be transplanted into pots in the greenhouse or on the windowsill. Leave any ungerminated seeds in the bag with the peat moss and return to the refrigerator for further germination. Germination will be irregular; more seed will sprout in a few weeks. When there are several small, ferny leaves and the plant becomes established in the pot, harden off the young seedlings and transplant them to the garden. Light frosts should not harm properly acclimated transplants.

Sweet cicely in bloom

HARVESTING AND PRESERVING
Harvest fresh leaves and flowers during spring and summer. Sweet cicely does not dry well for future use. Both leaves and flowers make a lovely anise-flavored cordial or syrup.

Origanum majorana

tender perennial, 12 to 18 inches tall

 hardy to zone 9b

 full sun

keep moist but not constantly wet

 well-drained gravelly or rocky loam, pH 6.9

SWEET MARJORAM

Origanum majorana

Perfumers describe the clean, sweet smell of sweet marjoram as a warm-spice, aromatic-camphoraceous, and woody scent reminiscent of nutmeg and cardamom. The small, gray-green, felty leaves and terminal heads of white flowers make the plant a delight in pots on the patio. It is also a kitchen favorite, combining a sweetness suggesting mild spice and green herb with savoriness akin to oregano though not as pungent. It has a well-rounded, pleasant flavor that is good in just about any dish. Use it in soups, sauces, with vegetables, pasta, grains, legumes, vinaigrettes, or with poultry, seafood, or meat.

Sweet marjoram is widely used in beverages, meats, baked goods, and condiments. Its leaves (1.9 to 9,946 ppm), essential oil (1 to 40 ppm), and oleoresin (37 to 75 ppm) are considered GRAS. The essential oil of sweet marjoram shows antimicrobial activity and is among the few *Origanum* oils that can be used in perfumery.

Only the straight species is available, as seeds and young seedlings. A selection known in the trade as Greek marjoram or compact Greek marjoram is grayer, hardier, and a bit more compact in habit. The so-called Italian oregano in American herb markets (*Origanum ×majoricum*) is a cross between *O. vulgare* subsp. *hirtum* (Greek oregano) and *O. majorana*, and has a bit of pungency tempered by the sweetness of marjoram. We find Italian oregano to be another well-rounded herb that can be used like sweet marjoram. Sometimes called hardy sweet marjoram or Sicilian oregano, this hybrid usually survives winters in zone 8.

CULTIVATION AND PROPAGATION

Since sweet marjoram is a tender perennial, it must be carried over in the greenhouse or treated as an annual in most North American or northern European gardens. Sweet marjoram is usually grown from seeds, but in the spring greenhouse or under lights indoors, plants often succumb to root and stem diseases. Plants grown from cuttings are less vulnerable to these problems.

HARVESTING AND PRESERVING

Harvest fresh leaves during spring and summer. Sweet marjoram leaves are easily dried on screens or when the stems are hung up. Convection drying at about 113°F preserves the best flavor for marjoram. Store dried leaves in labeled jars out of sunlight until the next season's harvest. Sweet marjoram makes a delicate, tasty herb butter and well-rounded vinegar.

Galium odoratum

| herbaceous perennial, to about 4 inches tall | routinely hardy to zone 4 | part shade | keep moist but not constantly wet | humusy soil, pH 5.7 to 7.5 |

SWEET WOODRUFF

Galium odoratum

Dried sweet woodruff has an odor similar to newly mown hay or to sweet vernal grass, holy grass, tonka, and numerous other coumarin sources. It has just a suggestion of vanilla. Sweet woodruff has traditionally been used to flavor May wine, a kind of alcoholic blood thinner in the spring. When the leaves and flowers are infused in beverages like white wine, they impart a vanilla and haylike flavor that is slightly ashy. The taste works well with strawberries and rhubarb.

The leaves of sweet woodruff are considered GRAS to 400 ppm but only in alcoholic beverages because of the coumarin content. Coumarin is widely used to flavor tobacco (tonka is used in pipe tobacco) and wine. Coumarin is also used as an adulterant in Mexican and Caribbean vanilla extracts. Although coumarin itself is not a really good blood-thinner, people already on anticoagulant medication should avoid it.

Despite all this controversy, we have enjoyed steeping a few wilted stems of sweet woodruff (after a brief time in a low oven) in a German white wine or white grape juice overnight. Using more woodruff or oversteeping can result in something that tastes of old tea bags. To prepare this traditional Maibowle spring punch, pour the wine in a large punch bowl, add champagne and sparkling water or ginger ale to taste (about an equal volume), mix in a pint of sliced strawberries that have been macerated in a few tablespoons of grenadine or a box of frozen, presweetened strawberries, float an ice ring (one made of ginger ale with Johnny-jump-ups or violets, woodruff flowers, and alpine strawberries is particularly attractive), and decorate with dianthus petals, Johnny-jump-ups, violets, sweet woodruff blooms, tiny fragrant rose petals, or sliced strawberries. Not only is it a pretty presentation, it is a tasty libation.

CULTIVATION AND PROPAGATION

Sweet woodruff is easy to grow and propagate from its abundant runners in the humusy soil of a wildflower garden. Seed is rarely available, so get a clump from a friend's garden, plant it in a partly shady spot, and you will have it forever. Growing is not the challenge, but you will have trouble controlling it in areas that it likes. Native to open forests in northern Europe, sweet woodruff can easily form a solid ground cover. It is an attractive low-growing ground cover with bright green, whorled leaves bedecked by tiny white flowers.

HARVESTING AND PRESERVING

Sweet woodruff can be used fresh, but for a really intense flavor, drying releases coumarin. Coumarin is normally bound to a sugar (called a glycoside) in the living plant and relatively tasteless, but drying ruptures the bond and releases the tasty free coumarin. Once dried, store sweet woodruff leaves in a labeled jar out of sunlight until next season's harvest.

Thymus vulgaris

| erect subshrub, to about 1 foot tall | hardy to zone 6 | full sun | keep moist but not constantly wet; can withstand drought when fully established | light loamy soil, average pH 6.3 |

THYME

Thymus species

Common thyme or garden thyme (*Thymus vulgaris*), native from the western Mediterranean to southeastern Italy, is widely used in cooking. *Thymus vulgaris* has wide variation, often not characterized by cultivar names, in its native range. Individual plants exhibit a large assortment of growth habits, leaf sizes, leaf colors, and scents. For culinary purposes, we prefer the ones that are high in thymol, which causes an odor that is similar to oregano though more subtle. The scent should be warm-herbaceous, somewhat spicy, with perhaps just a hint of citrus, and distinctly aromatic. The flavor should be warm, somewhat sweet and slightly biting but not bitter or tarry, and well rounded and pleasant.

Common thyme is indispensable in egg dishes, marinara sauces, and most foods of the Mediterranean. Its balanced flavor rounds out soups, sauces, vinaigrettes, ragouts, and marinades. It goes well with mushrooms, vegetables, grains, and beans, as well as poultry and

meat. If you are looking for an herb to add to a dish and not sure what to choose, use thyme; its taste works well with everything. The tiny purplish flowers are also edible and add an extra visual appeal when used fresh.

The flavored thymes, like lemon, caraway, and orange, have various levels of the flavor they are named, while the creeping and woolly thymes are not good culinary choices. Lemon thyme imparts a thymelike aroma and taste with overtones of sweet lemon to vinaigrettes, vegetables, salads, poultry, and fish, and can also be used in breads, muffins, cakes, and cookies.

Common thyme

'Narrow-Leaf French' thyme is the name given to the seed strain high in thymol, which is often offered as 'German Winter', 'French Summer', or 'Greek Gray'. In common parlance, this is *the* garden thyme or common thyme. 'Broad-Leaf English', which is often sold as common thyme, is attractive and

'Provençal' thyme looks and tastes similar to French thyme.

Wild thyme (*Thymus pulegioides*) is easy to grow.

'Broad-Leaf English' thyme is a handsome and popular herb.

will work in the kitchen, but we much prefer the aroma and flavor of French thyme. Many forms of 'Narrow-Leaf French' will not come completely true from seed. If you find a particularly favorable clone, propagate it by cuttings or layering. We also particularly like the culinary cultivar 'Provençal', which flowers more profusely than the French.

Many gardeners prefer *Thymus pulegioides*. Called wild thyme, mother-of-thyme, or Pennsylvania Dutch tea thyme, it superficially resembles pennyroyal (*Mentha pulegium*). Wild thyme is variable in height, leaf shape, and flower color, so, again, choose ones with a typical thyme odor, since you have to like the smell and taste if you are going to cook with it. This thyme is also more easily cultivated in a general vegetable garden and even reseeds itself into nearby flower beds and lawns, something that common thyme usually does not do.

Lemon thyme

Lemon thyme (*Thymus ×citri-odorus*) comes in green-leaved and golden-leaved forms with pink or lavender blooms. Rub the leaves and taste to see which one you prefer, or grow both.

CULTIVATION AND PROPAGATION

All thymes require well-drained, near-neutral soil and a position in full sun. At least 50 percent sand, gravel, or similar aggregate in the soil is beneficial because water is not retained for long periods of time and so the roots are less likely to rot. While common thyme may be directly seeded, the process is slow, which is true with most small-seeded perennial herbs. You will gain much time the first year by setting out transplants. Reproduction of favored thymes requires vegetative propagation by cuttings, layerings, or divisions.

HARVESTING AND PRESERVING

Harvest thyme as a fresh herb throughout the growing season. Thyme is easily dried over screens or by hanging. Store whole thyme leaves in labeled jars out of direct sunlight until the next season's harvest. Thyme makes a flavorful herb butter. Lemon thyme makes a delightful vinegar or syrup.

'Golden Lemon' thyme

'Green Lemon' thyme

Viola tricolor

VIOLA

Viola species

Happy little faces of viola blossoms are harbingers of spring. These common European wildflowers are traditionally used to garnish the May wine punch bowl and other beverages, desserts, tea sandwiches, and salads. They are used in making jellies, butters, and fancy desserts. The wild violets are separated in this discussion from the Johnny-jump-ups (*Viola tricolor*) and pansies, since they are generally found naturalized in the wild, in contrast to cultivated perennials. While all the colorful little blooms in this genus are safe to eat, the foliage of wild violets is edible whereas the leaves of "johnnies" and pansies are not eaten.

Wild violets

Violet (*Viola* species) most often refers to the wild purple-blue violets and white-flowering wood violets, sometimes called confederate violets (*V. sororia*, or *V. papilionacea* in the older literature), birdfoot violets (*V. pedata*), and sweet violets (*V. odorata*). Wild violet leaves are usually heart-shaped, except for the birdfoot, whose leaves look like what its name suggests. Violet blooms have

five petals, which are held up on long, thin stems above the foliage. The first two violets just mentioned have a mild scent, slightly sweet, and the taste is also very mild, sometimes a touch acidic. Sweet violet (*V. odorata*), however, is very fragrant with a strong, sweet perfume and tastes much more flowery. Generally, flowers with the stronger fragrance have more flavor, so they are used in beverages, syrups, cordials, pastilles, ice creams, and confections. They are also often candied and used to garnish fancy desserts.

Violet flowers and young leaves are eaten raw in salads; they contain a good amount of vitamins A and C. Leaves are cooked with other spring greens or added to stews as a thickening agent, since they have a slight mucilagenous quality. If eaten in large amounts, because of the saponin content, viola may cause nausea and a tonic cleansing effect.

Johnny-jump-up and pansy

Generally, the blooms of all the Johnny-jump-ups (*Viola tricolor*; also called heartsease) taste like a mild salad green, some with a hint of perfume. Both Johnny-jump-ups

Viola sororia

We delight in the whiskered faces of pansies.

and pansies (*V. ×wittrockiana*) have a pleasingly mild, sweet taste like baby lettuce. Some of them have a slight, mild hint of wintergreen, and a few bring bubblegum to mind. Smell and taste the blooms before using. We love the faces of these flowers and the huge variety of color combinations. Use them on salads: the whole bloom of Johnny-jump-ups and pansies can be used, or pull the petals from the calyx and sprinkle them on salads or canapés. The colored petals are lovely in herb butter, floating on a beverage, or scattered on frosted cakes or cupcakes. The flowers can be candied and used as a fancy edible garnish on desserts or as a confection. They are also quite lovely floating in May wine or embedded in an ice ring.

CULTIVATION AND PROPAGATION

Viola species grow best in a woodland environment. They favor shade to partial shade, though they will perform well in a sunny, herbaceous border with proper moisture and organic matter. Plants do not get much larger than 6 to 12 inches tall. The violet is a hardy perennial with large heart-shaped leaves and blooms in various shades of purple and white with purple veins. They are naturalized in lawns, fields, and woodland edges and will spread if allowed to do so.

Pansies and johnnies can be started from seed, and plants are widely available at garden centers and nurseries. Pansies are biennials to short-lived perennials, but are most often treated as an annual. Their blooms come in many colors, from white, yellow, orange, pink, lavender, and purple, to bi- and tri-colored. The short-lived perennial Johnny-jump-up or heartsease is usually lavender, purple, white, or yellow, or a combination thereof; their flowers are about the size of violets. They often self-sow, and will reappear in your garden or lawn every spring.

HARVESTING AND PRESERVING

Leaves of violets (not johnnies or pansies) can be harvested, washed and spun dry, and used as a salad green or cooked. They can also be dried for use in tea or soups. Pick viola flowers and put their stems in water until ready to use. Pinch the flowers from the stems and use small flowers whole. Use pansies whole as a garnish, or separate the petals to scatter them. Violets and Johnny-jump-ups are ideal for candying—which is the best way to preserve the bloom for eating—although they do press well in a flower press for crafting. Store candied blooms in a tightly closed container between layers of wax paper or parchment paper up to about six months. Violet syrup and butter can be made with fragrant violas.

Nasturtium officinale

hardy aquatic
perennial; 6 to
18 inches tall
when in bloom

hardy to zone 6;
can withstand
light frost

sun to light
shade

keep in fresh
running water or
wet soil

prefers wet,
sandy or loamy
soil, pH 7.2

WATERCRESS

Nasturtium officinale

The most common variety of cress, and the most popular, is watercress (*Nasturtium officinale*). Though watercress is not very aromatic when you casually smell it, its spicy, peppery flavor has added piquancy to salads and soups for hundreds of years. It offers interest to any green or vegetable salad and goes well with combination salads that include grains, potatoes, beets, pasta, fish, or chicken. It is delightful in a springtime salsa verde. Watercress is a versatile and tasty garnish. Try the bright green leaves in spring rolls or egg rolls, on sandwiches, or as a pizza topping. The white flowers are also an edible garnish and are quite spicy tasting, though the leaves tend to become bitter once the plant blooms. The pleasurable pungency of cress disappears when it is cooked as a potherb, and a different, though satisfying green vegetable taste comes through, with suggestions of spinach and mustard greens.

Native to Europe and Asia, watercress is the cress that is referred to in herb lore. The name "cress" comes from the Greek word *grastis*, for green fodder. Throughout history, Romans harvested wild cress for their salads, and when English peasants had no flour, they ate cress in place of bread.

We seek out clean springs and creeks where watercress has naturalized (to ensure safe eating, see details under Harvesting and Preserving, following). For herbs with similar peppery cress flavors, see Garden Cress, Nasturtium, and Wintercress.

CULTIVATION AND PROPAGATION
Watercress has become naturalized in many areas throughout the world and can be found floating or creeping in fresh water situations. To cultivate watercress, provide fresh running water, whether a spring, creek, stream, or brook. Rooted pieces of watercress can be transplanted easily along the water's edge about every foot or so. This is best done in spring or fall.

HARVESTING AND PRESERVING
When gathering watercress, be careful not to pull the plant out by the roots; just cut the tops from the mature shoots. If wild-harvesting watercress from streams or creeks, take caution: do not eat watercress unless you are sure that the flowing water has not been exposed to human or animal contamination and is free of pollutants. Plants growing in water that drains from fields where there is livestock, especially sheep, should not be eaten raw. It could be contaminated with liver fluke parasite. Cooking watercress kills the parasite, making the greens safe for consumption.

Barbarea vulgaris

hardy biennial or perennial, 1 to 2 feet tall with bloom

cold tolerant, hardy to zone 6

shade

keep moist but not wet

fertile soil, optimum pH 6.2

WINTERCRESS
Barbarea vulgaris

Wintercress, sometimes called yellow rocket, has a flavor and color very like watercress. In appearance, however, its glossy leaves are longer and more pointed, and its blooms are yellow like mustard blossoms rather than white. The pungency of wintercress is similar to a wild mustard and watercress, but it is much more bitter in flavor. Small leaves can be used on sandwiches and as a salad ingredient, though it is best to tear or chop them to distribute the bitter and peppery flavor. Larger leaves can be tough and stringy, so remove the center stem. Wintercress is native to temperate regions in the Northern Hemisphere.

Both the pungency and bitterness dissipate when you cook wintercress in boiling water, leaving a wilted green that tastes like a combination of parsley, spinach, and mustard greens; use this potherb as you would spinach. Steaming and sautéing the leaves, as well as the buds, does not get rid of the bitterness like boiling does. In the southern United States, this wild plant is known as "creasy greens," which in early spring are sought after, harvested, and cooked down, often with bacon fat. As flower buds form, they can be snipped from the tips of plant stalks and cooked like broccoli, though they are bitter like the leaves. The yellow flowers can also be eaten;

they are also somewhat bitter but have a sweeter floral note. Use them in tea or as a garnish.

The species *Barbarea vulgaris* grows wild in our gardens. Upland cress (*Barbarea verna*) is a close relative of wintercress and can be used in similar applications, though it is not as widely available. For herbs with similar peppery cress flavors, see Garden Cress, Nasturtium, and Watercress.

CULTIVATION AND PROPAGATION
This plant is very hardy, and often will winter over and remain green even in freezing temperatures. It returns to life after winter and sends out new growth, which is a good time to harvest the new leaves. It prefers some shade and loamy, moist soil. Since it self-sows and has naturalized around our gardens, backyards, and nearby fields, many of us do not need to sow this plant. It spreads by the many seeds it forms, dropping them near the mother plant. To establish wintercress in the home garden, directly sow seed in spring or autumn. It will germinate in just a few weeks, and you may never need to plant it again.

HARVESTING AND PRESERVING
Gather the leaves anytime during the growing season before the flower buds appear. Cut the buds at the tips, or harvest the flower stems to keep them cut back and then just use the tips since the stems are tough and stringy. Put the stems in water until ready to use the buds, and then snip them off when ready to cook. Flower stems are also tough, so pull off the flowers and scatter them over a salad.

Oxalis stricta

low-growing annual, 5 to 15 inches tall

hardy to zone 7

sun to shade

keep moist

rich soil, optimum pH 6.8

WOOD SORREL

Oxalis stricta

The most common wood sorrel, *Oxalis stricta*, has green leaves and yellow flowers and is sometimes called yellow sorrel, upright sorrel, or sourgrass. The leaves on first glance are often confused with clover (*Trifolium pratense*), because both have three leaflets atop a stem, but on closer inspection, they are very different. Clover leaflets are usually round or oval in shape, whereas wood sorrel leaflets are heart-shaped. The notched leaves are attached to the stem at the point of the heart and have a crease down the center. They fold downward in the evening, when it rains, or when it gets too hot.

The leaflets have a sour taste, similar to sorrel (*Rumex* species) but not quite as astringent. The leaves, flowers, and seedpods all share a pleasantly sour flavor, sort of a combination of tart lemon and green apple. Fresh leaves are added to salads or sandwiches, green sauces or butters. They are used to make a lemony infusion, which can be sweetened if desired, for wood sorrel lemonade. They can also be used as a potherb, added to soups or sauces, but when heated, they wilt down to almost nothing and turn the same army-green color that sorrel does.

While we most often gather the yellow-flowered *Oxalis stricta*, which is naturalized in our gardens, quite a few other oxalis species are also edible and come in different sizes and a variety of colors. *Oxalis corniculata* is very similar to *O. stricta*, and also has yellow flowers. *Oxalis montana*, often referred to as common sorrel, has light pink or white flowers with darker pink veins, while *O. violacea* has bright fuchsia to pink-purple petals, and *O. oregana*, which is found in the Pacific Northwest, is the largest-leaved wood sorrel.

CULTIVATION AND PROPAGATION

Oxalis stricta is a partial-shade to shade-loving plant that prefers somewhat moist soil. It grows in backyard gardens, woodlands, and meadows, or in places where the soil has been disturbed. If the climate is warm enough, it sometimes behaves like a perennial. The seedpods, which have an elongated shape like tiny okra or bananas, pop open when dried and cast seeds in the general vicinity. Wood sorrel seeds, gathered before dispersal and sown in a moist medium, will most likely germinate.

HARVESTING AND PRESERVING

Wood sorrel is a delightful snack to munch on in the garden or in the woods. Since the leaves and flowers wilt quickly once they are cut, be prepared when ready to harvest. Hold the long stems in one hand and cut them with garden scissors. Put them in a plastic bag and try to keep them moist and out of the sun until you are finished harvesting and get back to the kitchen. Trim and wash them as soon as possible, but if necessary, they can be kept in the refrigerator until ready to use.

When picked, the leaves fold up fairly quickly and the flowers close up right away, but they still taste good. Using scissors, trim the fibrous stems off, almost up to the leaves, leaving just a little piece. Do the same with flower stems and green seedpods.

GROWING HERBS

This raised spiral bed contains an herb garden with aromatherapy and culinary herbs. Brigit's Garden, Ireland.

THE IDEAL HERB GARDEN will sequester herbs in individual niches or pockets where they are happiest, from full blaring sun in relatively dry conditions to semishade with constant moisture. Except for some isolated gardens in past times—the Tudor era, apothecary gardens, and herb gardens of the colonial revival in North America (a re-created time in the twentieth century that was more idealized than practical)—herbs were not set off by themselves in dedicated herb gardens. Our ancestors realized that peppermint was happiest next to the water pump in the back of the house, while thyme would thrive in the dry, gravelly edges of the walkways out front. They didn't try to jam peppermint and thyme next to each other in an artificial ecological setting that would make extra work. And why make extra work for yourself today?

WHERE DID OUR FAVORITE HERBS ORIGINATE?

Many of the best known culinary herbs were first cultivated and used by the peoples of the eastern Mediterranean, later by the Greeks, and still later by the Romans. In the Middle Ages in Europe, herbs were cultivated in monasteries and home gardens. Because of this background, the plants that we know today as culinary herbs in the kitchen garden most often originated in one of three geographical regions: the Mediterranean region, northern and central Europe, or southeastern Europe and southwest Asia. As global exploration increased from the Renaissance onward, plants were added from Asia, Africa, and the New World. Each herb from those localities often requires specific environments for best health, depending on the species.

Herbs from the Mediterranean region

Herbs native to the Mediterranean region generally require full sun and a loose friable (easily crumbled) soil that is sub-acid to slightly alkaline (sweet, with pH 6.5 to 8.0). Many soils in the United States require the liberal addition of sand or gravel, and additional measures such as raised beds, may also be required to insure proper drainage. Many herbs from the Mediterranean will also frequently benefit from a light-colored mulch, such as gravel, sand, marble chips, or ground oyster shells, which will reflect light into the plant, rapidly drying them in the morning and thereby deterring fungal diseases, and often deterring insect pests. Avoid dark organic mulches, such as wood chips, which foster fungi and do not reflect light into the plants. After testing your soil for its pH, the addition of limestone may be required. Some woody-stemmed herbs from the Mediterranean that demand this treatment are lavender, oregano, rosemary, sage, savory, and thyme.

Sure, you can grow herbs of the Mediterranean region for a short time in deep, organic soils with dark colored mulches, coupled with overwatering and overfertilizing. But if you truly are interested in

Wheat straw is a good mulch for many herbs.

optimal health for these herbs and maximum flavor of your harvest, then you will look to their origins for tips for success.

Herbs from Europe

Herbs originally native to northern and central Europe generally require full to part sun, depending on the species, and a good garden loam that is slightly sour (pH 5.5) to slightly alkaline (pH 7.5). For these herbs, most soils in North America will benefit from the incorporation of good compost or other organic matter, and dark-colored mulches,

Well-drained raised beds with reflective gravel mulch are perfect for growing Mediterranean herbs. Ozark Folk Center, Arkansas.

such as wood chips or wheat straw, to contain moisture and control weeds. Herbs from northern and central Europe that thrive in these conditions include chives, dill, parsley, and French tarragon, among others.

Herbs from southeastern Europe and southwest Asia

Herbs originally native to southeastern Europe and southwest Asia run the gamut from conditions near to those of Mediterranean to those of northern and central Europe, although, generally, all relish a deep, organic soil, which has a pH more similar to the soils of the Mediterranean. A light mulch of straw may be beneficial to these herbs to help control weeds and moisture, and it breaks down into organic matter. But avoid a heavy, thick mulch of wood chips. Herbs from this region include chervil, coriander, and cumin, among others.

Herbs from Africa, Asia, and the New World

The herbs from Africa, Asia, and the New World require specific cultural conditions, and it is difficult to make generalizations. For example, basils, which are native to the tropics of both the Old and New World, are very sensitive to temperatures below 50°F. So you might plant it at the same time as tomatoes in your vegetable garden. On the other hand, lemon verbena will endure heavy frost, being native to colder areas in Argentina. The scented geraniums will flower best with a cool (but not freezing) winter, and generally prefer semidry conditions during dormancy. Each herb from these regions will require close attention to the factors of their original homes.

GETTING STARTED

Revisiting a plant's origins may be the most important journey a gardener takes. The herb's original environment often reveals the limits of a plant's ability to live on its own. The native habitat also provides important clues to methods of cultivation and to a plant's cold hardiness—environmental information on which the gardener will base many decisions.

What characteristics in the plant's native environment provide the most important cultivation clues? The essentials for plant growth are annual rainfall, amount of sun, minimum and maximum annual temperatures, and soil conditions. Also, an understanding of insects and diseases that a plant may encounter in its hometown is helpful, even when soil and climate seem perfect.

The closer we can reproduce the native conditions of the plants that we call culinary herbs, the better the chances of good growth. Plants have only a limited ability to adapt to conditions far removed from their origins, because their genes only allow a limited number of responses. Plants that have been widely cultivated for millennia will have a broader ability to adapt. Most culinary herbs do not have the millennia of adaptation that most major field crops do (such as wheat, cabbage, or corn), so we must pay heed to their origins.

Sun and air

Most of the herbs we cultivate today really benefit from both abundant sun and full air circulation—the conditions of their origins. Overcrowded herbs suffer from not enough air circulation and usually the more tenacious plants survive. For instance, tarragon is an herb that must have plenty of space around it or it will just shrivel up and turn brown if it is in the shade of larger, spreading herbs.

It is important to note the size of plants included in the plant profiles in this book.

You might start with seedlings or small plants in 3-inch pots, and when you transplant them, putting 1 foot of space between them, it might look like plenty. But if the plants grow to be 3 feet tall and 2 feet wide, then they will be crowding one another for air, sunshine, and nutrients, and they will not do well.

Shade and stale air can promote lax growth and devastating fungal growth. On the other hand, some herbs, such as those from forests in Europe, prefer some shade and water.

Soil and water

We try to abide by the simple adage that we learned when we first started gardening: "Plant a $1 plant in a $10 hole." Whatever beneficial supplements you incorporate into the soil where you first put a plant will reap untold benefits as that plant develops. It is so much easier to do this initially, rather than trying to retrofit the soil later on.

Before planting, really examine your soil. Can you easily break it apart with your hands? If it is friable, you are lucky. However, if like many gardeners, you initially encounter soil with the consistency of concrete or clay, then you have a job ahead of you. The addition of abundant sand and gravel, along with plenty of organic matter and mulches, will usually make your soil workable.

Heavy, compacted soils will drain poorly, which will kill most of the herbs from the Mediterranean. So, if your soil is so compacted it cannot be fixed, consider making raised beds. Some school gardens are built with raised beds on macadam, which is about as impenetrable as you can get in a garden situation. Building raised beds with friable soil high in organic matter on top of compacted soil will also have the benefit of encouraging earthworms, which will slowly but eventually do the job of increasing your soil tilth (physical condition of the soil, from compact to loose and friable) underneath.

Next, consider the chemical composition of your soil. Find where you can have a soil test done (in the

United States, contact the local USDA State Extension office). The cost of the test is usually minimal and is frequently subsidized by your tax dollars. Follow the directions for gathering a soil sample by taking small amounts from around your garden and combining them to get an average sample. The test results will be returned to you within a few weeks. Most herbs require the same amounts of nitrogen, phosphorus, and potassium as do many garden vegetables, so closely follow the agency's recommendations for additional fertilization (if needed) or pH adjustment.

Next, consider the bacterial and fungal composition of your soil. Many gardeners advocate adding good compost, because not only do you add critical nutrients and organic matter with compost to change the tilth of the soil, but the accompanying bacteria and fungi will determine the future of your soil. Lacking good compost, you can choose from a few good manufactured bacterial and mycorrhizal fungal preparations, usually of a pasteurized chicken manure base. These preparations increase the health of your garden soil, and they rejuvenate tired soils, especially in large pots.

About manures: not all manures are created equal. Cow, horse, and pig manures will promote sudden wilt fungi, such as *Phytophthora* (a sudden wilt fungus that attacks herbs), while chicken manure will promote fungi antagonistic to *Phytophthora*. Well-rotted chicken manure can be a blessing in the herb and vegetable garden, if you can obtain it. This could be a reason to raise your own chickens.

Cool-weather versus warm-weather conditions

Some herbs are adapted to cool weather. Annual, cool-weather herbs flower and fruit quickly and then die, such as chervil, cilantro, and dill. When planting these herbs, put in successive plantings at ten- to fourteen-day intervals to extend the harvest in both spring and fall. Other cool-weather herbs are perennial, such as good King Henry, French tarragon, and lovage. They just sit back and bide their time, not producing much new growth, from June to September until the weather gets cooler.

Most herbs are adapted to warm weather. When planting basil, wait until the weather reaches at least 60°F and there is no chance of frost. Basil just stops growing below 50°F and starts turning black. For the same reason, do not store basil in the refrigerator, but instead, keep it in a glass of water on the windowsill until ready to use.

For gardeners with a very short cool season, there are some warm-weather mimics of the cool-season herbs. For example, culantro (*Eryngium foetidum*) has a flavor comparable to the cool-season cilantro (*Coriandrum sativum*). And Mexican tarragon (*Tagetes lucida*) can serve as an alternative to French tarragon (*Artemisia dracunculus* 'Sativa').

CONTAINER GARDENING

Container gardening can be a useful approach to growing plants for many reasons. Perhaps you do not have a backyard, but you have a deck or patio where you can place some pots. Or maybe good soil is just not available to you, or the local soil was contaminated by leaking fuel oil, runoff from the driveway, or leached lead from old house paint. For older gardeners or gardeners with disabilities, containers serve to bring the plants closer to hand-eye level. Also pots are a wonderful way to get children involved in gardening: give them their own pots to plant and care for. Tender plants that cannot be carried over through the climate of a harsh winter are simply easier to maintain in pots, since you can bring them indoors in the cold weather. And sometimes, herbs just look great in that unusual pot you purchased as a last minute whimsy as you left the garden center.

Pots

We have found that very large pots are ideal for growing herbs, from arugula and miner's lettuce in spring to nasturtiums and basil in summer. We have used large plastic tubs (the ones often sold for under $10 for collecting building debris), drilled holes in the bottom, placed some upside-down broken pottery over the holes, and filled them with porous soil. These may fade in the sunlight over time, but you can easily paint them (Art uses a textured Monet blue paint). If the pots are ceramic (which can crack in the winter from frost expansion), then either place blocks of foam on the inside of the pot or simply turn the pots on their side in winter to prevent accumulation of water.

Clay pots, in our experience, require constant watering, sometimes more than once a day, and gradually flake over time, especially in winter. Concrete pots are ideal: while they are often very heavy, their thick walls, along with evaporation of water from the surface, help the soil to remain cool. But concrete pots will also require the blocks of foam or placing on their side in the winter where freezing occurs.

Most herbs grow well in containers.

Wooden whiskey barrels make good large containers if you drill extra drainage holes in the bottom. It takes lots of soil to fill one, so we place a broken cinderblock in the bottom (which adds lime to the mix). Mints thrive in the barrels and are kept confined from spreading. We have also used large metal pots, painted inside and out to prevent leaching of metal ions into the soil. These make it through winter without cracking. Old leaky galvanized aluminum washtubs, painted with a satin exterior paint, make good recycled plant containers.

Growing mediums

Soil in pots must be light and airy, since compacted soil will accumulate water and rot many herbs. We routinely use several soil conditioners, from perlite to terra-cotta frit to pottery pebbles. Perlite is steam-expanded obsidian that occurs in natural deposits; it resembles a white friable sandlike material and is easily crushed by hand to powder. Manufactured terra-cotta frit resembles finely broken pottery that is perhaps more aesthetically acceptable than perlite in a soil mixture. It is widely used by rock gardeners and for golf courses. Manufactured pottery pebbles are fired small pottery balls, and are routinely used in hydroponics. These products lighten up the soil and retain moisture between watering. Styrofoam beads, while unsightly, can also be used as a soil conditioner and have the benefit of withstanding frost expansion during the winter. Vermiculite is used as a soil conditioner for short-term soils, like those used for germination of seeds, and should be avoided for large pots because it quickly breaks down into individual slippery mica pieces. Sand, chicken grit (ground oyster shell), and gravel are also useful for increasing drainage but their weight in pots limits their usefulness.

Into the primary soil itself, we work in a range of organic soil amendments, from sphagnum peat moss to composted bark or household compost, to increase the water-holding capacity, permeability, and soil aggregation. We generally like to use one part sphagnum peat moss to one part pasteurized leaf mold or compost to two parts soil conditioner. Finally, similar to taking probiotics for our gut, we add a beneficial bacterial and mycorrhizal fungal product (for example, Espoma's Bio-tone).

Mix the soil ingredients when they are slightly moist but not totally dry or wet. Depending on the size and number of pots, you can mix soils easily in a bucket, but you might use a wheelbarrow or even a cement mixer.

Nutrients and moisture

Herbs of the Mediterranean will often survive with minimal moisture, but herbs of the other regions will require attention to moisture. All herbs require nutrients appropriate for a typical vegetable garden, and overfertilization is not necessary for proper growth and often results in reduced flavor.

Growing up, we remember many gardeners using "manure tea." A rain barrel was placed under a house gutter spout, and a large cloth bag of manure, usually cow manure, was suspended in it, or some folks mixed the solution in an old bathtub or livestock trough. Today, use of manure tea in the garden is limited because of concerns about pathogenic strains of bacteria, such as *Salmonella* species and *Escherizia coli* (*E. coli*), but if you can find a source of pasteurized, dehydrated manure, it is still worth trying.

As an alternative fertilizer, for pots (and general use in the garden), we prefer what is commonly called fish emulsion. Studies have compared fish emulsion with inorganic fertilizers and found them rather similar in the nutrition they provide. But with the fish emulsion, you also foster beneficial bacteria and fungi that are not necessarily favored by the inorganic fertilizers.

If you don't like the odor of fish emulsion, then controlled-release fertilizers are a lazy gardener's dream. Simply sprinkle the pellets onto the surface of the soil and water them in; they should last for months, depending upon the brand.

We also recommend seaweed or kelp extracts in the water at initial planting of seedlings and divisions. Seaweed or kelp extracts contain a number of plant hormones that promote cell division and therefore rapid root regeneration.

Whatever the source of nutrients, pay attention to the nutrient ratings. Nitrogen, phosphorous, and potassium (NPK) are considered the major primary nutrients for plant growth, so these are the principal materials rated in a fertilizer as percentages. A 5-10-5 fertilizer, for example, will have 5 percent nitrogen (N) as nitrate, 10 percent phosphorus (P) as phosphate, and 5 percent potassium (K) as potassium oxide by weight. Also pay attention to whether the fertilizer of choice has essential minor or trace elements, such as iron, molybdenum, boron, copper, manganese, zinc, and chlorine. Calcium and magnesium, for example, will facilitate the availability of nutrients (as well as alter the pH). We like to add these elements with a sprinkling of ground dolomitic limestone when we create our planting mediums (depending on the soil test results and the range of pH preferred by the particular herbs).

GROWING HERBS INDOORS

Sunlight and air circulation so necessary for the formation of the flavors and fragrances of herbs are difficult to mimic indoors unless you have a greenhouse. A bright, sunny, partially heated sun porch is an ideal alternative. Lacking these, the home gardener can often grow some herbs, such as basil, parsley, and chives, on a bright, sunny windowsill.

We are hesitant to recommend growing herbs under fluorescent lights because of the high capital investment necessary and the constantly changing equipment, as well as the increased electric bills. The hydroponic stores that are springing up with the new laws on medical marijuana can be a good source of information on growing some herbs indoors under lights.

In all these scenarios, pay attention to the air circulation, especially in winter. Stagnant air will foster diseases and insects. We recommend an overhead fan or several small, strategically placed fans.

MAINTAINING THE HEALTH OF HERBS

Herbs are susceptible to diseases, insects, and crowding out by weeds, so pay attention to each specific herb's origins and its needs regarding light, drainage, and soil. For example, herbs from the Mediterranean are notoriously finicky about low light, poor drainage, acidic soil, high humidity, and lack of air movement. Any or all of these conditions will encourage bacterial and fungal diseases if they don't kill the plant outright. Almost daily attention will produce the best herbs.

Typical health problems and treatments

In this section we summarize some of the health problems your herbs might experience, listed by symptoms, diagnosis, and treatment.

Symptom: Brown leaf tips.

DIAGNOSIS Uneven watering or overfertilization. Overwatering or underwatering is most often the culprit, but excessive fertilizing can also produce these symptoms, so be sure to read the fertilizer package instructions. Too much fluoride, copper, or boron in the water can produce the same appearance.

TREATMENT If improved watering and fertilizing techniques fail to alleviate conditions in new leaves, check water quality with a comprehensive test.

Symptom: Foliage is covered with a white powdery substance.

DIAGNOSIS Probably powdery mildew.

TREATMENT Plants are most susceptible to powdery mildew when subjected to high humidity, temperatures below 80°F, and poor airflow. Leaf dampness and low light conditions also promote mildew growth, which is why plants like rosemary can become infected when they are brought into the house for winter. Powdery mildew is usually not a problem when plants are outdoors in the open, especially when afternoon temperatures are above 86°F and air is continually circulating through the foliage. If this problem occurs indoors, install a small fan nearby to increase the air circulation. If changing the growing conditions does not alter the symptoms, combat the infection with sprays of a solution of 2 tablespoons of baking soda in 1 quart of water. It may take two or three applications to completely get rid of the powdery mildew. If this fails, try sprays of garden sulfur. Use caution, though, because high temperatures combined with sulfur sprays can sometimes be toxic to plants.

Symptom: Leaves have an oily, greasy appearance or have water-soaked spots; plant stems wilt and blacken.

DIAGNOSIS Probably a bacterial disease.

TREATMENT Destroy the infected plants and throw them in the trash. Do not put on the compost pile or reuse their soil. Space healthy plants so that air can circulate around and through them. Do not wet the foliage when watering. Keep plants in as much sunshine as they can withstand in order to create strong leaf tissue. If this problem occurs indoors, consider placing a small fan nearby to increase air circulation.

Symptom: Plant roots are brown to black instead of their usual firm consistency and light or white color.

DIAGNOSIS This could be root rot.

TREATMENT Roots need air. When they are irrigated, water fills the small holes in the growing mediums that contain air. If plants are watered too often or given too much water, air cannot reach the roots, and they begin to die. It is sometimes helpful to test how long a plant can go without water before it shows signs of stress, and then adjust the quantity and frequency of watering.

Symptom: Leaves and stems of new and old tissues are covered with a gray or brown mold.

DIAGNOSIS Likely culprit: *Botrytis*.

TREATMENT *Botrytis*, a fungus with gray or brown fuzzy growth, is encouraged by cool, damp weather and other conditions that stress plants. Provide plants with plenty of sun or longer hours of indoor plant lights. Be careful not to overwater; instead, toughen plant tissue by withholding water. Do not crowd plants, so that air can circulate through and around them. Indoors, use a fan to gently push air through the plants.

Symptom: Dead leaves hang on branches low to the soil, while upper leaves are healthy.

DIAGNOSIS Probably fungus disease.

TREATMENT The disease is spread by moisture and reduced airflow. Remove infected, dead, yellowing, and damaged foliage and put into the trash. Increase air circulation within and around the plant by judicious pruning and increased spacing. Add a pea-gravel mulch or white sand to reflect heat into the plant and help keep leaves dry.

Symptom: Lower leaves wilt, yellow, and die. Process proceeds up the plant. Plants may suddenly wilt and die.

DIAGNOSIS There's a good chance the soil is infected with *Pseudomonas*, *Verticillium*, or *Fusarium* fungi that cause sudden wilts of young, succulent plant tissue.

TREATMENT Remove plants and put them into the trash. Plant resistant varieties or set new, disease-free plants in uncontaminated soil.

Symptom: Plant suddenly collapses or wilts when adequate irrigation is available.

DIAGNOSIS Could be infected with *Phytophthora*, *Fusarium*, *Verticillium*, or *Pythium*, which are soil mold diseases that attack many herbs native to the Mediterranean basin and their cultivars. These diseases clog the plants' vascular tissue and reduce the transmission of water. The diseases are often caused by overwatering, poor drainage, and inadequate air circulation.

TREATMENT Copper foliar sprays are sometimes effective on infected plants. These diseases are often accelerated by overwatering, poor soil drainage, or inadequate air circulation. Changing the plant's location may be helpful, but a fresh start with new plants is desirable. Incorporate abundant sand and gravel into the soil—enough to raise the planting bed's level above the rest of the garden. Consider a light-colored mulch of sand, gravel, marble chips, or ground oyster shells to reflect heat back into the plant. Mycorrhizal (beneficial) fungal dips may be helpful in some instances, if the plants are small.

Symptom: Chive shoots in early spring are covered with black insects.

DIAGNOSIS Black aphid infestation.

TREATMENT Aphids are among the most common garden pests; there are more than 4,400 species. They feed by sucking plant sap, and a heavy infestation can stunt and deform their host. In addition, about 60 percent of plant viruses are transplanted by these little insects. Aphids are often seasonal in the garden, especially during periods of cool nights.

Light aphid infestations in the garden can be handled with a strong spray of water that knocks the insects from the plants. If the garden or greenhouse is overrun, spray a combination of insecticidal soap. Biological controls include ladybugs, lacewings, parasitic wasps, and insect-pathogenic fungi.

Symptom: Bay tree leaves feel sticky and are covered with a sootlike substance.

DIAGNOSIS Most likely an infestation of scale, a tiny sucking insect commonly found on bay plants (and quite often on citrus plants), especially if the bay tree was summered outdoors and brought in for the winter.

TREATMENT Coating the plant with a fine horticultural oil mixed with water and applied either by spraying or dipping (if the plants are small) suffocates the insects and gives the plant a healthy shine.

Symptom: Tiny flies float around potted plants.

DIAGNOSIS Fungus gnats, probably.

TREATMENT In greenhouses, stores, and homes where light levels are low and soil moisture is high, fungus gnats are likely inhabitants. The adults are merely unsightly, but their offspring burrow into

roots and stems and often transmit diseases such as *Pythium*, *Fusarium*, *Phoma*, and *Verticillium*. Drench the soil with *Bacillus thuringiensis* (BT), a spore-forming bacterium that destroys the larvae of fungus gnats.

Symptom: Green or yellowing leaves show pinhead discolorations.

DIAGNOSIS Thrips or spider mites. Thrips leave an irregular, discolored pattern that looks like the pigment has been sucked from small areas of the leaves. Spider mites leave many tiny, round marks on leaves from their feeding, where the color has been drawn. Minute webbing with tiny insects scooting over it may be visible during major infestations of spider mites.

TREATMENT Sprays of insecticidal soap and rotenone every three days for two weeks can break the insect life cycle and control the pests, if not totally eradicate them.

Symptom: Wiggly discoloration through leaf surfaces, especially sorrel.

DIAGNOSIS Probably leaf miners, the larvae of the flying adult. Little clusters of eggs are often clearly visible on the undersides of leaves.

TREATMENT Create a barrier to prevent the adults from laying eggs by protecting foliage with a floating row cover of spun-bonded polypropylene fabric, especially in spring and fall.

Symptom: Ragged holes in leaves or leaf margins, particularly basil and sorrel.

DIAGNOSIS Probably night-foraging slugs, which spend their days under layers of mulch, large stones, and sidewalks—wherever there is darkness and moisture. If you look, there should be a shiny slug trail around the plant. Also look for caterpillars, which usually feed during daylight hours.

TREATMENT Seek out and destroy these pests'

resting places. Trap the pests by placing flat pieces of wood or inverted, scooped-out melon shells on the soil—a veritable slug hotel—during the day, and then destroy the guests. Some sprinkle diatomaceous earth around the plants in peril, because the small particles are jagged and sharp so the slugs don't cross over it or it will cut them; it needs to be replaced after rain. A 4-inch-high copper flashing pushed into the soil on its edge makes an impervious slug fence. Some mail-order garden supply companies sell copper material to block slug attacks, and copper flashing is available at roofing supply firms. Recent tests of beer as a bait and trap for slugs showed that beer was not effective at significantly reducing slug predation of strawberries, and the beer-baited traps are effective for only a few feet.

Symptom: Poor growth, yellowing leaves, dying growing tips.

DIAGNOSIS After ruling out pH imbalance, poor drainage, and lack of nutrients, consider microscopic soil insects called nematodes. These pests burrow into roots, causing raised nodes, interfering with nutrient uptake, and slowly killing the crop. Nematode-infested roots can spread the critters to previously uncontaminated areas, particularly when field-grown plants are dug and sold or new plants are created from divisions. Nematodes also promote the spread of soil-borne fungi.

TREATMENT Soil enriched with grass clippings destroys most nematodes. If infestation is severe, turn to container gardening, and use a growing medium containing equal parts of peat moss and perlite.

PROPAGATION

Many herbs can be grown easily from seeds, but some (like named cultivars of rosemary and lavender) must be propagated by cuttings or other vegetative means. For example, planting seeds of 'Hidcote' lavender will not produce 'Hidcote' lavender. If anything, the resulting product could be described as 'Hidcote'-derived, but it certainly would not be 'Hidcote'. Actually, most offerings of 'Hidcote' seeds currently on the commercial market have a mixture of light to dark flowers, and range from dwarf size to tall growth—in other words, a potpourri of lavenders, not 'Hidcote'.

In addition, some herbs are simply seed-sterile. Peppermint (*Mentha ×piperita*) is a sterile hybrid of two fertile species, sort of a mule among herbs. Yes, you will see offerings of "peppermint" seed in catalogs and at your local garden center, but these germinate to a rank-odored spearmint, not peppermint. Likewise, true French tarragon (*Artemisia dracunculus* 'Sativa') was a sterile, high-estragole selection

(with an odor a bit like anise) from sometime in the Middle Ages and does not produce flowers or seeds. Again, offerings of "tarragon" seeds from the current commercial market will produce the parental Russian tarragon (*A. dracunculus*), smelling a bit of shoe leather—not what you want for a successful béarnaise sauce.

Growing herbs from seed

Because many of us want to grow herbs from seeds started indoors, the choice of a soilless medium or pasteurized soil mixture is important. Lack of good air circulation and light will promote fungi and bacteria, so the less spores that you start with, the better.

As previously discussed, we generally like to use one part sphagnum peat moss to one part pasteurized leaf mold or compost to two parts soil conditioner. The leaf mold that is sold packaged at garden centers as "humus" or "garden soil" is generally pasteurized leaf mold from city collections. Perlite is a good soil conditioner to use with this material, and the final mixture will be 50 percent perlite.

There's something sacred to us about the terra-cotta clay pot. Like most home gardeners, we prefer the old-fashioned terra-cotta clay pot over large plastic trays. We do use large plastic trays when we are growing hundreds of plants for sale. But for growing just a few plants for your garden, the terra-cotta pot 5 to 8 inches in diameter can't be beat. Start by placing a piece of broken terra cotta in the bottom of the pot, concave side down. Then fill the pot with the moistened planting medium. (If you are using seed flats, follow the basic directions for a pot.)

In a separate container, mix sterile play sand, milled sphagnum moss, and fine vermiculite. This mixture provides just the right amount of drainage, and the milled sphagnum moss inhibits fungi such as *Pythium*, which will cause seedlings to wilt just as they emerge. Sprinkle about ⅛ inch of this mix on top of the soil medium, and then sow the seeds. Seeds will need to be covered with about twice the narrow width of the seed: In other words, if the narrow width of your bean seed is ¼ inch, then it will have to be covered with ½ inch of the mix. Very fine seeds can be simply sifted over the surface with no further covering.

Place the terra-cotta pot in a saucer of water at least ½ inch deep and gently water, being careful not to dislodge the seeds. (Or water a flat very gently with a fine mist.) Keep the potted seeds at near room temperature and constantly moist. At this stage, until seedlings emerge, a thin cover or plastic wrap will help to retain moisture but should be immediately removed upon germination to avoid fungal wilt.

After germination, seedlings should be carefully separated and planted in new soil. You can transplant seedlings to pots or into warm soil in the garden when the plants' first true leaves are well developed and the second leaves begin to emerge. Crowding prior to transplanting will allow fungi, such as

Arugula seeds are being started in a sphagnum and perlite mix.

These dill seedlings are ready to be transplanted.

These amaranth plants are
ready to be planted outdoors.

Pythium, to grow, resulting in wilted seedlings. We
find that seedlings should be "pricked out" in groups
of three or more, because less root damage seems
to occur when seedlings are transplanted in groups
rather than individually. After seedlings show growth
in the new soil, a diluted general fertilizer may be
used, but make sure to provide even moisture coupled with good air circulation, which are of utmost
importance.

Growing herbs by layering and cuttings

For propagating woody perennials, such as sage and
lavandin, the home gardener will find that the easiest
method is layering. Simply choose a side branch,
scrape off some bark, apply a little rooting hormone
to the scraped area to hasten rooting, and either
weigh the branch down with a rock or brick or hold
it down with a U-shaped hook bent from an old wire
coat hanger. Maintain even moisture. This method is
slow, however; the production of a good root system

will require months before the new plant can be
severed and transplanted.

For quicker propagation of a number of plants, cuttings are the preferred choice. Rooting from cuttings
can range from extremely simple to elaborate, from
only one cutting to thousands. But first, you should
pay attention to the type of parent plant. Plants that
grow in very moist situations generally can be rooted
in water. Plants that grow in dry environments will
rot in water and require more attention.

We have a preference for "heel" cuttings. Choose
a side branch near the tip that is 1 to 3 inches long.
With a sharp downward pull, remove the branch,
pulling off some older tissue of the parent stem (and
the base of the cutting will resemble the heel of a
foot). Then remove the basal leaves. Dip the bottom
of the branch in rooting hormone, and then gently
place into moist medium.

Perhaps the simplest method we have used with
cuttings is florist foam. Small blocks of foam can

Rosemary is easily started from rooted cuttings.

easily be carried in small, clear plastic bags. Merely take the cutting, place into wet florist foam, and put into the plastic bag. At home, place the bag on a windowsill that receives full light but no direct sunlight and keep the florist foam moist but not wet. When roots appear, gradually peel back the plastic bag, and eventually transplant to soil. This method works very well with most herbs that require moist soil. Since it uses the essentially sterile medium of florist foam, the chance of fungal rot is severely reduced until transplanting to soil.

For herbs that require drier soil, the growing medium must be carefully prepared. Taking lavender and lavandin as examples, prepare pots or trays with 1 part perlite to 1 part sphagnum peat moss. Moisten the medium and place where the pots or trays have good drainage in indirect light; a 50 percent shade cloth works for us in the greenhouse or outdoors. Place the pots or trays in a spot that is free from strong winds but still has some exchange of air. Gently cover with thin, clear plastic without sealing, to retain some moisture but still allow air exchange. Water frequently, from every day to at least every other day, depending on the temperatures and wind. After about two weeks, gently tug the cuttings to see if roots are forming. When a good, healthy root system has developed, remove the plastic and expose the seedling to more air and light, and eventually transplant.

PRESERVING
THE HERBAL HARVEST

Bringing in the herbal harvest is among the greatest pleasures for the gardener.

This thyme is ready to harvest.

AS GARDENERS AND COOKS, we look forward to the growing season with great anticipation. We celebrate our garden bounty daily. We delight in warm, sun-ripened tomatoes with fresh basil, just-picked green beans with a piquant, savory vinaigrette, and sprigs of spearmint muddled in lime juice with rum for the perfect mojito. Because of the season's abundance, we suppose we take it for granted. We don't need to bemoan the fact that there are no fresh herbs to brighten our cooking in the cold weather—because we have preserved them during the season.

In this chapter, we share the very best methods and recipes for harvesting and preserving your garden's herbs so you can enjoy them year round. From our years of experience, these simple instructions will guide you in harvesting, drying, and freezing herbs.

Herbs are at their finest when they are fresh and in season. They reach their peak of flavor and essential oil production in summer, especially when flowering. During the growing season, we harvest herbs as

Harvest herbs at their
peak on a sunny day.

needed for whatever dish we might be preparing. We bring fresh herbs into the kitchen, give their stem ends a fresh snip, and put them in a jar of water. They will keep on the kitchen counter out of direct sunlight for at least five days, maybe longer—especially if the water is changed every couple of days.

When ready to use the herbs in a recipe, rinse them if needed and pat or spin dry. Often, when we harvest herbs, especially if it has just rained, they don't need to be rinsed. But if they are even slightly dirty or gritty, they must be washed. If herbs are very dirty, put a few tablespoons of vinegar in the washing water and the grit will fall to the bottom of the container. Then dry them well before combining with oil (oil and water do not mix). We do this in a salad spinner and then place the herbs on a kitchen towel to air dry, or direct a fan on them until all water is evaporated.

To have a year-round supply of herbs, you will want to preserve some of summer's bounty for the winter months. Gather the herbs "while ye may" and preserve them in your pantry and freezer. Take pleasure in the time spent preserving your herbs, knowing how satisfying it will be to have their flavor and nutritious benefits all year.

HARVESTING HERBS

Pick borage blossoms when they are in full bloom.

For best flavor, most herbs should be harvested from just before the plants form flower buds to mid-flowering, unless you want the blooms. Herbs do vary as to when to harvest. Some perennials, like oregano, thyme, and other woody-stemmed herbs, are often harvested about mid-blossom time at the maximum oil production. Basil is best harvested before the bloom, since the leaves tend to become bitter once the essential oils are concentrated in the flowers. On the other hand, you may want dill to flower so that you can save the seed. To know when to harvest, usually you can allow your eyes and nose to be your guide. And in the herb profiles, we recommend individual harvest times.

Ideally, choose a sunny day for harvesting, and cut the herbs in the mid-morning after the morning dew has evaporated. Avoid harvesting herbs when they are wet, since this can inhibit the drying process as well as encourage mold. Herb oils are strongest in the leaves on a sunny day; in fact, harvesting on a cloudy day will not yield as much flavor. If the herbs seem gritty or dirty, try to plan ahead, and the day before you want to harvest, rinse the plants with water by spraying lightly with the hose. Both annual and perennial herbs can be harvested at least a few times during the summer season. Pruning them about once a month during the growing season will encourage new growth and yield, maximizing leaf harvest.

A rule of thumb is that annual plants like basil or cilantro can be cut back to just above the bottom two sets of leaves. This approach results in more stems, new leaf growth, and a much larger harvest the next time, and, if continued, at least a few more harvests. While harvesting herbs, keep the just-cut stems out of direct sunlight or they will wilt. Take them to a shady place for sorting and picking over or tying into bundles. For the final harvest of the season, pull up whole annual plants, tidying up the garden for winter and gathering the bounty at the same time. Or, cut annuals just above the bottom set of leaves.

Woody-stemmed, perennial herbs like oregano or rosemary can be pruned to about one-third of their height. Do not prune perennials too late in the fall, if you live in the north where the winters are cold, since this weakens the plants' resistance to cold. Six to eight weeks before a hard freeze, take your last cuttings, so that the plants have time to harden off and put out some new growth.

If you have pulled up entire annual plants, trim the roots off. Before bringing the herbs indoors, pick over the leaves and remove any wilted, brown, spotted, or bug-eaten ones. Brush away any dirt or grit and remove webs, insect eggs, or cocoons. If the herbs are dirty and you must wash them, rinse them quickly and pat or spin dry. To remove excess moisture quickly, lay them on a kitchen cloth in front of a fan.

Flowers should be harvested at their peak and, if necessary, swished in a bowl of water to remove any insects or grit. They can then be candied, dried, made into decorative ice cubes, or used in herb butter or herb vinegar.

Harvest sprigs of summer savory back to above the bottom two sets of leaves.

Plants harvested close to the ground, such as small salad seedlings when you are thinning, carry the risk of bacterial contamination from soil. For the leafy mustards and all harvested salad herbs grown in a highly organic soil, we recommend spritzing with household white vinegar and then household hydrogen peroxide, and then rinsing. The sequence will kill 99 percent of any bacteria, but don't combine the two into one disinfectant.

Hang herbs
to dry in small
bunches, out of
direct sunlight.

DRYING HERBS

Herbs can be dried by hanging them in bunches, or by laying them on screens and in shallow baskets. For hanging them, gather the stems into small bundles and fasten them with twine, string, or rubber bands. Lavender growers routinely use rubber bands because, as the stems shrink from drying, the band tightens, which won't happen with string, so the bunches can slip out and fall to the ground. They also twist a paper clip into a hook to hang the rubber-banded bunch from lines. Don't make too large a bunch or they won't dry: use three to seven stems per bunch, depending on how large the stalks are and how many leaves are on them. Select a well-ventilated place out of the sun and hang them to dry from a nail, peg, or hook; even pushpins work. Rafters in the house, an attic, or garden shed are good spots for drying herbs, as long as they are out of direct light.

If you use baskets or screens, the leaves of small-leaved herbs, such as thyme or sweet marjoram, along with savory or rosemary, which have thin, needlelike leaves, can be left on their stems and laid out to dry. For larger leaved herbs, like basil or nettles (wear gloves when handling the latter), pluck the leaves from their stalks and arrange them in a single layer on the screens or in baskets.

When drying flowers, pluck or cut them at their peak and spread them on baskets or trays to dry. We dry some flowers whole like chamomile blooms, lavender and anise hyssop spikes, dandelions, shungiku, and daylily buds. Depending on what we are doing with them, sometimes we dry whole calendula flower heads, and we often pull the petals from the center disks of calendula for faster drying. Generally, we remove the delicate petals from calendula, monarda, and pineapple sage, and dry them on baking sheets in the oven with just the oven light on (or a pilot light, if a gas oven). Ideally, dry the flowers quickly, so they don't lose their flavor and color. Store the dried flowers in labeled jars in a dark place and use before the next harvest season.

Just-harvested nasturtium seeds are ready for drying.

If drying herbs for seed, be sure that the seed heads are mature. Dill, fennel, and coriander seeds should be turning from green to tan or light brown. So should nasturtiums; since their seeds are much bigger, spread them in a basket in a warm place until they are dry.

Use the same directions for hanging herbs for seed. However, since the seeds tend to drop as they dry, it is wise to hang the seed heads over a screen or basket that will catch the seed. For tied bunches, place each one into a paper bag with a few air holes cut in it, hang it, and the seeds will fall into the bottom of the bag.

Depending on where you live, the air humidity, and the weather conditions, it could take a couple of

Just-harvested herbs are ready for preserving.

days to a few weeks for the herb leaves, seeds, and flowers to dry. Try to test the herbs daily. In humid weather, if they are left for too long, they tend to lose their green color (as well as flavor) and turn brown. A dried leaf or petal should crackle and crumble when rubbed between your fingers. If a leaf or flower is not crisp and it bends, it still contains moisture. To remove the last bit of excess moisture, place the leaves, flowers, or seeds on baking sheets, and put in the oven with a pilot light or just the oven light on. This raises the temperature to 110 to 115°F and will remove excess moisture without overheating the plant material.

Alternatively, preheat the oven to the lowest temperature possible, not over 200°F, and turn the oven off. Place the almost-dried herbs on baking sheets and put in the warmed oven for about 5 minutes. Check to see if they crumble and crackle, and repeat if necessary. Do not overheat them or they will lose their flavor and turn brown.

Although we have practiced these processes of drying herbs for many years, there is more than one way to dry herbs. Our friend, herbalist Tina Marie Wilcox, successfully dries some of her herbs in the refrigerator. Sicilian oregano (*Origanum ×majoricum*), marjoram (*O. majorana*), thyme, rosemary, dill, and cilantro dry green and fragrant with this method. Here's what to do. Herb sprigs should be completely

dry. Put small bunches in labeled, lunch-sized paper bags. Fold the top of the bags down and lay them flat on a free refrigerator shelf. Every day, turn the bags and shake gently so that air will circulate around the leaves. The cool air in the refrigerator keeps the volatile oils from evaporating. Drying time varies; the process can take two to three weeks. This process must be done in a refrigerator that isn't crowded, because it needs some air circulation to work.

We also know some herb farmers, Andrea and Matthias Reisen in New York state, who showed us some bright green, wonderfully aromatic lemon balm they dried in 24 to 48 hours, spread out in sunlight in their greenhouses, covered with a shade cloth, and with a fan running. The quality of their dried herbs convinced us to try that method, so we dried Italian oregano with great results. Drying in sunlight in a covered greenhouse protects the plants from burning and losing their essential oils, though it should be done quickly so they retain their bright color and flavor. Drying can be done in an attic, shed, or any place where there is good air circulation; warm temperatures aid in faster drying, while humidity hinders drying.

When the herbs are dried and ready to store, working over a large bowl or newspaper, carefully strip the whole leaves from the stems. Transfer the whole leaves into clean jars with tight-fitting lids, preferably with dark glass. When handling, do not crush the leaves, since this releases their essential oils; take care to gently pack the leaves whole to keep the best flavor. (The idea is to crumble the leaves into the dish you are making, to then release the essential oils and flavor.) Herbs will mold and spoil if they are not completely dried when you pack them in jars. Since dried herbs tend to look alike, be sure to label the jars after they are filled. Stored away from light and heat, home-dried herbs can be kept in jars or tins for a year, or until next season's crop comes in.

Gently pack completely
dried herbs into airtight
jars, label, and store out
of direct light.

Aromatic herbal pastes are a wonderful way to capture herbal essence.

FREEZING HERBS

Generally, freezing most herbs does not yield great results. When herb leaves are frozen, the low temperature breaks down the cellular structure, and the leaves become mushy and turn dark. We often see recipes for freezing chopped herbs in water in ice cube trays; we do not prefer this method since it accentuates this result. Ice crystals often form on the more tender leaved herbs, which makes them watery after a month or two in the freezer. We prefer to dry the woody-stemmed perennials, such as rosemary and sage, for texture and flavor. Herbs like tarragon are better preserved in vinegar, since tarragon loses its flavor when dried.

For our favorite way to freeze herbs, we find that making a paste with the fresh chopped herb leaves and oil yields a far superior product. The oil surrounds the herb and captures its essence and keeps it from turning dark. This process also has a longer shelf life than freezing herb leaves on their own or in water. (See page 306, Aromatic Herbal Pastes.)

However, if you want to freeze herbs on their own, harvest and clean the herbs as instructed for drying. For the best flavor, the easiest method is to freeze whole leaves. Annual herbs with thin leaves tend to freeze better than the woody ones: try parsley, cilantro, dill sprigs, salad burnet, and basil. Remove the leaves from the stems and place them in one layer on baking sheets. "Flash freeze" these for about 30 minutes until they are hard, and then pack them in small, airtight freezer containers or pint freezer bags, and label. Frozen this way, they tend to keep their green color a little better and they don't stick together in a frozen mass. Remove the leaves as you need them, adding them to your recipe while still frozen. The bright green color will turn dark once they are thawed.

MASTER

RECIPES

USING CULINARY HERBS

Herbal syrups are a delightful, sweet way to capture the flavor of herbs.

OUR MASTER RECIPES WILL guide you in using your fresh herbs in inspired infusions such as herbal vinegars for sublime salad dressings as well as in herb syrups that can be used to fashion a libation or to glaze your favorite cake. We also discuss how to prepare herb butters to have on hand for seasoning winter vegetables or adding a finishing touch to homemade biscuits. And regarding freezing your herbs—don't just freeze them. Capture their essence in an aromatic herbal paste, which can be frozen and used as needed to add fresh, bright flavor to sauces (like basil paste to be used for pesto), soups, and baked goods. These basic, easy-to-follow recipes will have you enjoying your harvested herbs in every season.

▶ FRESH HERBS TO USE FOR SYRUPS

The amounts of herbs and flowers used in herb syrups vary, depending on the flavor of each herb. The listed herbs are calculated in sprigs, most 4 to 5 inches long, which will yield the appropriate amount for the Simple Herb Syrup recipe. Sprigs of shorter herbs like sweet woodruff or thyme might only be 3 to 4 inches long. These amounts of herbs and flowers will produce a well-balanced, nicely flavored syrup. You can use more herbs or flowers, but you will get a more concentrated syrup, which may need to be diluted, depending on its use.

Anise hyssop: 6 to 8 sprigs with flowers, or a handful of flowers

Basil: about 8 sprigs of anise, cinnamon, green, or lemon basil, or a handful of flowers

Bay: 6 to 8 leaves

Chamomile: about 2 tablespoons fresh flowers

Gingerroot: one 3- to 4-inch piece sliced thinly into coins

Lavender: 8 to 10 flower spikes, or 1 scant tablespoon fresh flowers

Lemon balm, lemon thyme, or lemon verbena: 10 to 12 sprigs

Lemongrass: about ½ cup minced stems

Mint: about 12 sprigs of orange mint, peppermint, or spearmint, or a handful of flowers

Rosemary: 5 to 6 sprigs, or a handful of flowers

Rose petals: a large handful of fresh petals (these vary in flavor, so taste first or use recommended cultivars)

Sage: about 4 common sage sprigs, or 6 fruit-scented or pineapple sage sprigs

Scented geraniums: a handful of flowers, or 12 to 15 leaves (can be bitter)

Tarragon or Mexican tarragon: 7 to 8 sprigs

Violas: violets or pansies, use a large handful of fresh flowers

Herb seeds: about 1 tablespoon bruised anise, coriander, or fennel seeds (slightly green are best; they should be simmered gently in syrup for ten minutes)

Herb syrups are delightful essences on fruit or in beverages.

Simple Herb Syrup

MAKES ABOUT 2 CUPS

A simple syrup is generally made with a one-to-one ratio of water to sugar. For a rich herb syrup, the sugar is doubled, so the ratio would be one part water to two parts sugar, which will result in a thicker, much sweeter syrup.

1½ cups water
1½ cups organic sugar
8 to 10 herb sprigs or a large handful of herb
  leaves

We have been capturing the essence of herbs in herb syrups for many decades. Syrups are a gratifying and easy way to enjoy seasonal herbs and to preserve them throughout the year. Once you have these syrups on hand, you will find all sorts of ways to use them. We create delightful beverages with them from natural sodas to luscious libations. Herb-flavored syrups are wonderful in fruit salads or used to perk up a not-so-ripe melon or pineapple. Drizzle these herbal essences over desserts from ice cream to cake, waffles and pancakes, yogurt, or baked goods just out of the oven like poppy seed muffins or pound cake. We use them in place of the liquid in cakes, pie fillings, ice creams, and sorbets. Make these syrups when you have fresh herbs in abundance. Their flavor and aroma will bring a brightness to many dishes throughout the year.

Any kind of sugar can be used in making herb syrups, but we prefer organic cane sugar. Darker sugars, honey, and maple syrup can also be used, but these sweeteners have strong flavors that may dominate the flavor of the herbs. Stevia will sweeten, but it is an herb leaf and the result will be like an infusion rather than a syrup consistency; it would have to be refrigerated and used within two days.

Combine the water and sugar in a small saucepan, and bring to a simmer over medium heat, stirring constantly with a spoon. When the sugar has dissolved, remove the pan from the heat and add the herbs. Bruise the herbs against the side of the pan with the back of the spoon. Cover the pan and let stand for at least thirty minutes, or until cool. Using a slotted spoon or strainer, gather the leaves and squeeze them to extract their essence into the syrup, then discard the leaves. Pour into clean, airtight containers and label. This syrup can be kept in the refrigerator for ten to fourteen days.

We often freeze herbal syrups in pint or quart canning jars. When freezing, leave a generous 1-inch headspace in the jar, since the liquid will expand when frozen. Label the jars, because the contents tend to look alike once frozen. Store in the freezer up to one year. If using the whole jar, just remove it from the freezer and let it thaw on the counter at room temperature. If you need just a bit (say, enough to glaze a batch of muffins), place the jar in a bowl of warm water (not hot) until partially melted. Pour off what you need and put the jar back in the freezer.

HERB VINEGARS

Creating herbal infusions is a pleasure for the herb gardener, and is a simple, straightforward way to concentrate herb flavor and store it for a year. Harvesting leaves and flowers of your favorite herbs when the plants are at their aromatic peak and soaking them in good-quality vinegar for four to six weeks are all that is necessary to accomplish this agreeable task. Part of the fun of making vinegars is experimenting with different herbs. Often, a combination of two or three herbs offers a pleasant surprise. The herbal vinegars you make will enhance salads and sauces for months to come.

Some good choices of herbs for making vinegars are anise hyssop; basil, especially the purple varieties since they tinge the vinegar a gorgeous ruby-red color; chive with chive blossoms, since the flowers will also give clear vinegar a lavender hue; dill; lavender; all of the lemon herbs; lovage; mints; oregano; tarragon; and savory. A few favorite combinations are chile peppers with cilantro, oregano, sage, or thyme; a blend of some of the lemon herbs including lemon balm, lemongrass, lemon thyme, or lemon verbena with fresh gingerroot; and chives and dill with nasturtium flowers or blends of fines herbes or herbes de Provence. Generally, we recommend combining no more than three to four herbs in a vinegar, because the flavors become muddled and you can no longer detect the individual herbs.

We do not use distilled vinegar for making herb vinegars, since it is highly processed. We recommend using vinegars that come from natural food sources, like apple cider vinegar, white and red wine vinegars, balsamic vinegars from grapes, rice wine vinegar from rice, and ume vinegar (from umeboshi plums).

We choose organic apple cider vinegar or good quality white wine or rice vinegar to make the best herb vinegars. Apple cider vinegar and umeboshi vinegars are good choices, but they do not give the clean, bright colors that a clear vinegar does. For the clearest vinegars, white wine vinegar and rice wine

Herb vinegars add brightness to salads, sauces, and pickles.

vinegar are good choices. The strong tastes of red wine and balsamic vinegars generally overpower the flavor of botanicals in a vinegar. Some people, however, prefer robust herbs such as oregano, rosemary, or even chiles combined with red wine vinegar, and we have sampled a tasty chile pepper vinegar made with sherry vinegar. Experiment with whatever vinegars and herbs appeal to you.

Herb Vinegar
MAKES 1 QUART

For herb vinegar, harvest the fresh herbs of your choice on a sunny morning, rinse the sprigs if necessary, and pat dry. You will need one clean quart glass jar with a lid or two clean pint glass jars with lids. Use plastic lids; metal lids for vinegar solutions will corrode over time. Or before you screw the metal lids on, cover the mouth of the jars with plastic wrap.

For many years, we as well as other herbalists set the jars out in the herb garden for two to four weeks, and let the sun do its work to infuse the herbs and vinegar. But we have found that the infusion in the dark has a full herb flavor and is less acidic and sharp than the sun-infused vinegar.

2 to 3 cups fresh herb leaves and/or flowers, loosely packed

1 scant quart of your choice of vinegar

Fill one 1-quart jar or 2 pint jars half to three-quarters full with the herbs you have chosen. Pour the vinegar over the herbs to cover them. Cover the jars tightly and put in your pantry or a cool, dark place, and shake them daily, if you think of it.

After two to three weeks, open the jars and taste the vinegar. If you are happy with the flavor, strain the herbs from the vinegar and discard. Or, if you want a stronger flavor, re-cover and leave for another week or so. Pour the vinegar into attractive bottles, adding a fresh sprig of the herb if desired, and label. Store the vinegars in a cool, dark place and use within one year.

AROMATIC HERBAL PASTES

Herbal pastes are one of our favorite ways of storing summer's bounty.

Many herbs freeze well when chopped and moistened with a little oil. This process is good for preserving savory herb pastes (such as pesto or salsa verde) for cooking and baking. We use this process most often with basil, since fresh basil tastes so different from dried. When dried, basil loses its bouquet—that wonderful aroma—and also loses flavor. We prefer the simplicity of freezing an herbal paste over preparing and freezing pesto, because the ingredients in pesto, like garlic, pine nuts, and Parmesan cheese, do not freeze well. For optimum flavor, add these other ingredients fresh when preparing the final dish. When making herbal pastes, you can add small amounts of other herbs like marjoram or oregano to make a blend of herbs, but we usually just use one herb, and then perhaps combine a few pastes when cooking.

Savory Herb Paste

MAKES 1 TO 2 CUPS, DEPENDING ON HERBS USED

The yield for this recipe varies. Thin-leaved herbs like dill or thyme will process down to a much smaller amount than bulkier leaves like basil or mint. If you have washed the herbs for a paste, they must be completely dried before combining with oil (oil and water do not mix).

About 4 cups herb leaves, cleaned and patted or spun completely dry, stems removed
¼ to ⅓ cup extra-virgin olive oil

Coarsely chop the herb leaves in a food processor (or blender) by pulsing with about 2 tablespoons of the olive oil. Continue pulsing, adding just enough oil to coat the herbs and make a paste, but not so the herbs are floating in oil. There should still be some texture to the herbs and they should not be puréed.

Frozen herb-oil pastes are best stored in airtight, half-cup to cup-sized freezer containers. Fill containers with the herb paste, leaving a 1-inch headspace for expansion when frozen. We often use heavy-duty ziplock freezer bags: add ½ or 1 cup of the herb paste, flatten the bag to spread the contents evenly, remove the air, and zip closed. Be sure to label the freezer containers or bags with a permanent marker (they will all look similar when frozen). Place the containers in the freezer and stack. These herbs in oil will keep in the refrigerator up to one week and in the freezer until the next season's harvest.

When we need some of the herbal paste for a recipe, we take a container or bag from the freezer, and if not using the entire package, we use a spoon to scoop some from the container, or break off a chunk from the bag, and drop it into a soup or defrost it to make a sauce.

Sweet Herb Paste

For making a sweet herbal paste, use the preceding Savory Herb Paste recipe with this difference: herbal pastes for sweet recipes vary from savory aromatic herbal pastes only in the herbs chosen and the kind of oil used. For baking, we make pastes of summer herbs, such as the mints, lemon balm, lemon basil, lemon verbena, anise hyssop, and monarda, to maintain their bright, fresh flavor. Rather than olive oil, choose from more neutral expeller or cold-pressed vegetable or nut or seed oils; we especially like sunflower seed oil. Or you can use softened butter, which will solidify when frozen, or a combination of half oil and half butter, which will not freeze as hard as just butter.

During the cold-weather months, you will have these pastes to use when making freshly baked scones and biscuits, lemon poppy seed muffins, pound cakes, chocolate mint brownies, buttermint cookies, fudge sauce, and more.

HERB BUTTERS

Herb butters are easy to make and can be quite delicious. They can be used to add herbal flavor to vegetables, breads, sauces, egg dishes, and much more. Herb butters are usually made with savory herbs, but they can also be made with the sweeter herbs and used on pancakes, waffles, muffins, biscuits, and scones. Herb butters can be refrigerated, and they also freeze well and don't take up much room. Be sure to label the herb butters, since they all look alike when wrapped in the refrigerator or freezer.

When making herb butters, keep in mind that less is more. If using more than one herb, use one to three, maybe four, herbs for flavor. Too many herbs will make the taste muddled and dull. Use less of the stronger, perennial herbs like rosemary or oregano, and more of mild-flavored herbs like chervil or lemon basil. Herb flower petals add attractive dashes of color.

Some herbs that we like for savory herb butters are basil, calendula, chervil, chives and chive flowers, dill, fennel, marjoram, nasturtium flowers, oregano, parsley, rosemary, tarragon, and thyme. Combinations such as fines herbes and herbes de Provence make flavorful butters. We often add a clove of minced or pressed garlic or about 1 tablespoon finely minced shallot to flavor savory herb butters. We also like to add a little lemon or lime zest.

For sweet herb butters, the lemon herbs like lemon balm, lemon basil, lemon verbena, and lemon thyme are quite lovely, and spearmint or orange mint work well. Colorful flower petals from anise hyssop, calendula, lavender, or rose petals are appealing to the eye as well as the palate. Citrus zest also adds a tasty note.

Herb Butter

MAKES ½ CUP

For herb butter, harvest fresh herbs on a sunny morning, rinse the sprigs if necessary, and pat dry. You will need wax paper or plastic wrap to roll the herb butter logs, or you can use airtight freezer containers.

> 8 ounces (1 stick) unsalted butter, at room temperature
> 2 to 6 tablespoons minced fresh herbs and/or flower petals
> 1 tablespoon olive oil or other expeller or cold-pressed oil (optional)

Put the soft butter in a medium bowl. Add 2 to 6 tablespoons of the herbs, depending on what strength you want, and mix well with a spatula. If you want to make a butter that doesn't freeze quite so hard, add the olive oil.

On the work surface, place a square of wax paper or plastic wrap. Scoop out the herb butter mixture and put it in the center of the wax paper. Form it into a log, and wrap tightly. Or pack the herb butter into ½-cup glass or ceramic containers and cover tightly with plastic wrap. Store in the refrigerator as is, or put the wrapped butter log or containers into a freezer ziplock bag for storing in the freezer. Be sure to label.

Herbal butters keep for up to two weeks in the refrigerator and six months in the freezer. To thaw frozen butters, put in the refrigerator for a few hours. The log-shaped butter can be sliced once it has hardened. Refrigerate the frozen herb butter for at least ½ hour before using, to allow the flavors to develop.

Herb butters can also be packed into containers.

Herb butters can be rolled into logs, wrapped tightly, and refrigerated or frozen.

METRIC CONVERSIONS

Length

INCHES	CM		FEET	M
¼	0.6		1	0.3
½	1.0		2	0.6
1	2.5		3	0.9
2	5.0		4	1.2
3	7.5		5	1.5
4	10		6	1.8
5	12		7	2.1
6	15		8	2.4
7	17		9	2.7
8	20		10	3
9	23		12	3.6
10	25		15	4.6
12	30.5		20	6
15	38			
20	50			

Temperatures

°F	°C
10	−12.2
20	−6.6
30	−1.1
40	4.4
50	10
70	21
80	27
100	38
200	95
300	150
400	200

$$°C = \tfrac{5}{9} \times (°F - 32)$$

$$°F = (\tfrac{9}{5} \times °C) + 32$$

Weight

0.002 ounce	50 milligrams
½ ounce	15 grams
1 ounce	30 grams
2 ounces	60 grams
3 ounces	85 grams
½ pound (8 ounces)	225 grams
¾ pound (12 ounces)	340 grams
1 pound (16 ounces)	454 grams
2 pounds	910 kilograms
8 pounds	3.6 kilograms
10 pounds	4.5 kilograms

SOME FOOD ITEMS, VOLUME/WEIGHT

1½ cups sugar/300 grams
1½ cups water/340 grams
2 tablespoons minced herbs/5.3 grams
½ cup minced lemongrass stems/55 grams
2 cups grated horseradish/200 grams
4 cups herb leaves, loosely packed/180 grams

Volume

1 teaspoon	5 milliliters
1 tablespoon (3 teaspoons)	15 milliliters
¼ cup (4 tablespoons)	60 milliliters
⅓ cup (2½ fluid ounces)	75 milliliters
½ cup (4 fluid ounces)	125 milliliters
1 cup (8 fluid ounces)	250 milliliters
1 pint (2 cups)	500 milliliters
1 quart (4 cups)	approx. 1 liter

SOURCES

These sources are herbal businesses that we have used throughout the years. Some sell just plants, others just seeds, and some both.

ABUNDANT LIFE SEEDS
P.O. Box 157
Saginaw, OR 97472-0157
541-767-9606
abundantlifeseeds.com
  (seeds of herbs and potherbs)

W. ATLEE BURPEE & CO.
300 Park Avenue
Warminster, PA 18974
800-888-1447
FAX 800-487-5539
burpee.com
  (seeds of herbs and potherbs)

BAKER CREEK HEIRLOOM SEEDS
2278 Baker Creek Road
Mansfield, MO 65704
417-924-8917
rareseeds.com
  (heirloom seeds)

COOKS GARDEN SEED
P.O. Box 535
Londonderry, VT 05148
802-824-3400
cooksgarden.com
  (herb seeds and plants)

DEBAGGIO'S HERB FARM & NURSERY
43494 Mountain View Drive
Chantilly, VA 20152
703-327-6976
debaggioherbs.com
  (wide selection of herb plants; does not ship)

FOREST FARM
P.O. Box 1
Williams, OR 97544
541-846-7268
FAX 541-846-6963
forestfarm.com
  (herbal trees and shrubs)

HORIZON HERBS
P.O. Box 69
Williams, OR 97544-0069
541-846-6704
FAX 541-846-6233
horizonherbs.com
  (herb plants and seeds)

J. L. HUDSON, SEEDSMAN
P.O. Box 337
La Honda, CA 94020-0337
jlhudsonseeds.com
  (wide selection of seeds)

JOHNNY'S SELECTED SEEDS
955 Benton Avenue
Winslow, ME 04901-2601
877-564-6697
FAX 800-738-6314
johnnyseeds.com
 (wide selection of herb seeds, especially potherbs)

KITAZAWA SEED CO.
201 4th Street, #206
Oakland, CA 94607
510-595-1188
FAX 510-595-1860
kitazawaseed.com
 (Asian herbs and vegetables)

NATIVE SEED/SEARCH
526 North Fourth Avenue
Tucson, AZ 85705
520-622-5561
nativeseeds.org
 (seeds of herbs, chiles, and potherbs)

NICHOLS GARDEN NURSERY
190 Old Salem Road NE
Albany, OR 97321-4580
800-422-3985
nicholsgardennursery.com
 (herb seeds, some plants)

PARK SEED
One Parkton Avenue
Greenwood, SC 29647-0001
800-845-3369
FAX 800-275-9941
parkseed.com
 (seeds of herbs and potherbs)

RENEE'S GARDEN SEEDS
6116 Highway 9
Felton, CA 95018
888-880-7228
reneesgarden.com
 (herb seeds, chiles, and potherbs)

RICHTERS HERBS
357 Highway 47
Goodwood, ON
L0C 1A0 Canada
905-640-6677
FAX 905-640-6641
richters.com
 (herb plants and seeds)

SEEDS OF CHANGE
P.O. Box 152
Spicer, MN 56288
888-762-7333
FAX 320-796-6036
seedsofchange.com
 (heirloom seeds)

SEED SAVERS EXCHANGE
3094 North Winn Road
Decorah, IA 52101
563-382-5990
FAX 563-382-6511
seedsavers.org
 (heirloom seeds)

TERRITORIAL SEED CO.
P.O. Box 158
Cottage Grove, OR 97424-0061
800-626-3131
FAX 888-657-3131
territorialseed.com
 (seeds of herbs and potherbs)

WELL-SWEEP HERB FARM
205 Mount Bethel Road
Port Murray, NJ 07865-4147
908-852-5390
FAX 908-852-1649
wellsweep.com
 (herb plants)

ZACK WOODS HERB FARM
278 Mead Road
Hyde Park, VT 05655
zackwoodsherbs.com
 (certified organic herb plants)

SUGGESTED READING

In this reading list, you will find books both new and old. Some we reach for often on our reference shelves, and some are just old favorites. These books have influenced our lives as herbalists, gardeners, and cooks.

Arndt, Alice. *Seasoning Savvy*. Binghamton, NY: Haworth Herbal Press, 1999.

Belsinger, Susan. *Flowers in the Kitchen*. Loveland, CO: Interweave Press, 1991.

Belsinger, Susan, and Carolyn Dille. *The Greens Book*. Loveland, CO: Interweave Press, 1995.

Belsinger, Susan, and Tina Marie Wilcox. *The Creative Herbal Home*. Brookeville, MD: Herbspirit, 2007.

Bown, Deni. *Encyclopedia of Herbs and Their Uses*. New York: Dorling Kindersley, 1995.

Crocker, Pat. *The Healing Herbs Cookbook*. Toronto: Robert Rose Inc., 1999.

DeBaggio, Thomas, and Susan Belsinger. *Basil: An Herb Lover's Guide*. Loveland, CO: Interweave Press, 1996.

Elliott, Doug. *Wild Roots*. Rochester, VT: Healing Arts Press, 1995.

Falconi, Dina. *Foraging and Feasting: A Field Guide and Wild Food Cookbook*. Accord, NY: Botanical Arts Press, 2013.

Foster, Steven, and James A. Duke. *A Field Guide to Medicinal Plants: Eastern and Central North America*. Boston: Houghton Mifflin, 1990.

Foster, Steven, and Rebecca L. Johnston. *National Geographic Desk Reference to Nature's Medicine*. Washington, DC: National Geographic, 2006.

Gladstar, Rosemary. *Family Herbal: A Guide to Living Life with Energy, Health and Vitality*. North Adams, MA: Storey Books, 2001.

Hill, Madalene, and Gwen Barclay. *Southern Herb Growing*. Fredricksburg, TX: Shearer, 1987.

Johnson, Wendy. *Gardening at the Dragon's Gate*. New York: Bantam Dell, 2008.

Kallas, John. *Edible Wild Plants: Wild Foods from Dirt to Plate.* Layton, UT: Gibbs Smith, 2010.

Larkom, Joy. *The Salad Garden.* New York: Viking, 1984.

Laws, Bill. *Fifty Plants that Changed the Course of History.* Buffalo, NY: Firefly Books, 2010.

Madison, Deborah. *Vegetable Literacy.* Berkeley, CA: Ten Speed Press, 2013.

———. *Vegetarian Cooking for Everyone.* New York: Broadway Books, 1997.

Peterson, Lee Allen. *A Field Guide to Edible Wild Plants: Eastern/Central North America.* Boston: Houghton Mifflin, 1999.

Phillips, Roger. *Wild Foods.* Boston: Little, Brown, 1986.

Rose, Jeanne. *Herbs and Things.* New York, NY: Grosset & Dunlap, 1974.

Soule, Deb. *How to Move Like a Gardener.* Rockport, ME: Under the Willow Press, 2013.

Thayer, Samuel. *Nature's Garden: A Guide to Identifying, Harvesting, and Preparing Edible Wild Plants.* Birchwood, WI: Forager's Harvest Press, 2010.

Traunfeld, Jerry. *The Herbal Kitchen: Cooking with Fragrance and Flavor.* New York: William Morrow, 2005.

Tucker, Arthur O., and Thomas DeBaggio. *The Encyclopedia of Herbs.* Portland, OR: Timber Press, 2009.

Wood, Rebecca. *The New Whole Foods Encyclopedia.* New York: Penguin Books, 2010.

ACKNOWLEDGMENTS

Many thanks to Pat Kenny, for taking the authors' photo; she is truly one of our herbal heroes. We appreciate the continued enthusiasm and assistance of our friends who garden and grow the herbs for us: Francesco DeBaggio, Deborah Hall, Denise Sharp, and Tina Marie Wilcox and thank Linda Cunningham, Henry Flowers, Andrea and Matthias Reisen, for shipping herb specimens that we needed for photographs. We both thank our respective families and friends for their continued patience and support while writing this book. Verily, we are passionate about what we do, because we get to share our findings with our herbal cohorts and colleagues.

We would also like to thank our editors throughout the long process of making this book, Juree Sondker, Eve Goodman, and Ellen Wheat. Our appreciation also goes to farmer Josh Volk for cultivating the herbs in the book's photographs, and photographer Shawn Linehan for capturing the herbal images.

PHOTOGRAPHY CREDITS

INDEX

PAT KENNY

Shawn Linehan photographs small farms and farmers mostly around the Portland, Oregon, area. With a journalist's sense of narrative and an artist's eye, she creates intimate, authentic images that celebrate the lives of our environmental stewards.

Susan Belsinger has been teaching, lecturing, and writing about gardening and cooking for more than forty years. As a food writer, editor, and photographer, she has written and edited more than twenty-five books, hundreds of articles, and numerous calendars. Described as a flavor artist, Susan delights in kitchen alchemy—the blending of harmonious foods, herbs, and spices—to create real, delicious food and libations that nourish our bodies and spirits and titillate our senses. Her website is susanbelsinger.com

Arthur O. Tucker has spent more than fifty years using, researching, and publishing on herbs in both popular and scientific media. His book *The Encyclopedia of Herbs*, co-authored with Tom DeBaggio, was published by Timber Press in 2009. This update and the previous edition, *Big Book of Herbs*, were the first books that attempted to digest the voluminous scientific information on herbs for the general public. His cottage garden was featured on the cover of *Southern Living* for April 2003. Now emeritus professor at Delaware State University, he continues to love herbs and has started a second life as a concrete artist.